The Ocean of Grace

Tributes to Amma's all-embracing love

Volume 1

The Ocean of Grace

Tributes to Amma's all-embracing love

Volume 1

Edited by Ramana Erickson

Co-edited by Julius Heyne

Mata Amritanandamayi Center
San Ramon, California, USA

Ocean of Grace – Volume 1

Tributes to Amma's all-embracing love

Edited by Ramana Erickson
Co-edited by Julius Heyne

Published by:
Mata Amritanandamayi Center
P.O. Box 613
San Ramon, CA 94583-0613, USA

In India:
www.amritapuri.org
inform@amritapuri.org

In Europe:
www.amma-europe.org

In US:
www.amma.org

Contents

Preface 7

Grace and Surrender 11
A message from Amma

1. Amma — Indweller of the Heart 13
Sarvaga - USA

2. Śhraddhā 25
Akshay - Germany

3. Grace in my Life 37
Dr. Shyamasundaran - India

4. Amma: Our Divine Lifeguard 50
Rasya - USA

5. The Three Rare Gifts 62
Vinod - Italy

6. Why Sad? No Need 74
Medhini - Lebanon

7. A Householder's Journey through Life with Amma 86
Anita Sreekumar - India

8. The Guru's Sandals 98
Sadānand - USA

9. Satsang and Sēvā in my Life 110
Nihsima M Sandhu - USA

10. The Center of My Spiritual World — Amma's Divine Embrace 122
Susi - Germany

11. Form and Formless Worship 134
Sugata Duygu Akartuna - Türkiye

12. Ahaṅkāra — The Ego 147
Dr. Sriram Ananthanarayanan - India

13. **Selflessness** 159
Sahaja - Australia

14. **From Banking World to Amma's World — A Devotee's Journey** 171
Daya Chandrahas - India

15. **This Precious Life** 182
Tejasvini - USA

16. **Overcoming Suffering with Amma's Love** 193
Purnima - Germany

17. **Creation and Creator are not Two, but One** 206
Prasadini - Germany

18. **From Untruth to Truth, Darkness to Light, Death to Immortality** 218
Varenya - Spain

19. **Arise, O Scorcher of Foes** 229
Rudran - USA

20. **Humility** 240
Malathi - France

21. **Amma — the Guide, the Path, and the Goal** 252
Sahaja - France

22. **Amma, the Love that Vanquishes All Fear** 261
Vimala Purcell - USA

23. **Amma, PhD, and Beyond!** 272
Dr. Shyam Nath - Mauritius

24. **The Mystery of Faith** 279
Janani - Poland

25. **Becoming an Instrument** 291
Gautam - USA

Glossary 303

Pronunciation Guide 319

Acknowledgments 320

Preface

Sanātana dharma[1] has divided life into four stages known as āśhramas. The life of a student is called *brahmachāryāśhrama* ('brahmachārya' for short). During the householder stage of life known as *gṛihasthāśhrama* ('gṛihastha'), a person acquires wealth and fulfills desires while leading a virtuous life. Once the children are grown, the husband and wife hand over their worldly responsibilities and concentrate on propagating *dharma* and performing spiritual practices. This is called the *vānaprasthāśhrama* ('vānaprastha') or retirement stage. *Sannyāsāśhrama* ('sannyāsa') is the final stage of life. It is marked by total renunciation and detachment from all worldly ties. The *sannyāsī* focuses on *mōkṣha* (liberation) and leads a solitary life.

There are three paths one can take to arrive at the final stage of sannyāsa: upon fulfilling one's duties and responsibilities as a gṛihastha, a person can directly enter sannyāsa; or else one can take up sannyāsa after the vānaprastha stage. The third way is if one gains total detachment early on, one can take sannyāsa without ever having entered into the life of a gṛihastha. The brahmachārīs and brahmachāriṇīs who reside in Amritapuri have no desire for householder life. Therefore, Amma initiates them directly into sannyāsa, bypassing the gṛihastha and vānaprastha stages.

After many years Amritapuri witnessed a grand *yajña* — a *mahāyajña* — a great sacred ceremony on Friday, March 13, 2020. More than fifty brahmachārīs and brahmachāriṇīs were initiated into sannyāsa. On that same day, over 200 āśhram residents took brahmachārya *dīkṣhā* (initiation) as well. Amma had given

[1] The 'Eternal Religion' or 'Eternal Way of Life,' the original and traditional name of Hinduism.

strict instructions that all the renunciates living in the various branch āśhrams and institutions should immediately come to Amritapuri to participate in the dīkṣhā ceremony. At the time, only Amma knew her reasons for issuing such strict directions. However, Amma's foreknowledge concerning what was about to happen on a global scale soon became clear, and her urgent instructions were then understood.

A few days after the sannyāsa initiation ceremony, the Covid-19 pandemic forced the entire country into lockdown. People were confined to their homes, and travel became impossible. The gates of the āśhram that were usually open twenty-four hours a day, all year round were suddenly closed in compliance with orders from the government. Amma's devotees were devastated. How could Amma not listen to their call?

Since Amma could no longer travel, the āśhram residents once again performed their spiritual practices in Amma's physical presence, like in the early days of the āśhram. Meditation, *satsangs* (spiritual discourses), and *bhajans* (devotional songs) were streamed online in webcasts. Using this modern technology, Amma entered the homes of her children worldwide, while they were in lockdown due to Covid-19. The inner strength and relief they gained due to these webcasts cannot be expressed in words.

During this time, Amma instructed the āśhram residents to start giving half-hour long satsangs every day at the evening programs, after meditation. The resultant satsang series started on March 30, 2020, and continues to this day. Once the Covid-19 travel restrictions were lifted, Amma's gṛihasthāśhrami children also started participating.

This is the first volume of a compilation of satsangs that were given by Amma's non-monastic children as they related their experiences in person while sitting beside Amma.

Reading about these devotees' various experiences with Amma, the transformation in their lives after they met her, and the difference in their attitudes and outlook as they deal with individuals and situations will refresh and energize our minds. The rocky paths often traveled were not limited to their own experiences; we too can relate to them. When we read and reflect upon the experiences of others, we are able to lay down the burdens of our past and move forward with renewed vigor and purpose.

The small lamp we hold in our hand as we traverse a pitch-dark path sheds light not only for us, but for all those who are walking along that same path. Likewise, when we read about the experiences of devotees across the world, we will realize that the strength Amma gave to them is being imparted to us too. We will experience that the light Amma shed in their lives, also removes our darkness. When each person draws word pictures of their individual experiences, we see different facets of Amma. We wonder at Her various forms and *bhāvas* or divine moods.

There is no doubt that this book will guide us in our journey to Self- realization. Let us pray to Amma for her grace.

Swāmī Jñānāmṛitānanda Puri

Grace and Surrender

A message from Amma

Children, we strive for many things every day. Of these, we succeed in getting only a few. We might drive very carefully. Yet, if there is a careless or drunk driver coming from the opposite side, he might crash into us. Similarly, even if a student prepares thoroughly before an examination, she might not get the marks she deserves if the examiner grading the paper is careless. Why do such things happen? No matter how talented or hardworking we may be, our efforts will be crowned with success only if God's grace is with us.

One day, Bhīma was walking alone in the forest. Suddenly, he spotted a pregnant doe in the distance. The deer started at the sight of Bhīma. She glanced in the four directions and stood petrified. When Bhīma looked all around, he understood why the deer was behaving this way. A lion was waiting in front to pounce on her. It was waiting because there was a hunter behind her, his arrow trained on her. To her right was a rapid river, and to her left, a forest fire was blazing brightly. The deer was surrounded on all four sides by dangers.

Seeing the doe's plight, Bhīma's heart melted, but he was helpless. If he tried to chase the hunter away, the frightened deer would run straight into the jaws of the lion. If he tried to put out the forest fire, the doe would leap into the river in a panic and become submerged by its swift currents. Seeing no way to save her, Bhima finally called out to God: "O Lord, I'm totally helpless. Only you can save the deer. Please save her!"

The very next moment, dark rainclouds gathered and there was a loud clap of thunder. Heavy rains began pouring down. The hunter was struck by lightning and fell unconscious. The rain extinguished the forest fire. The lion ran away, frightened. As soon as the threats around her disappeared, the deer fled to safety. Seeing all this, Bhima stood transfixed in astonishment.

When we understand the limits of our abilities and appreciate God's infinite glory, we will realize that only divine grace can make our efforts fruitful. Bhīma became befitting of God's grace because of his compassion for the deer and his surrender to the Divine. When effort, compassion and surrender come together, God will definitely shower His grace.

1

Amma — Indweller of the Heart

Sarvaga - USA

We all know that attempting to describe Amma's love, or the depth of our relationship to her, seems almost impossible. Yet her compassion is so great, that even in trying to describe her — we are uplifted. Listening to the stories of her grace — we are purified.

For each one of us, who are so seemingly different from each other, it is Amma that exists as the indweller of our hearts. The very center point of our existence. Amma shines as that radiant Self that unifies all beings. When we listen deeply to each other with open hearts and minds, without judgment, it awakens that inner center point of our oneness. True understanding, true compassion, and true love all meet at that point.

Real listening can only happen when the mind becomes silent. In those moments of silence, we can experience a taste of our unity. Watching Amma give *darśhan* (Amma's divine embrace), we witness the flow of her unconditional love.

Sometimes unknowingly we identify with the person being held in her arms. We may also laugh with their laughter or shed tears with their pain. Amma's entire life is a living demonstration of oneness, and she is always guiding us towards this expansive experience.

Oneness is the secret of Amma's perfect language of love, the language of silence. Like how a mother understands the heart of her child with no need for words. This is the deep experience of each one of us when in her embrace.

It is with this same language of love that Amma understands the hearts of all creatures. A friend of mine had a pet turtle that she would always bring for darśhan. One time, Amma told her that the little turtle was lonely and needed a companion to share his heart with. So she got another little turtle, and brought the two together for her next darśhan. Amma happily blessed the turtles and asked my friend to let them go free. She released them onto her property, and after that she never saw them.

One year later, when Amma was coming again, my friend went to her garden to pick vegetables for an offering. Suddenly she saw the two little turtles looking up at her expectantly. They had come back after one whole year, on the exact day of Amma's program! They wanted to see the mother that understood their hearts. She picked them up and brought them for Amma's darśhan.

***

Once Amma asked me to teach a group of hearing-impaired children to perform bhajans using sign language. After practicing, the children sang for Amma for the very first time. Not with their voices — but with the silent language of their hands and hearts.

I hid on the stage so that the children could see me in case they forgot the signs. Suddenly, Amma asked me to stand up. She stopped the darśhan and watched all of us attentively. I let go of my shyness and felt just as if I were one with the children. At that moment, Amma loudly called my name for the very first time. This call went deep into my heart. My name '*Sarvaga*' means 'all pervading.' I always felt Amma gave me this name to point me towards oneness, to the truth of who we really are; beyond our limited names and forms.

Thousands of years ago, God revealed through the *Bhagavad Gītā* his promise to rescue his devotees from all suffering. For Amma's children, this promise has become a living reality. There is nothing in the history of this world that can compare to the glory of the Divine Mother descending to Earth to save her children; to return them to their oneness with her.

We can never imagine the sacrifice and compassion that keeps Amma on this Earth. Amma once told me, "Amma is like a helium balloon. At any moment, she can rise up. But she keeps herself down on this Earth, only to uplift her children."

***

The little story of my life is like one among the uncountable grains of sand that have been sanctified by the touch of Amma's feet.

I was born into a poor Jewish family, in a cabin next to a river, on the other side of the world. Yet Amma found me there. A few days after I was born, my father was unexpectedly given an idol of Lord Kṛiṣhṇa. He performed a ceremony, placed me at the feet of the Lord, and sincerely offered the life of his newborn to God. In this way, I always felt my life was offered to Amma from birth itself.

My earliest memory is when that cabin by the river burned to the ground when I was only three-years old. My mother was home alone with five small children including my infant sister, whom she had to run into the burning home to save. Whatever little possessions we had and our two dogs were lost, but we all got out unscathed.

My most profound memory was going through the ruins the next day. I clearly remember my father pulling two large books from beneath the ash. Only the hard covers had been burned. They were the only things that had not been destroyed, and still remain with me to this day. These two books were the *Bhagavad Gītā* and the Śhrīmad *Bhāgavatam.*

It was my very first lesson in life, and one of the most fundamental on the spiritual path: Only God is indestructible and will always remain with us. It is this living God, our Amma, who will carry us, protect us and console us as we face the various fires of life — our compassionate mother who will finally save us from this impermanent world of birth and death.

The second major fire in my life came when I was seventeen. My mother was diagnosed with a terminal illness and given a prognosis of only six months to live. It was during this time that I came to Amma in 1997. At the first sight of Amma, I was filled with the knowing that she was the Divine Mother. I received Amma's *mantra*, and gained the inner strength to care for my mom during the last months of her life. I felt in the depth of my heart that my mother's form was only returning to my true mother. Amma had come into my life, making sure that I was not even a moment on this earth without a mother.

The day after my mom died, I was bedridden with a high fever. Amma's would be returning soon, and I was praying intensely for the strength to go see her.

Suddenly the fever cleared completely. A few days later I traveled to see Amma. The moment I was held in her arms, Amma called out with deep concern, "Fever! Fever!" She took a large amount of sandalwood paste, and with a love I had never known existed, gently applied it all over my face.

As I sobbed in her embrace, all the pain from my mom dying left me. I was filled with the deep experience that Amma is the all-knowing Divine Mother and I am her child. From that moment, I knew I could not be separated from my true mother and by her grace I have spent my life in the refuge of her shade.

***

I made the journey to India only a few months later. It was my first time leaving home. Waiting to reach Amma, I wrote the following poem:

What am I
but a leaf in the wind
Who am I?
I am carried by the currents to Your feet
Watching this mind
nothing seems real
but the tears that tremble
to the brim of my heart
waiting to fall into your ocean
What is real
but this blind calling
to abandon myself at your doorstep
Mother imbibe me
with the strength of Surrender
the grace of perseverance
Mother I am coming
to offer myself to You
Please accept this offering
Embracing this child
Open my heart
to who I truly am

I'll never forget crossing the backwaters in a little boat under a star-filled sky. Tears streamed continuously so that I could hardly see. Finally reaching Amma's lap, I wondered if she would remember to call me her daughter. After darśhan, as I stood in front of her, she gazed into my eyes and called out very loudly, "My daughter! My daughter!" I felt as if Amma was announcing that her daughter had finally reached home.

Soon after my arrival, Amma came one day to the pool. After swimming with all of us, Amma lay on her back in full lotus posture in the water, and entered into *samādhi* – the state of union with God. Her hands were held in *mudras.* She lay absolutely still, yet her body moved gently around the pool, propelled by her divine śhakti.

I was in the pool at the edge, gazing at Amma, spellbound. Amma began to move towards me. I kept moving away until I reached the very corner, but Amma kept coming towards me. She moved so that her head was only a few inches from my heart. Then she simply remained there.

I gazed down at her face. Never had I seen anything so enchanting. Her face was glowing like the full moon, a radiant smile of absolute bliss and indescribable peace was on her lips, and pure light poured out from beneath the thick lashes of her half-closed eyes. I can never quite describe what happened with words. Gazing at Amma's beautiful face, radiant with unearthly peace, I saw the face of my own biological mother. Her face was somehow merged in the radiant, blissful countenance of Amma.

I burst into tears of shock. Amma stayed near me, her head at my heart for a long time as I cried loudly like a child. When I became peaceful, she floated away. It was as if the river of my mom's deep suffering merged forever into the ocean of Amma's radiant peace.

In that moment a deep merging also happened within my heart. Even if the fire of *māyā*, the cosmic illusion, can take away the physical form of a mother, what remains is our real mother, shining upon us with her immortal love. Though our lives may be filled with fires, Amma always guides us towards an inner refuge that remains untouched.

Through all the experiences of her grace, one of her greatest miracles is to slowly develop faith and surrender within us. We may face tests in life in which we feel we are failing to surrender, and find ourselves pulled under by waves of sorrow. Yet, when we call out for Amma in absolute helplessness, she comes to our rescue.

Eleven years ago, a series of procedures at Amma's AIMS hospital showed that I was exhibiting signs of a rare, terminal liver disease. The testing was inconclusive and continued for many months. Even though Amma told me not to worry until we knew the results, I found myself faced with an overwhelming fear of death.

I was shocked at my own lack of faith. I felt so unprepared. Yet no matter how scared I was, I could never pray to Amma to take away the disease or to change the outcome. I could only pray for the strength to surrender. I could only pray that whenever my death was meant to come, that filled with surrender and love, I would be ready to merge in Amma forever.

Finally, seeing my distress, Amma herself called for the head doctor at AIMS and asked him to arrange the decisive procedure. Waking up from the anesthesia, I felt as if I had been lying in Amma's arms. I felt a tangible wave of Amma's grace wash over me as they told me I did not have the disease.

When I told Amma the results, she held her hands to her heart and breathed a deep sigh of relief. Then she held her hands to the sky, showing the sign that it was God's grace. Amma's humble way of showing it is HER grace alone. I pray to use this life, given through her grace, in true preparation to surrender fully in love.

When we carry the weight of our fears of the future, or the heaviness of the past, we might find ourselves collapsing. Yet, when we surrender these burdens, we find Amma giving us the strength to face the present moment. If we feel surrender is only for some future moment, when we will let go of all of our attachments and ego, we may become afraid. Imagining that it is beyond our capacity, we will continue to cling out of fear.

Yet Amma understands our weaknesses. She understands our capacity for surrender at each moment in our lives. Amma says that surrender is acceptance. This acceptance is a moment to moment opportunity given to us by Amma. Each and every situation that arises in life, is Amma's invitation to practice acceptance.

Amma often speaks of this as *prasāda buddhi* — accepting everything that comes as God's gift. Yet for this attitude to become natural for us, we also have to practice *pūjā manō bhāvam* — offering all that we do, offering our own Self, with awareness and love.

Slowly, as Amma develops the awareness, love, and faith within us, she will take us to the final state of surrender, to merge forever in her immortal love. Amma's compassion is so great, that she herself builds this faith in our hearts by giving us experiences of her all-knowing presence.

***

Another series of fires came into my life when my father was diagnosed with the same terminal illness my mom had died from. Yet Amma was there to save us from the flames of every fire; extending my father's life in ways that would take a book to describe. After many years, my dad's health deteriorated to the point where I needed to move to the U.S. to care for him.

Witnessing his constant pain, not knowing how long he would survive, and being separated from Amma physically, was the hardest challenge I had ever faced. At one point, he seemed to have developed pneumonia. It was unbearable to see him suffering and I felt he was near the end. I was all alone with him and deeply feeling the pain of my separation from Amma.

One afternoon I brought some soup for him, even though he had already stopped eating. As I approached his bed, the bowl suddenly fell from my hands onto the floor and broke into many pieces. In that moment, it felt as if my heart had shattered. I suddenly felt that all my strength had left me. I ran outside into the forest, crying uncontrollably. I screamed out to Amma from the depths of my heart, "Amma! Can you hear me? Amma! Are you with me? Amma, I need you so much right now!" It was a cry of pure desperation.

After crying my heart out, I felt some peace and renewed courage. I knew that Amma had heard me. I went back to clean up the shattered bowl, and served my dad the best I could. Late that night, deeply exhausted, I finally went to bed.

I was soon awakened by the phone ringing. Startled, I grabbed the phone. What I heard made my heart leap. It was Amma's beautiful voice! She asked in English if my father was ok. When I came to my senses, I told her that I was afraid my dad might have pneumonia.

Amma comforted me and said that she had been thinking of me while she was in her room between the programs that afternoon. I realized later that this was the exact same period of time when I had been calling out for her in the forest. I was overwhelmed by the realization that Amma had not only heard me, but had physically responded to me during one of the most desperate moments of my life.

My father recovered by morning and gradually his condition improved. Amma continued to support our entire family, slowly helping us to develop the strength to face each situation that arose with acceptance.

When we reflect, we see clearly how much we suffer when we resist what is happening in the present moment and we recognize the flow of grace and peace that comes when we accept.

Amma continuously teaches us how to be joyful and peaceful along this unpredictable journey of life. She shows us the way to transcend sorrow through acceptance and faith.

In meditation everyday, Amma tells us that awakening our inner child means to invoke the principle of surrender and love. The child has absolute faith in its mother. As our faith and love deepen, surrender becomes natural. Otherwise, we will cling to the way we think things should be — to our attachments, to avoiding pain, to our likes and dislikes.

With faith, we will understand that Amma is taking on an unimaginable portion of our *prārabdha karma,* the results from our past actions. We will accept that what we must experience is meant to purify and strengthen us. We will trust that Amma is guiding everything to free us from all sorrow and merge us into her.

One of the greatest spiritual teachings that Amma has given me, came in the form of my father's last words before he died. He had indicated that he had one final message to give. All of us children gathered around his bed. He struggled for a very long time to stay conscious long enough to speak. It was as if all he had learned in his entire life had to be shared in this one message.

Finally, with an intensity and love that seemed like God was asking him to speak, he said loudly and clearly, "BE WHO YOU ARE!" These words sank into the depths of my heart. I felt it was Amma's own words coming through him.

Soon I was with Amma again. One day, Amma suddenly looked at me and asked, "What were your father's last words?"

I told Amma that he had said, "Be who you are."

Amma said nothing more, but looked deeply into my eyes and smiled knowingly. She was clearly affirming that it was indeed her own message.

There was a profound sense of urgency when my father spoke these words. Why? 'To be who you are' can only happen in this present moment. One who is at the doorstep of death will understand the urgency; the need to live each moment with the awareness of God.

The reality of who we truly are is covered by our identification with what we are not — the ever-changing thoughts, emotions, and ego. In each moment, we can shine the spotlight of awareness into our own hearts. Then Amma's grace will light the path that leads us to our own true Self.

Inquiring deeply into my own heart, is to clearly see all of my weaknesses and false identifications. What is left is an overwhelming longing to experience my own true Self. Not knowing my own Self, I can only cry out to Amma. Amma who is that radiant Self, manifested for each one of us out of pure compassion.

As an orphaned child always longs to reunite with its mother, the same is the longing to be free from all suffering, and to merge in Amma. Once, Amma looked into my eyes and said, "Amma can never say that *bhakti* (devotion) is less than *jñāna* (knowledge), because they lead to the same Truth." Through this I have understood that the pain and tears of longing for Amma will purify us, revealing the truth of who we really are.

I found another poem I had written as a teenage girl during that first journey to India so long ago. I offer this as a prayer for each one of us:

Mother — Source of all compassion
I bow before You
I pray allow Your Love
To radiate — from each touch of my hands
Your clarity — to center my mind
Let my heart be a spring

From which You are the Source
Dawn on me — the light of Awareness
So that I might see to walk
With humbleness and care
Give me the strength — to surrender
Knowing it is You Who carries all burdens
Give me willingness to Share the suffering of others
So that I might find true joy
Give me faith — to accept my own suffering
As your gift to know the peace Of equanimity
Give me the vision to see — In all situations
The keys you offer — To unlocking the inner treasure
Take from my mind — The winds of agitation
So that in stillness I may reflect You
Grant me the innocence And faith of a child
So that I might come to know My True Nature
Merging in You forever

2

Śhraddhā

Akshay – Germany

I heard about a great miracle I'd like to share with you. There was once a young man studying in Berlin. His life was divided between attending to his university studies, and enjoying life to the fullest. Like many of you, he was following a philosophy, but his philosophy was neither *Dvaita* (dualist philosophy), *Sāṅkhya* (foundational philosophy of yōga), nor *Advaita* (non-dualist philosophy); his philosophy was *carpe diem.*

Carpe diem is a Latin phrase. Carpe means 'pluck' and diem means 'day.' So, it means 'Seize the day,' or 'enjoy the moment.' To this university student, carpe diem meant, 'Enjoy what you can, when you can, while you can.'

By some strange twist of fate, this young man was drawn to India. During the cold, gray German winter, the sunny beaches, exotic flair, and excessive dance parties in Goa seemed very enticing. And so, on break from university, he traveled to India.

It was after one of those parties on the beaches of Goa, that he first heard about Amma. Sitting with a group of friends he'd met, people were sharing some of the experiences they had had during their travels. They talked about the Gurus they had visited, the yōga classes they had taken, and the temples they had seen.

His attention was caught when someone started elaborating about Amma's āśhram. He had already planned to travel all the way down to India's southern tip, and thought this would be the perfect time to visit Amma's āśhram.

He traveled on the Alappuzha - Kollam tourist boat that meandered down the backwaters, until it made a stop on its way to Kollam to let him and other tourists off at the āśhram boat dock. The boat captain assured him he could finish the trip to Kollam on the same ticket after staying at the āśhram for a night or two.

Delighted and curious, this young man got off the boat to find out about Amma. He had no idea that meeting Amma would transform him overnight into a new person. He had no idea that stepping off that boat onto the sand sanctified by Amma's *tapas* (austerities) would burn up all of his bad habits. He had no idea that for the rest of his life, that second half of his boat ticket to Kollam would go unclaimed.

In the āśhram, I started studying Malayalam and could soon recognize some sentences that Amma used frequently. One of these sentences was, 'Ī *nimiśham mātrame nammaḷude kaiyyil ullu*' - 'Only this moment is in our hands.' This may sound similar to carpe diem, but Amma doesn't mean, 'Only this moment is in our hands, so let's go to the next bar.' Or, 'Only this moment is in our hands, so let's spend all our cash on the latest fashion.' What Amma means is: we should live in the present moment with the utmost *śhraddhā*.

Śhraddhā! This is another word that I learned early on. In Malayalam, it means alertness, attention, focus, concentration, and even one-pointedness (ēkāgrata in Sanskrit). I'll give you a couple of examples of when I heard Amma say this:

Once, I was helping with crowd control on Amma's India Tour, and I pulled so hard that one person almost fell face forward onto the floor. "Akshaya!" Amma called out, "*Ninte śhraddhā evide*?" - "Where is your attention!"

Or while serving french fries at a tour stop, after giving clear instructions to serve exactly ten fries per plate, Amma exclaimed, "Akshaya, there are only five fries! Ninte śhraddhā evide?" – "Where is your attention?" Then a few minutes later, "*Eṭā! Ippōl patinañju fries* āyi*! Nī* śhraddhikkēndē? – "Hey! Now there are fifteen fries! Shouldn't you be concentrating?"

'Śhraddhā' and 'Ī nimiṣham mātrame…' Amma uses these two expressions over and over again. The Guru's words of today are the scriptures of tomorrow. So, we have to treat them as such and contemplate upon them to understand their depth. Amma herself says that to truly understand her words, we have to study the scriptures. Therefore, I would like to explain Amma's words using an ancient text known as the *Yōga Sūtras* of Sage Patañjali.

The word yōga comes from '*yuj samādhau*' – the Sanskrit root 'yuj' as the achievement of '*samādhi*' – 'perfect concentration.' The very first line of Sage Vyāsa's commentary on the Yōga Sūtras reads: '*yōga samādhiḥ*.' It means, 'Yōga is perfect concentration;' 'yōga is one-pointedness;' or 'yōga is śhraddhā.' Thus, the *Yōga Sūtras* are the perfect scripture to shed light on Amma's meaning of the word śhraddhā.

***

From childhood we have been told to concentrate, but we have never been taught to concentrate. To teach us about this, the *Yōga Sūtras* first explain the nature of the mind.

The mind is structured in such a way that we can only be aware of one thought at a time. It is like a chair on which only one person can sit at a time. As soon as that person gets up, another one can take his or her place. In this way, many different thoughts can arise and subside in the mind within seconds. We think about the amazing inauguration of Kamala Harris; then about the Covid-19 vaccine; from there to the vaccine conspiracy theory, that Kanye West thinks Bill Gates has Dr. Fauci implanting us all with liquid chips so that the lizard people can track us and send our geo-location to the aliens in space and then aaaahhhh! More or less, everyone knows about this nature of the mind.

Commenting on the Yōga Sūtras, sage Vyāsa describes this aspect of mind as: *sarvārthatā chitta dharmaḥ* – 'Distraction is the nature of the mind.' Learning this, we may think, "Oh, well! I guess this is just the mind's nature. There is no hope." But to our relief, a second nature of the mind is revealed to us: ēkāgratāpi *chitta dharmaḥ* – 'One-pointedness is also the nature of the mind.' This second nature of mind is the foundation for any success.

How do we maintain śhraddhā, and prevent other thoughts from coming in? In India, if you go to a train station to purchase a ticket, people stand in such a tight queue that no one from outside the queue can squeeze in. If we want to focus on something, then our thoughts should also come in such a tight queue.

A good example of this is when we repeat the 'Meditation on Amma' prayer, reflecting on each part of it, one phrase at a time:

> *dhyāyāmō – we meditate on the one,*
> *dhavalāvaguṇṭhanavatīm – her head covered with a white sāri,*
> *tējōmayīm – who is effulgent,*
> *naiṣhṭikīm – who is ever established in truth,*
> *snigdhāpāṅga vilōkinīm – who glances with loving eyes.*

Et cetera.

Therefore, concentration doesn't mean just repeating a single thought. It means we should be able to focus on one object – in this case Amma – by sending a continuous stream of different thoughts towards her, creating that tight queue.

In yōga this is called *nirōdha* (restraint). Nirodha is achieved not by trying to push unwanted thoughts down or out of the way, but by ēkāgrata – by maintaining thoughts that are in line with our chosen subject of focus.

Now it becomes even more interesting. Any thought that we repeatedly entertain becomes stronger. Once repeated, it will resurface. When it resurfaces again and again, these thoughts form our *saṁskāras* – our habitual mental tendencies.

Whether we cultivate positive thoughts that produce positive saṁskāras, or we cultivate negative thoughts producing negative saṁskāras is up to us. To succeed in mental restraint, all we need is practice. As Lord Kṛiṣhṇa says in Chapter 6, verse 35 of the *Bhagavad Gītā:*

> *asaṁśhayaṁ mahā-bāhō manō durnigrahaṁ chalam*
> *abhyāsēna tu kauntēya vairāgyēṇa cha gṛihyatē*
> 'Undoubtedly, O mighty-armed Arjuna, the mind is difficult to control and restless; but by practice and by dispassion, it may be restrained.'

Practice starts with *dhāraṇā* (concentration). Chapter 3, verse 1 of the *Yōga Sūtras* defines dhāraṇā as:

> *dēśhabandhaśhchittasya dhāraṇā*
> 'Focusing on a particular point is dhāraṇā.'

When Amma tells us during guided meditation to imagine a triangle on our forehead and focus on the self-luminous white pearl, that is dhāraṇā.

The next step is *dhyānam.*

Yōga Sūtras Chapter 3, verse 2 states:

> *tatra pratyayaikatānatā dhyānam*
> 'An unbroken flow of knowledge toward that object is dhyānam.'

The sage Vyāsa in his commentary on this sūtra explains it further as:

> 'Dhyānam is a constant flow of similar thoughts towards the object of meditation.'

Amma always tells us, our practice of yōga shouldn't stop after we get up from meditation. It should continue throughout the day. Since yōga means "one-pointedness," any action that we perform with utmost śhraddhā becomes yōga. Like this, our *archana* (repetition of divine names) becomes yōga, our *bhajans* (devotional singing) become yōga and our work becomes yōga.

***

For many years, I was involved in serving the āśhram food. At that time, the kitchen was where the *brahmachāriṇī's* dining hall is at present. We had to transfer the food out of big cooking pots into smaller serving vessels, bring them to the dining hall, serve everyone, and then bring the vessels back to the kitchen for washing.

To avoid wasting food, we were supposed to scrape all the leftover food out first. One night when we had just closed the serving line, and had brought all the pots back to the kitchen, Amma suddenly appeared inside the kitchen. She was on a mission. She went straight to the washing area and inspected all the pots we had just placed there. Many of them contained small portions of leftover rice.

Amma started to slowly and carefully clean out all the pots with her hand, and collect all the rice onto a plate. When she was done, she had a heaping plate of rice. She handed the plate to me and said, "Akshaya! Ninte śhraddhā evide?" – "Where is your alertness? There are people living in this world that don't have food, and you are wasting it here!"

From this experience on, I tried my very best to focus on my sēvā with maximum śhraddhā. Many times I failed, but sometimes I succeeded.

During Amma's 2019 U.S. Tour, at one of the chai stops, a small boy asked Amma if we could have pizza. Amma agreed, and instructed me to have pizzas ready for when we arrived in Boston.

Making pizza for 400 people was a big challenge, and I put maximum śhraddhā into it. While the final evening program was going on in the ballroom of the hotel in New York, we were working hard to prepare and pre-bake about fifty huge pizzas. We needed to cool them down, pack them, and load them into our kitchen van.

The minute the program ended, we jumped in our van and raced to Boston. Upon reaching the hotel there, we had to unload everything; heat up the pizzas; make french fries; load all the food into warmers; and then transport everything to the Boston āśhram. All this had to happen before Amma came out for group meditation with the staff.

Along with the pizzas, we had prepared french fries, ice cream, and even provided colorful candy topping for the ice cream. Yum! Amazingly, everything had arrived in time, and everything was ready. I was feeling pretty proud of myself.

However, when Amma started serving the food, she called me over to her. She was quite upset, saying, "Why did you make all this food? I only asked you to make pizza. Don't you know that there should be a balanced diet? How can you serve only junk food? There should be some variety – some vegetables, something with vitamins. You should eat to nourish your body, not to indulge. Only by renouncing the taste of the tongue can you experience the blissful taste of the Self."

I stood there with my head bowed low. Even though I had been focused and did my best, my efforts failed. Even though I had practiced śhraddhā, things went wrong. I had not listened to and understood Amma's words properly.

In Sanskrit, listening is called śhravaṇam. It is a very essential quality. Śhravaṇam is not mere listening, but also understanding and imbibing the teaching. Amma makes a gesture pointing from the ear to the heart when she says śhravaṇam. So, in addition to śhraddhā, we need to do śhravaṇam. This proper understanding of the Guru's words can be difficult. Sometimes we need to be able to read between the lines to grasp the true meaning.

***

On March 1st of 2020, I went for *darśhan.* I told Amma that I was going to Europe to get my visa renewed, and to work for three weeks. Amma said, "Oh! There are also Covid-19 cases in Germany." I replied that I was not going to be in Germany, as the three-week job I had committed to doing was in Switzerland.

Amma asked when my visa would expire. I said in two days. Amma gave me some *prasād*[1] candy, and I left. I could see that Amma was concerned, but since I was only planning to be away for twenty-six days, I thought everything would be fine. Little did I know that those twenty-six days would turn into 260 days.

While I was stuck in Europe, I received a lot of support from my parents, friends, and devotees. They generously shared their homes with me, and I feel very grateful to them. However, wherever I stayed, after a few weeks a feeling of sadness and despair would come over me. Amritapuri is my home, and I have

[1] A blessed offering or gift from a holy person or temple, often in the form of food.

never stayed away from Amma for more than a month at a time since I became a resident in 1996.

At the end of every month, I would check the Indian Foreign Ministry website, looking for any signs of change in entry policy, and at the end of every month, I would get more depressed. On March 31st 2020 it went from Lockdown 1.0 to Lockdown 2.0. By April 30th, it had gone from lockdown 2.0 to Lockdown 3.0, and so on.

The only place I felt any real happiness and contentment was when I spent time in nature. I had a small tent and stove, and started hiking through the Alps. Altogether I spent about three months walking through the German, Austrian, Italian, Swiss, and French mountains.

I saw some wonderful scenery and amazing wildlife. Many years ago, Amma told me that to calm my mind I should look at the flowers; look at the moon. So, the flowers and the moon became my meditation. It is an effortless way to practice dhāraṇā and dhyānam.

I would look at the moon, and then console myself that it is the same moon shining in Amritapuri on Amma as well. I know that many people who are listening to this online today are still stuck physically away from Amma. My heart knows your pain, and as looking at and thinking about the moon in this way brought me some consolation and peace during my ten months locked away from Amma, I recommend trying this same practice. We can all take Amma's advice, "Look at the flowers; look at the moon."

I loved traveling over the high mountain passes that were still covered in snow. Snow makes everything feel pure and magical, like stepping into another world. I felt small and humble hiking between mountains that towered thousands of feet above me, with majestic glaciers below my feet. I sometimes hiked for days without seeing any other person, yet I never felt lonely. I felt like I was walking on Dēvī's (Divine Mother's) lap or on the palm of God's hand.

The only company I had was my *mantra*. Sometimes I chanted the *mahāmṛityuñjaya mantra*,[2] imagining Amma being with me in Śhiva *Bhāva* (assuming the mood and dress of Śhiva) with her hair tied up in a top knot, and yellow prayer shawl tied together behind her neck.

Once when I was walking through Switzerland, I had to cross a big mountain range. The most challenging section to cross was the 'Nollen Ice Cliff.' The light-weight crampons I wore on my shoes weren't biting into the ice. So I had to start cutting small steps with my ice pick to be able to place my feet and hands. I would cut the handhold, cut the foothold, then hit the ice pick as hard as I could into the ice above my head and pull myself up, then repeat the process.

I didn't even notice the passing of time. Only when I reached the top, did I realize that two hours had passed. Though the task was extremely simple and repetitive, I was able to focus on it for more than two hours. I was able to do so because I knew that if I made a mistake, it could be my last. I had so much śhraddhā during that climb that there was absolutely no space for fear or other negative thoughts to jump in the queue.

Later I wondered, why can't I always have such śhraddhā? The truth is, even just sitting here, our next breath could be our last. We could catch Covid; we could die in a car accident on our next journey; we could die of a heart attack simply walking down the stairs. When Amma says things like this, perhaps we think it is just some story Amma makes up to scare us. No. All of us know that this can and does happen.

---

[2] Famous mantra of Lord Śhiva, conqueror of death.

Amma gives the example of a clock that goes tick-tock, tick-tock. With every tick and every tock, death is moving one step closer. If you cannot hear the clock, put your hand on your heart. With every beat Death is coming one step closer, and we have no idea how many beats we have left before we meet him. The future is not in our hands; the only guarantee we have is this moment now.

In Amma's bhajan *'Kāḷī Mahēśhvariyē,'* it says:

> *kāḷī-mahēśhvariyē jaganmātē kaitozhām ende ammē*
> *ōrō nimiṣham eṇṇi-inchiñchāyi chattu tulayuvōril*
> *hanta ñānum tulayum enna chinta nalkāttorammē tozhām*
> 'I bow down to you Divine Mother, who hides from us the thought, Oh, I too will die, even though I see people dying all around constantly.'

On the day I climbed the ice wall, I realized what a huge difference it makes when we live with full śhraddhā. I tapped into a potential that is usually hidden, and when I went to sleep that night, I knew that I had given my best. But how many times have I been able to feel that way in my day-to-day life? That potential is always inside us, but for whatever reason, we are not able to invoke it.

The sands of time are running through our fingers, and many times I feel like I'm merely crawling through life – not even attempting to climb the mountains in my way. Why am I unable to do my best while chanting archana? Why am I unable to give my best during śhāstra (scripture) class? Why am I unable to be my best while performing my work?

My point is not that we should be *the* best, but we should be *our* best. Who in this room can say that they give their very best in every situation? Well... I know only one person.

Not only today but everyday throughout her entire life, Amma gives her best. Her life is like a documentary on śhraddhā. Amma shows us through her example what living in the present truly means.

Every evening in the mountains, I sat in my tent, turned on my headlamp, and meticulously planned the next day. I would check the map: how much distance do I have to cover? How difficult is the terrain? Is there any danger of rockslide or avalanche? How is the weather going to be? Et cetera.

Amma says that in spiritual life, we need to do the same thing. We need to be aware of what we want to achieve. What are my goals in life? What are my goals for this month? What is my goal for today?

It is śhravaṇam that helps us to define these goals, and śhraddhā that helps us to achieve them. While śhravaṇam gives us direction, śhraddhā is the engine that propels the rocket of our life forward. Śhraddhā and śhravaṇam go hand in hand. Śhraddhā and śhravaṇam are what enable us to truly "live in the present moment." They in fact are what allow us to truly understand the meaning of carpe diem.

That meaning is: this moment is invaluably precious. We must use it to realize our true nature. Carpe diem! Seize the day! Ī nimiśham mātrame nammaḷude kaiyyil ullu!

3

Grace in my Life

Dr. Shyamasundaran – India

Lord Kṛiṣhṇa and his warrior-disciple Arjuna were once walking along a riverbank. Kṛiṣhṇa asked Arjuna, "Who is the greatest warrior in this world?" Without hesitation, Arjuna replied, "I am!" Hearing Arjuna's response, Kṛiṣhṇa was taken aback and said, "How can you be so egoistic about your abilities?"

Arjuna replied, "Why not *Bhagavān* (Lord)? What stops me from being the greatest warrior when I am an instrument in your hands?" Here, Arjuna recognized Kṛiṣhṇa's divinity and was aware of how fortunate he was. In my case, for a long time, I remained ignorant of the fortunes and opportunities I had received throughout life. It took Amma to finally open my eyes to them.

Many flowers are used for worship in our āśhram every day. Some really lucky flowers are offered for the evening ārati[3] for which Amma is physically present. Those flowers ultimately make it to Amma's holy feet.

Also, when the prasād lunch plates are passed via Amma's hands during Tuesday's prasād-day program, how lucky those plates are to be experiencing Amma's divine touch. In both instances, neither the flowers nor the plates are aware of their great fortune.

I think in my case, I am both one of the lunch plates, as well as one of those luckiest of flowers, because though I have not made much effort, and until recently was unaware of my great

---

3 Ārati is a traditional ritual involving the waving of a lighted lamp to the Guru or deity usually done towards the end of *pūjā* or worship.

fortune, our all-knowing Amma has been most generous in choosing me as one of her sons, giving me the opportunity to taste eternal bliss.

Our family has known Amma since I was a child, and I've received her darśhan many times. I also attended *bhajans* (devotional songs), *satsangs* (spiritual discourses), *sēvā* (selfless service), etc., but I never realized how precious those moments were, and I went through all those experiences mechanically.

I took all such experiences as normal, and mostly just followed what others did. I didn't have a strong bond with Amma... I mean the bond from my side. I had no idea how to pray to Amma from the depths of my heart, and I never cried for Amma. Well, perhaps I did during difficult situations, but I never cried just for Amma without some other reason. Amma has chosen me and lavished her love on me despite all of this.

***

The topic of my satsang is *kṛipā* — grace — in my life.

To obtain *Gurukṛipā* (Guru's grace) we need three things:

- The seeker must be a devotee of the Guru.
- The seeker should work in service of the Guru.
- The seeker should be dedicated to a spiritual path.

The Guru bestows grace by intention, or simply by the power of his presence.

Grace is like the fragrance of a flower. One cannot explain it; it can only be experienced. As Amma says, "One cannot experience the sweetness of honey just by licking the word 'honey' written on a piece of paper. To experience honey, you must taste honey."

Therefore, it's not enough just to think about or talk about grace. Only when we directly experience it will we have an understanding of what it is. If we have a stuffy nose, the fragrance of a flower does not attract us. In the same way, if we are too full of ego, we may miss the grace flowing toward us.

In reality, we are always immersed in grace. We need to develop the ability to draw on it; develop the ability to see the grace in everything and in every experience, be it positive or negative.

Amma often says that fragrant lotuses bloom due to the sustenance they draw from the mud below. I was ignorant about the grace in my life and was living according to my *vāsanās,* the latent tendencies of my mind. However, underneath it all, Amma has always been, and continues to be the guiding light in my life. Hence, I consider her presence itself to be a tremendous source of grace and love.

I remember an incident in my life that shows how I experienced Amma's grace in disguise:

After I graduated high school from Amrita Vidyalayam, Kodungallur, I wanted to continue my higher education at one of Amma's educational institutions as well. At the same time, I had a long-cherished desire to stay in the āśhram. I thought that if I secured a place at Amma's Āyurvēda[4] college here at *Amritapuri,* I could live in the āśhram.

Unfortunately that didn't happen, and I had to go to Karnataka to complete my Bachelor of Ayurvedic Medicine and Surgery (BAMS) and Doctor of Medicine (MD) degrees. During that time, Amma provided her guidance whenever I came to receive her *darśhan.* After I got my MD, I thought I might be able to work at Amma's Āyurvēda college, and even Amma agreed that I should apply for a job there.

I envisioned finally living in the āśhram, and that I'd be able to take part in Amma's tours; cherish lovely moments with Amma like going for "room darśhans," which are special private

---

[4] Ancient Indian system of medicine.

darśhans for āśhram residents; swim with her in the swimming pool; witness Amma's *masālā dōsā*[5] dinner celebrations; and so on...

As fate would have it, at that time, there was no opening for someone with my specialization, with no certainty as to when a position would open up! With no other choice, I went to Gujarat to work at an Āyurvēda medical college there. Fifteen days later, I got a call from Amma's Āyurvēda college saying that a position had just become available!

Unfortunately, the college in Gujarat wouldn't allow me to break my contract so soon after joining, so I missed a golden opportunity! I felt very sad about this, but had no choice but to continue working in Gujarat.

After working there for about a year and a half, the director of the institute called me to his office, threatening to fire me, as someone had complained about me not doing my work. This shocked me as I had good relations with all my colleagues, and I had been working to the best of my ability. I got angry, and strongly responded saying, "I quit!" When I reflect on this, I am indeed astounded at how I reacted. I'm not usually like that — to reply so sharply. I don't know what came over me. Leaving his office, I was at a loss at what to do.

I composed myself, called Swāmī Śhankarāmṛtānandajī , the director of Amma's Āyurvēda college, and told him about my decision to resign. I was astonished when he offered me a position at the college right there and then! My happiness knew no bounds! Finally I was able to move to Amritapuri.

Looking back on this experience, there was no reason for such an incident to happen the way it did. I realize now that Amma created the entire situation to bring me back home.

---

[5] A typical south Indian savory pancake with filling.

I also realize that I was initially attached to my choices. Only when I let go and accepted whatever result may come, did I receive Amma's grace. When I opened my closed doors, Amma's grace which was already there, flooded in.

Like Arjuna on the battlefield, I was also confused and was left with no choice but to surrender to Amma. By surrendering, I became an instrument in my beloved Amma's hand. As Kṛiṣhṇa says to Arjuna in the *Bhagavad Gītā* Chapter 11, verse 33:

> *nimitta-mātraṁ bhava savya-sāchin*
> 'O expert archer, become only an instrument.'

However, I feel there is a difference between my case and Arjuna's. Kṛiṣhṇa addresses Arjuna as '*savyasāchin*,' which means 'expert archer.' On the other hand, I am no 'life expert,' so Amma had to smooth out my sharp edges by making me face challenges in life as they came, and to learn from experiences that I otherwise would have totally missed.

Though still not a complete 'expert,' Amma has shown me the way to become one. When we become a compliant instrument in Amma's hands — letting go of attachment to our choices — Amma is able to guide us to the state of 'savyasāchin.' I pray to Amma for many such opportunities to learn to become her true instrument. The path to happiness is already laid out for each of us. It is up to us to choose when we take that path, what we want to learn from it, and how eager we are to reach the goal.

The *Charaka Saṁhitā*[6] says in the *Sūtrasthānam*, Chapter 9, verses 24 and 26:

> *śhāstraṁ jyōtiḥ prakāśhārthaṁ darśhanaṁ buddhirātmanaḥ*
> *tābhyāṁ bhiṣhak suyuktābhyāṁ chikitsannāparādhyati*

---

[6] An ancient Sanskrit text that comprehensively covers the principles and practices of Ayurvedic medicine.

> 'The śhāstra (scripture) is like a lantern and the buddhi (intellect) is like the eye. When a vaidya (medical doctor) is equipped with both of these, he never fails in his treatment.'
>
> *maitrī kāruṇyamārtēṣhu śhakyē prītirupēkṣhaṇam*
> *prakṛitisthēṣhu bhūtēṣhu vaidyavṛittiśhchaturvidhēti*
> 'The vaidya should possess [some indispensable qualities like] *maitrī* (friendliness), kāruṇya (compassion), love towards patients, and discernment in judgment. Only then, will he succeed in his profession.'

Thus, knowledge of the scriptures is very much required for a vaidya to work in the right way. This is known as śhāstra *kṛipā* (grace of the scriptures).

Āyurvēda is not merely the oldest medical science in the world, but also a shāstra that has been passed down through generations by a great lineage of *ṛiṣhis.*[7] Āyurvēda focuses on the attainment and maintenance of good health, thereby supporting the ultimate goal of life — Self realization. Āyurvēda's practices are rooted in virtues, and it believes that only through such a wholesome approach can one heal others.

I remember an experience related to this:

One night in 2012 when I was working the night shift at a 350-bed hospital, it was a very busy night and all the beds were full. I had to attend to many patients. Among them was a middle-aged lady who repeatedly called me for help. She suffered from chronic insomnia. The other night-duty doctors found her difficult, because she repeatedly called for them throughout the night, always asking for something more to help her sleep.

She was given many types of medication and therapies, but nothing seemed to work very well. I felt sorry for her condition

[7] Sages or seers to whom mantras are revealed in deep meditation.

and wanted to find some way to help her get some sleep. On the other hand, I also felt sorry for myself, as many types of medications had already been administered, and now it was my turn to do something... I was at a loss as to what to try!

I knew that if I didn't succeed, she would constantly call me away from attending to other patients, so it was a difficult situation. Finally, I had an idea. I chose a medicine that was much milder in strength than the ones she was currently taking, as the other doctors had already exhausted the usual list of medicines and treatments used to treat her problem. I went over to the patient, held the medicine in my hand, closed my eyes and prayed to Amma. I then handed it to her and told her to take it. She also prayed before taking the medicine.

I then told her to go back to bed, and confidently stated that she would be asleep within fifteen to twenty minutes. She did as I told her, and I left her room with fingers crossed. I attended to some other patients, and by early morning I still hadn't heard from her. I was surprised and curious to see if my 'magic pill' had worked.

I quietly peeked through the door of her room and there she was, sleeping like a baby! I felt very happy and thanked Amma for this amazing result. I now realize who gave me the confidence to tell her so assuredly that she would quickly fall asleep. The next day when the patient's consulting physician came to do his rounds, she told him that she had slept very peacefully that night for the first time in many months!

Her doctor was very curious to know what magic pill I had given her. When he heard what it was, he and everyone else on the floor were surprised, because it was a very mild and simple medicine. From then on, her doctor kept that medicine as part of her prescription, and she continued sleeping very well.

I narrate this story not to boast about how clever I was, but to point out that this entire situation was nothing but Amma's *līlā* (divine play).

Amma says that it is not enough to only trust in a doctor, or take the prescribed medicine to overcome a disease. Along with that, one must also follow *pathyam* — a proper regimen of food and lifestyle suitable to treating the disease. However, what I learned from this experience is that along with all these, divine grace is most essential.

Amma says, "Compassion resides within everyone, but it is difficult to experience it, and express it in all our actions. We must turn inwards to search deep within ourselves if we want to bring peace to the external world. First, our inner world needs to be at peace."

When I had the intense desire to help that patient, by inwardly tuning-in to Amma she made me her instrument, reaching out with compassion, and giving me a taste of inner peace and satisfaction at the same time.

***

I'd also like to relate an experience I had when I felt Amma's grace in the form of Saraswatī Dēvī's[8] blessing:

When I was in high school at Amrita Vidyalayam, there was a time when I was struggling with my studies. I didn't do well in tests even after putting in a lot of effort, and I was unhappy about it.

Journaling was part of the school curriculum. We would write daily in our diaries, and submit what we'd written to Swāminī Gurupriyāmṛita Prāṇajī. She would personally read all of them and make comments or suggestions about what we'd written. We were free to write about anything. Once, I wrote about the

---

[8] Goddess of learning and the arts.

difficulty I was having of not being able to concentrate or do well in exams.

In reply, Swāminī told me to keep trying, and surprisingly, she added that I should help take care of the school's cows! I was delighted by this because I love cows. At Amrita Vidyalayam, we lived by a very strict timetable. Taking care of the cows had to be done between classes, meals, and our spiritual practices. Though we got extra credit for doing it, it was hard work.

We had to clean the cowshed, bathe the cows, take them out to pasture to graze, feed them, etc. I loved doing cow sēvā. Looking back, I realize now that cow sēvā helped solve many of my problems. It wasn't the total reason, but once I started doing this sēvā, I was indeed able to study better, and perform better at exams. Saraswatī's blessing in this way was a new lesson for me!

When we do our actions with *satbhāva* — the right attitude, with utmost sincerity, and accept whatever results may come with *prasāda buddhi* — accepting whatever happens as God's will, it becomes *karma yōga* (the yōga or path of selfless action). It helps us evolve. Studies also say that taking care of cows reduces stress and increases positive thinking, it has become a therapy!

I bow down to all the *brahmachāriṇī* school teachers at Amrita Vidyalayam who took care of us like we were their own children, and instilled moral values in us. I am indeed indebted to them.

Another type of grace is called ātmā *kṛipā* (Self grace). While I was in Gujarat, I had an unusual experience concerning this Self grace. Within a month's time, I witnessed three traffic accidents. Each time, there were only a few other people around, and I ran to assist the victims. For each accident, I had to initiate the rescue response and call for an ambulance.

Others joined in to help once I started attending to the victims. In two of the incidents, by Amma's grace, all of the victims were saved. I felt strongly that I was an instrument used to help in those dire situations, and I learned precious lessons. First, it made me understand how fragile and uncertain life is. Secondly, I learned that anyone may get chances in life to become an instrument, but it is up to each of us to act first, thereby drawing God's grace to us. Perhaps this is what Amma means by ātmā kṛipā or *svayam kṛipā* — Self grace or one's own grace.

***

Amma's grace also entered my life in the form of my parents. I am lucky to have such lovely parents, and I owe them a lot. My father is a refined person and very accommodating in nature. My mother has deep faith and love for Amma. She was the first of our family to move to Amritapuri. She adheres strictly to the āśhram schedule, and has inspired me to be punctual and systematic in life.

***

I think I was in the third or fourth grade when we first met Amma. We were living in Bangalore then, and though Amma's program there was very crowded, we found a place to sit, and I watched Amma as she sang bhajans. Later, we stood in a long queue and got darśhan. After that, we saw Amma whenever she came to Bangalore.

There was no *Brahmasthānam*[9] temple or Amrita Vidyalayam school in Bangalore at that time. We attended bhajan gatherings at other devotee homes, and visited Amritapuri once a year.

On one such visit, we met an older devotee, Sri. Padmanabhan Achan (lovingly called Pappettan), who recommended that I attend Amrita Vidyalayam in Kodungallur. His suggestion

---

[9] Literally 'Abode of Brahman,' Amma's unique consecrated temples in India and Mauritius.

marked a significant change in our lives and deepened my relationship with Amma. This is how Amma brought me closer to her.

The Covid lockdown in the āśhram proved to be an excellent experience for me. Before Covid, even though I was living in the āśhram, I hadn't had a chance to be involved much with the various activities going on there. I just went back and forth from the āśhram to my work at the Āyurvēda college. However, the pandemic afforded me many opportunities to be actively involved in āśhram sēvā, and I enjoyed doing it.

I got to know many other āśhram residents through these sēvā opportunities, and we all became like family. I thank Amma for these opportunities and for being able to connect with other āśhramites. By Amma's grace, we now have a solid team of volunteers involved in various sēvā activities.

***

I had another experience of grace in my life that I'd like to share:

Once during a group darśhan with other āśhram residents during the lockdown, I got to sit very close to Amma. Amma was enquiring about the health of the āśhramites and the Covid precautions being taken.

Amma looked right into my eyes and seemed to be speaking directly to me the whole time. I felt as though Amma was addressing everyone through me. It made me think about how Yaśhōdā may have felt when she saw the universe in baby Kṛiṣhṇa's mouth; or how Arjuna might have felt when he saw Kṛiṣhṇa's universal form; or how Śhabarī might have felt when she finally met Lord Rāma.

Thank you Amma for that memorable experience. I had never had the opportunity before then to be in Amma's presence for so long.

In Chapter 9, verse 22 of the *Bhagavad Gītā*, Lord Kṛishṇa says:

ananyāśhchintayantō māṁ yē janāḥ paryupāsatē
tēṣhām nityābhiyuktānāṁ yōgakṣhēmaṁ vahāmyaham
'For those who always think of me, worship me, and are ever absorbed in me, I provide whatever they lack and preserve what they already possess.'

If we surrender to the divine in the form of our Guru, she will guide our life decisions, help alleviate our problems, and share in our happiness.

Amma has taken care of all the details of my life. Amma looked for a marriage partner for me for a long time, and I thought I was willing to marry whomever Amma chose. However, each time a proposal came, I found myself being judgmental. I was holding on to my preferences, and had not surrendered to Amma in this matter. I realized how difficult it can be to trust in Amma's will; how difficult it can be to surrender to Amma! Ultimately, our compassionate Amma came down to my level and fulfilled all my desires. I now have a very loving and understanding wife. Amma, thank you for your infinite grace.

I'll conclude with a short prayer in Hindi:

har karm mērā hē prabhū
pūjā tērī ban jāyē
kadam baḍhe nit rāḥ par
tujh se milan karāyē
'Let every action of mine become an offering to you, may I march towards you and merge in you.'

Amma, may everyone become more 'grace sensitive,' and learn to take things positively so that everyone's hearts open, and we all invoke that infinite kṛipā — the grace in which we eternally dwell.

4

Amma: Our Divine Lifeguard

Rasya – USA

Many years ago, we were sitting in an airport with Amma at the end of a tour. She was about to go back to India and those of us not going with her were feeling really sad. Amma sat there, without speaking, lovingly gazing at each one of us. Someone sitting near me broke the silence, "I miss you so much when you are gone Amma, and sometimes I have to admit that I just don't feel you are with me."

Amma reached out and took the young man's hand. She said, "In truth, Amma cannot ever be separated from her children, but it is you who have to wake up to the reality of this oneness." Maybe knowing that most of us were not ready to digest this *advaitic* (non-dual) truth she continued to explain, "Take it as a practice."

She continued, "Whatever you are doing, imagine that Amma is there next to you, doing it with you. Think: What would Amma do? What would Amma say? Try to see the world through Amma's eyes. Remembering her like this, know that Amma is always with you as you go through each moment of life." Looking around at us, everyone's eyes filled with tears...Amma added softly, "How can I *not* be with you?"

Lord Kṛiṣhṇa (God incarnate) says the same thing in Chapter 6, verse 30 of the *Bhagavad Gītā*:

yō māṁ paśhyati sarvatra sarvaṁ cha mayi paśhyati
tasyāhaṁ na praṇaśhyāmi sa cha mē na praṇaśhyati

> 'For those who see me everywhere and see all things in me, I am never lost, nor are they ever lost to me.'

Amma's advice that day in the airport and this verse are like an invitation to see the divine in all experiences of life. Amma has said that there isn't a spiritual life (sitting in front of our altar) and a separate worldly life (like going to work). There is only one life. If we understand this then every event in our life can become our practice and our path to God.

***

I met Amma in 1987 when I was fifteen-years old. But actually, the how-I-met-Amma story starts twenty years earlier, before I was born.

In the mid 1960's my mom came to India to study philosophy at Madras University and at the same time became a student of haṭha yōga with the yōga master Kṛiṣhṇamāchārya. It was there that she met my dad, a wandering hippie searching for the meaning of life. For several years my parents traveled back and forth from India to the U.S., and whenever my mom returned to America, she always taught yōga.

One of my mom's eighteen-year-old yōga students was thirsty for everything she had to offer in her classes. My mom introduced this young man to *Sanātana Dharma,*[10] and gave him his first copy of the *Bhagavad Gītā* which they would discuss after class. She told him, "You should go to India; you would make a great monk." Some of you will recognize this young man's name — Neal Rosner. Neal did make his way to India, and eventually became one of Amma's first western disciples, now Swāmī Paramātmānanda Puri.

---

[10] The 'eternal law or principle.' The original name of Hinduism.

When Amma's First World Tour was being planned, Nealu Swāmī (as he was called then) asked my parents if they would help host Amma's program. They agreed. Amma came to the U.S. in May 1987, and literally arrived at my doorstep.

Amma and the *swāmīs* stayed in our house in the Wisconsin countryside on that first tour. Amma gave the morning *darśhan* in our living room. Our farm also had a big traditional red barn standing empty.

Since Amma was scheduled to give *Dēvī Bhāva*[11] *darśhan* at the farm, and the living room was already full during the regular darśhan programs, we had to figure out a bigger space for the program. It was decided that we would use the big empty barn.

It was not a place fit to receive the Queen of the Universe, but all Amma wanted was a place to receive her children. Mom and dad took out all the Indian cloth and wall hangings they had brought from their last trip to India, and with many people's help, fashioned a Dēvī Bhāva temple inside the barn.

That night the sleepy country road which was normally empty, was lined with cars in both directions for a kilometer. The barn was full, and people were also happily sitting on the green grass under the stars.

When talking about me, Amma told my mom that first year, "Thank you for raising her." Poor Amma is still trying to finish off the job...this is one big baby!

Each year Amma came to the U.S., I became more and more attached to her. Early on I bought a photo of Amma and kept it in my locker at school. During exams she traveled with me in my backpack from classroom to classroom. During these moments of tension I knew I wasn't alone.

---

[11] 'The divine mood of Dēvī' – an occasion when Amma reveals her oneness with the Divine Mother.

I finished high school, and my photo of Amma and I went off to college to study acting. I didn't make the transition to college well, and I realized that this was not at all the life that I wanted. I would sit on my bed in the dorm and cry to Amma's photo, "Amma please help me!"

During Amma's next tour, I asked her about moving into the San Ramon āśhram (called M.A. Center). She said yes, and that I needed to finish college. So I enrolled in university in California to study education, and moved into M.A. Center in August 1990. I was eighteen. And guess who was the swāmī in residence? Nealu Swāmī! When he was eighteen my mother had played such an instrumental role in his spiritual journey, and now here I was eighteen, and under his care. Each day we had scripture class and *bhajans* with the future Swāmī Paramātmānandajī!

Little did I know that I would live and grow at M.A. Center for over 20 years!

***

I began to travel with Amma on the western tours, and visited Amritapuri for the first time in 1992. A whole new world opened for me. Those memories are treasures: darśhan in the thatched hut; watching old spiritual movies at night with Amma in the garden beneath her room; learning how to make garlands from *Acchamma,* Amma's grandmother, in the temple every Dēvī Bhāva day. She would call me over and flash me her big toothless smile, gesture for me to sit next to her, and hand me the thread...no words exchanged or needed.

Her garlands were a tradition: She was always the first one in line for darśhan. I remember her small form, bent over with age, reaching up to be able to get the *mālā* (garland) over Amma's crown, and Amma bending forward to receive it.

At the end of one of my visits to India, Amma told me to go back and get my Master's degree. I told Amma I was afraid of going back to America, going back to school, and losing focus on my spiritual life. She looked at me with such kindness and said, "Amma knows that it is very difficult to not be affected by the pulls of the world." Then fixing her eyes on me with a mischievous smile, she slowly tied the end of her sāri to the end of my sāri so we were connected, and said, "Don't worry daughter, Amma will never let you drown."

One thing about me is that I can't swim. My swimming education ended abruptly when I was eight. I refused to jump in the water, so the swimming instructor pushed me into the pool to prove to me that I wouldn't sink. Well, she was wrong. I sank to the bottom...And so began my life long fear of water. Going back to school in America was like me trying to swim in deep water with choppy waves, so Amma's words were my lifeboat. Her words "Amma will never let you drown" gradually awoke an inner confidence in me.

I returned to school and threw myself into *sēvā* (selfless service) at M.A. Center. I feel strongly that it was the magic of sēvā that helped create a deep bond with Amma even though I was so often away from her physically.

Amma was saying, "You want to be happy? Then give love and attention to others." She told me once, "Don't be like a beggar for love with upturned hands, instead be someone who gives love, hands downturned."

***

Amma brought Haran, my husband, into my life early on, and we grew up together in the āśhram. In 2011, we asked Amma about moving from the heavenly battlefield of M.A. Center to Amritapuri. We got a happy head nod and a smiling, "OK!" Amma welcomed us here into the big Amritapuri family with so much kindness and care.

Amma sometimes describes the Guru as a master sculptor who brings out the divine form inherent in rock. Amma doesn't need to sit and personally chisel away at each one of us. A lot of the Guru's work is done by simply putting us all together, and we chip away at each other's rough edges for her! All of us sharp stones, full of likes and dislikes, are put in one container knocking against each other until we become smooth and polished, and our true inner beauty comes out... then Voila! The Guru's rock tumbler has done its job. This is one of Amma's favorite metaphors when talking about the spiritual process.

Knocking into each other's likes and dislikes can be uncomfortable, but it becomes a perfect vehicle for transformation if we use it to become more aware.

To explain further, let me present a small drama:

This play is called 'The Amritapuri Rock Tumbler,' and contains lots of different kinds of 'Ōm *Namaḥ* Śhivāyas'[12] that one might hear in a day in the āśhram.

Just imagine:

I rush out of my room, and arrive quite late to my sēvā hoping no one will notice, but my supervisor spots me right away and scolds me in front of everyone, "Namaḥ Śhivāya, Rasya you're late again!" "Namaḥ Śhivāya!" (It wasn't my fault!) After sēvā, I go to the café for a nice piece of chocolate cake.

Just before taking my first bite, I get distracted for a moment and the next thing I know someone is shouting "Namaḥ Śhivaay-ya!!!" I turn to see my cake flying away, in the beak of a very happy crow. I head back to my flat and wait in a long line for the elevator. Finally, it's my turn. As I'm about to step inside,

---

[12] Literally, 'I bow to Śhiva the supreme truth,' often used as a greeting in the āśhram.

someone carrying large boxes pushes ahead of me, saying "Step aside! sēvā – sēvā – Namaḥ Śhivāya, Namaḥ Śhivāya!" As the elevator doors close in front of my nose, they smile and wave, "Thank you! Namaḥ Śhivāya!" (Achh, I give up!) I go to the stage to sit with Amma for a little while for some peace. I am seated behind a very tall person. They are swaying back and forth to the beat of the bhajans... Ōm Namaḥ Śhivāya!

When I adjust so that I can finally see a bit of Amma's head, the stage monitor comes up so sweetly, "Namaḥ Śhivāya? Please give your space to someone else now. Namaḥ Śhivāya!"

I get up, and as I leave the hall the crow pays me another visit...he returns my cake, this time in liquid form! "Namaḥ Śhivāya!"

Exhausted and frustrated I start to blame others. Why can't I find any peace around here? What is wrong with all of these people?

But then I remember an example Amma tells, about the shopkeeper who at the end of each day, takes careful inventory of what he has sold, and counts up his income and expenses. Each day he tries to cut his losses and increase his profits.

In the same way, Amma says that the practice of taking self-inventory is vital for spiritual progress...I take an honest look at myself. Why did these situations bother me so much? I couldn't have changed any of the external situations today. Amma says happiness is a choice, so how can I start choosing to be happy?

I start reflecting...

Hmm...This morning my sēvā supervisor was right, today was the third time I've come late. I don't give enough importance to punctuality. I will make a resolve not to be late again.

Hmmmm...The man carrying those boxes to the elevator did seem really out of breath...they must have been heavy... I guess

I'm happy I was able to help him in a small way. And that crow? I should have had more *śhraddhā* (alertness, attention) with the cake. And the crow's "blessing" from above? Well, nothing to do but accept. In either case I can't blame the crow... I start to accept what I can't change.

When I start to think about others, my heart cracks open a little bit. I realize every moment I have a choice. I can either react to all the situations that life presents, or I can pause, look inside, and try to see the situation through Amma's eyes — those compassionate eyes.

To recognize that we have a choice, we need awareness. Amma says that awareness is like light cutting through darkness. It allows us to see thoughts and emotions rising up before we express them as words and actions. We can make a tiny gap. Like pressing pause on a remote control. We can choose. Will these words be helpful to improve the situation or will they make it worse?

That day, I had heard the divine sounds, "Ōm Namaḥ Śhivāya" so many times, but I had totally forgotten to remember the sublime meaning of this *mantra*, "I bow down to the supreme truth that resides in all beings." Every time we say and hear, "Ōm Namaḥ Śhivāya" it is a reminder to see and feel Amma in everything.

Amma says, "Try to see God in everything. People blame either God or others for their sufferings, but is there really any meaning in doing so? It is only our own attitude that is the cause of our sufferings."

***

Blaming and judging is one of the main ways I make myself suffer. I remember many years ago, Amma arrived for her programs at M.A. Center. Even though she had given darśhan throughout the whole previous night, and then had traveled the whole following day, as soon as she arrived, she wanted to serve dinner to all the devotees. Everyone rushed to set up the meal service in the garden of the house where Amma was staying.

As Amma served the meal, I looked around in shock, noticing that the garden looked half dead. I was annoyed and embarrassed. Why didn't the people in charge of garden maintenance do their job? Such a lack of śhraddhā!

The next day during darśhan, I marched up to the side of Amma's chair and told Amma how sorry and embarrassed I was. I went on and on – is this how we greet Amma?

Amma didn't interrupt me. She just looked at me and patiently waited until I had finished. I stood there feeling pretty good about myself. I was sure that Amma would be so impressed by my incredible dedication and devotion! Instead Amma stopped giving darśhan, turned to me and said,

"Daughter, never look at what others are doing." She continued, "There is no point in saying over and over what a mess the world is. You become a living example. Change yourself! This will inspire others. Always think, 'What can I do?'"

And so I try to make Amma's words a daily practice. I can't expect others to change. In fact, waiting for others to change can just be a tricky way to avoid changing myself.

"What can I do?" I can introspect, I can take personal inventory, increase my self-awareness, and transform my mental attitude.

***

Whether swimming through difficult experiences or through the waves of my mind, Amma has always been there. She will never let me drown.

This reminds me of an incident from the 1996 North India Tour that I will never forget:

It was a travel day, and Amma had stopped with all of us at the *Narmadā* river for a swim. I timidly entered the water, and got in line with the other girls to get my face washed by Amma. She would get her hand all soapy, and then once our eyes were tightly closed, she would tenderly wash each of our faces. It was quite motherly, and for me also symbolic of the inner purification that I hoped was going on.

Then Amma started chanting prayers in the water with the girls. As Amma moved through the water, she noticed the riverbed getting deeper with sudden drop offs, so she told anyone who didn't know how to swim to move back immediately to the shore. I didn't have to be told twice, but some of the *brahmachāriṇīs* who didn't know how to swim, kept following Amma on the shifting riverbed, like iron filings towards a magnet.

Some of the brahmachāriṇīs slipped and went under water. Amma immediately responded, diving down herself to pull them up from below. Some other expert swimmers rushed over to help. They managed to pull the girls out. Amma, in a very intense mood, told everyone to get out of the water immediately.

Everyone quickly got out and assembled around Amma's chair. Amma sat there, her bright eyes scanning the crowd one by one. She was in a worried mood. Even though it seemed that we were all safe and accounted for, Amma kept saying, "One of my children is still in the water!"

Amma sent some good swimmers back into the river immediately, and as Amma had known, one brahmachāriṇī was found happily sitting at the bottom of the river...still holding her breath!

They pulled her to safety, but Amma continued to look concerned. She seemed out of breath. Then Amma sat perfectly still, her eyes fixed on the horizon for a long time. We all sat quietly gazing at Amma in this absorbed state. After a while Amma came back to our world, sang some bhajans, served us dinner, and then we boarded the buses to complete our journey.

However, the story is not over...

When we finally arrived at our destination, I got an urgent message from the local organizer that I needed to call my father right away. I immediately went to the nearest phone booth and called him. He was on vacation in Costa Rica at the time.

He told me that about twelve hours earlier he had gone swimming in the ocean, and had gotten caught in a rip tide. My dad is an excellent swimmer. He grew up surfing. But no matter how much he used his skills and knowledge of the ocean, the strong current kept pulling him out further and further from shore.

Overwhelmed, he became physically exhausted. At one point, he couldn't even lift his arms anymore, and realized that this was the end. He was going to drown. At that moment, one thought came to his mind. He called out to Amma...Ammaaa! The next thing he remembered was waking up on the beach.

He called to ask me to thank Amma for saving his life. Suddenly everything clicked in my mind...the times matched perfectly. Amma's protection and love was not only saving the life of her brahmachāriṇī daughter here at the Narmadā river, but also simultaneously saving her son, my father, struggling in the ocean on the other side of the globe.

He had called out to Amma and she was there for him instantly. Distance cannot separate Amma from her children. Amma says that where there is love, there is no distance. And Amma is the fountain of love. As she told us long ago at the airport, "How can I not be with you?"

Amma says, "Don't think that you are physically away from Amma, or that you have not seen Amma in a long time. These are only the doubts of the mind. Stop listening to your mind and you will feel Amma right in your heart. You will realize that Amma has never left you; that you have always existed in her and always will."

It is with great gratitude that I sit here knowing that Amma is teaching me how to swim in this ocean of life; that she is here for all of us, watching and protecting us through the ups and downs of life.

5

The Three Rare Gifts

Vinod - Italy

By Amma's grace I have spent almost half of my life in *Amritapuri.* For this *satsang* I will describe my early days here, including relating several teachings that Amma gave me while performing my *sēvā.*

It is said that there are three rare gifts that living beings can attain.

Today, inspired by our most beloved Amma, I'd like to share how all three came into my life.

The third verse of *Vivēkachūḍāmaṇi*[13] states:

'There are three things which are rare indeed and are due to the grace of God, namely, *manuṣhyatvam* — a human birth, *mumukṣhutvam* — the longing for Liberation, and *mahāpuruṣha saṃśhrayaḥ* — taking refuge in a perfect master.'

The First Rare Gift — Human Birth

How many of us were aware of the gift of human birth when it happened? Our Amma as a baby was an exception, but for the majority of us like myself, we only became aware of being an individual by the age of four or maybe five. Yet something was there. What was it? Whatever it was, it was alive — consciousness in its purest state, untouched by the contamination of the sense of I and mine.

This is why Amma says, "If you want to see God, look into the eyes of a baby." Later on, we wrongly associate the sense of

---

[13] A sanskrit text written by Ādi Śhaṅkarāchārya, chief proponent of the non-dual Advaita philosophy.

"I-am-ness" with the body and mind, and we fail to understand that they are merely instruments.

I was fortunate to be born into a family that was not obsessed with politics and religion. My parents were *dharmic* and very loving towards me. However, because I was not exposed to spirituality, I had no clue that a human birth was a gift and that there were two more great gifts to come.

Longing for the Truth

From my elementary school days, I had the feeling that something was missing. This is why I just stared at the books without reading them. Later, I went to high school for a while but quit after one year. My father warned me about the consequences of ending my studies, but I found them just too boring, and always had the feeling that the teachers were trying to brainwash me.

Instead, I joined my father working in his bakery. After a few years, I became interested in cake decoration. One time, a friend of mine who is now Amma's Italian pastry chef, made a cake for my mother that had Amma's picture printed on it. The photo consists of food coloring on a thin layer of sugar. We ate it together until only the slice with Amma's face on it remained.

How could we dare to eat Amma?

Then I remembered the *bhajan* that says:

'Oh, Mother Kāḷī, when will I devour you?'

To eat Kāḷī actually means to imbibe and assimilate her divine qualities within.

As a professional baker, I enjoyed the artistic side of it. You might think that the most important aspect of baking is in the taste, but actually each *indriya* (sense organ) wants to enjoy it — taste, smell, touch, sound, and sight.

Sometimes my cake decorations were a real masterpiece. However, one day I started wondering why I should put in so much effort, dedication, and concentration into making cakes?

It takes at least two days to complete a wedding cake, and then what was the masterpiece's destiny? The cake that was made with so much care, no matter how artistically beautiful it was, would end up in the toilet! What was the point of making it perfect? Did eternal perfection actually exist?

Self Inquiry

I always thought that perfection is related to the result of our work.

Once I was standing behind Amma with a camera doing my video sēvā. In those days, one of the ashram kids used to come and sing before the swāmīs' bhajan sessions. He had created a new song and asked if Amma would like to hear it. Amma said yes.

After finishing the song, he ran up to the stage and got an apple from Amma and asked, "Did you like it?"

"Yes," replied Amma.

The interaction that followed is still imprinted on my heart. In those days, Aikyam only spoke French, so I was lucky enough to be his official translator.

While giving *darśhan* to people at the same time, Amma asked Aikyam, "Tell me, who created the song?"

"I created it," Aikyam replied.

Then Amma asked, "And who is this I?"

A bit surprised, Aikyam said, "It's me."

Then Amma said, "And who is this me?"

Touching his body, he said, "Me me, the body, don't you see Amma?"

"Oh, the body. And which part of the body did it come from?" asked Amma.

Aikyam was a bit perplexed; he looked at his body and then replied, "It came from the head."

"Are you sure?"

"Yes yes, um. Actually no, it comes from the heart."

"Are you sure?"

"Yes yes," Aikyam replied.

Then Amma paused from giving darśhan, turned to Aikyam and said, "No Aikyam, it doesn't come from the heart. It comes from God."

Karma Yōga (the path of selfless action)

As we all know, God as supreme consciousness doesn't perform any action. The body and mind function, and the heart muscle pumps blood only because they are enlivened by the power of consciousness. In terms of action, all actions inevitably create impressions and trap us in the cycle of *saṁsāra*,[14] all except one kind — selfless action.

Karma Yōga states that there are four requirements for making any action truly selfless, thereby neutralizing the karma:

- The action must be performed as an offering to the divine, implying that the body and mind are mere instruments surrendered to the divine.
- Absolute renunciation of ownership of 'my' action and 'my' result. The sense of 'mine' must be surrendered to the divine unconditionally. There is no ownership.
- Absolute renunciation of doership; the notion that 'I am doing.' There is no doership.
- No reaction is allowed, but response is permitted if needed. This is the most difficult requirement. A reaction due to our likes and dislikes, like getting angry, excited or upset, will compromise the very purpose of neutralizing the karma, and will create new karma instead.

[14] Cycle of birth and death; the world of flux; the wheel of birth, decay, death and rebirth.

A reaction implies ownership, identification with the 'I' and attachment to 'mine,' which ultimately leads to bondage.

In this context, in Chapter 5, verse 12 of the *Bhagavad Gītā*, Lord Kṛiṣhṇa advises his devotee Arjuna as follows:

> *yuktaḥ karma-phalaṁ tyaktvā śhāntimāpnōti naiṣhṭikīm*
> *ayuktaḥ kāma-kārēṇa phalē saktō nibadhyatē*
> 'One who is united with the divine, who has given up the results of action, attains everlasting peace. One who is not united with the divine, who has attachment to results due to desires, gets bound.'

However, out of compassion, Amma takes up part of our karma, including from our daily actions. Sometimes people ask how they can make Amma happy? This could be one way — to stop loading Amma with our karma, even though she doesn't mind.

The Second Rare Gift — The Longing for Liberation

I would have liked to have known from a young age what perfection is. Unfortunately, this is not what you hear about or experience in the world.

Disappointed in life, I completely threw myself into the worldly 'supermarket,' as Amma often calls it, enjoying each and every item. The few friends I had were more balanced, since they had projects, family, and business plans. However, since I wanted to know the real meaning of life, all that didn't make any sense to me.

Unable to find an answer, I started traveling. After two years with a few breaks in between where I worked for a few months to make money, I ended up on the island of Kopanghan, Thailand. I enjoyed the travel, the supermarket, until even that didn't make sense any more.

I felt so empty and scared at that point in my life. I experienced a fear that I had never felt before. I had the feeling that I had reached the edge of existence, and I could see nothing beyond that. I felt like a hamster endlessly running over and over on the same wheel.

You may think, "Come on! You always had your daily meals and shelter." Yes...true. But if that was my meaning in life, at least I would know what to search for. When you lack nothing, so to say, having received all the values and love from your parents, but still feel empty, not knowing what is missing, what you are searching for, then who can help you?

I overcame many small fears in life: passing school exams; my first job interview; the shock of a car accident where I almost died; traveling in unknown, dangerous areas; being threatened by soldiers in the middle of Amazonia while sailing down the Rios; and being surrounded at night by wild dingos while crossing the Australian desert. Yet nothing could compare to the abyss that now faced me.

One day in Thailand, I entered a tiny book store and among the Thai and English books, I found one book in my native language, Italian. I got the book only because of that. Little did I know, that book would change my life forever. It was *Autobiography of a Yogi* by Paramahansa Yogananda. Now if you ask me what was so good about that book, I can say, "it's a great spiritual book among many other great books by many other masters. Each one is unique in conveying the highest truth."

However after reading that book, I was no longer the same person. For someone born into a spiritual environment reading a spiritual book is a common thing. But for someone like me, to read such a book, at that time of my life when I had no idea about spirituality, it was like an explosion. I wasn't reading but drinking in each word.

The more I read, the more happy I felt until I was so happy that I could barely contain it. My joy knew no bounds. My entire being was pervaded by peace. All of a sudden, my attachment to the supermarket fell away, and a few months later I became a vegetarian. The search was over. By divine grace, I had found the second rare gift — mumukṣhutvam — the desire for liberation.

From that day on, the desire for liberation became my only reason for living. As it is said in the very first verse of the *Brahma Sūtras*:

> *athāto brahmajijñāsā*
> 'Now, from here, the desire to know *Brahman* (the Absolute).'

The impact on me was such that for the first time in my life, I didn't have to depend on external objects or relationships in order to be happy. I was so fulfilled and content that I didn't even look for any meditation or community centers. It was like stepping out from a dream.

Like Arjuna said in Chapter 18 verse 73 of the *Bhagavad Gītā*:

> *smṛitir labdhā*
> 'Oh Lord, I have regained memory.'

Always Alone

Externally nothing changed. I went back and resumed my job and spent the weekends in the mountains all alone. I was astonished to notice that I was constantly overwhelmed by peace and joy for no reason. For some time, I kept visiting my friends, sharing their company but soon we realized that we were living in two completely different worlds.

Once somebody asked Amma, "Why isn't everyone inclined towards spirituality?"

Amma said, "We all are spiritual beings. However, the spiritual saṁskāra may still be absent in some; it has not yet been sown."

Then I thought, this is why at the end of darśhan Amma checks very carefully to make sure everyone, especially newcomers, have received Amma's hug. Even if they don't come back, at least they received Amma's spiritual seed, which at the proper time will sprout... such is Amma's infinite compassion.

Not only that, once someone asked Amma why she looks all around while traveling, when she instructs us to focus on the *mantra*, and to not be distracted by our surroundings. Amma explained that her gaze was not a mere gaze, but a blessing to whoever received it. In fact, we all want Amma to look at us because we feel something very special in her eyes, in her gaze. But is there anyone behind those eyes?

I remember many years back during the European tour in Munich, I filmed an interview given by national media television during darśhan. The reporter asked, "Amma, how do you feel being in a crowd every day? How do you manage? Can you share what you feel about being surrounded by thousands of people?"

Amma replied: "Alone."

"What? What do you mean? How can you feel alone when they are all here for you?" asked the reporter.

Then Amma explained, "I am alone because in every person who comes for darśhan I only see myself."

Needless to say, the reporter was a bit confused...Astonished. But what about us, or me? Do I really understand what Amma means? Do I always see everyone as myself?

The first thing that comes to my mind is, "Oh, Amma must see so many Ammas all around." As Amma repeatedly states, "I'm not confined to this body." Amma isn't referring to her body when she says, "I see only myself."

The scriptures clearly state that the Self can't be seen, touched, heard, or smelled by the sense organs. It is *na rūpa* — it has no form. If that is the case, what does Amma see? When Amma doesn't look at me, should I feel sad? If so, who feels sad? Me, the body that can be seen, or me the Self that cannot be seen? Isn't the Self one and the same. This is what the *ṛiṣhis* realized after years of intense austerity. In the *upaniṣhads,* the knowledge portion of the *Vēdas*, the ṛiṣhi states:

> *atmaivēdam sarvam*
> 'Consciousness is all there is.'

Therefore, who is looking at whom? Often, we hear Amma say, "Be a zero to become a hero." In other words, zero form, zero color, zero thoughts, zero desires. Maybe then, in that zero, we may have a glimpse of the hero, of what Amma means by saying, "I feel alone. I always see myself."

I have been alone most of my life, but the sense of otherness was always present. Right now, with all of you looking at me, I may feel a bit uneasy. But what if the sense of otherness disappears all of a sudden, and I realize that those thousand eyes looking at me are none but my own eyes? Would I feel fine? If not, then maybe it's scary to realize that out there, there is nobody other than myself.

The Third Rare Gift — Taking Refuge in a Perfect Master

Almost two years after reading the *Autobiography of a Yogi*, I was still feeling inner joy in my heart, yet I wondered how it was possible that no one else was feeling the same. I guess they were so engrossed and dependent on the external world for happiness that they never tried to turn inward. How could they, if no one had ever explained what that means?

I tried to explain this to my friends, but it was in vain. I was starting to feel like an alien on an alien planet. The worst part was that I once again began to feel the pull of the world. That was like an alarm bell going off! I felt something was wrong.

I couldn't imagine depending once again on worldly objects for happiness. It was then that for the first time in my life, I prayed to God. I will explain what I mean by this statement later. I was praying for a hint, whispering, "God, I don't know how to pray, but I know you exist. Please don't leave me alone. Don't let the world pull me back." A few tears were flowing from my eyes, which is unusual for me. Then I fell silent, totally empty, and after some time one word consisting of only five letters crossed my mind: I–N–D–I–A. India.

No doubt, there was nothing left to be done other than to go to India. And the reason was super clear — to search for a guru — the third rare gift. This time the journey was one way only.

In November 1997 I landed at Trivandrum airport. I was really excited to begin my search. It took Yogananda many years to find his Guru, so I was wondering how many months or years it would take me to find mine.

A western lady was standing in front of me in the immigration line. I took the opportunity to ask if it was her first visit to India. She said no, that she had been coming every year for one reason only — to see Amma. Then she placed her hand upon her chest and said, "Oh I can't wait!"

The airport is a neutral zone. Only after passing through the immigration checkpoint are you officially allowed to enter the country. So I hadn't even set foot in the holy land of India before Amma came to get me! The search hadn't begun before it was already over. Looking back, I see that this was the answer to my prayer. Before that moment, I had spent thirty years of longing. Therefore, I kindly request Amma, "Next lifetime, if there is one, please don't let me play for so long in the supermarket."

Prayer

At that time Amma was on tour, so I decided to spend three days in Amritapuri. To be honest, I felt a bit uneasy, and now I understand why. I had been living my whole life for my own sake. I had never been in a spiritual community, and now all of a sudden here I was amongst a thousand people practicing *sādhanā* (spiritual practices) and doing sēvā.

The energy produced was tangible. People were more committed to giving than to receiving. It made quite an impact on me to all at once see a completely different way of life. Amritapuri is definitely an island on this planet that continuously generates a huge wave of love that benefits the world, thanks to all of Amma's children, and Amma's constant sacrifice.

Let me explain what I meant before when I said, "I prayed to God for the first time in my life." You may wonder, "Really?" As a child I was told to pray, but to me God was a meaningless word. I had no clue what I was doing. It was based on a belief system, but to pray to God from the heart like this was really a first time for me. After reading the book by Swami Yogananda, God was no more a mere belief, but a reality that I have felt within ever since.

And after meeting Amma, God was not just a word written down in the scriptures, but the manifestation of God's love in human form. Although even in Amma's presence we sometimes go through pain, think of those who are also in pain but don't even know Amma. At times we forget how blessed we are.

Once the three rare gifts have been attained, can there be any other goal than Self-realization? I used to pray for it, but then I realized how foolish that was. It was like placing a mango seed on an altar and then praying for a mango fruit to sprout. It doesn't work. The seed needs to be sown. The second rare gift — the desire for liberation — is the seed! The seed that needs to be sown through our daily practice.

Amma is our third rare lovely gift — our mother and master who will guide us through the entire process. We may wonder how our life would be if we realized the Self. It's enough to see someone who is established in that state, and we don't need to look far. Amma is the example here with us. And what has Amma been doing since her childhood? She has been joyfully serving and loving everyone unconditionally. This is how our life will be once we have realized the Self. But the real question is...Do we need to wait to realize the Self to love and serve everyone?

6

Why Sad? No Need

Medhini – Lebanon

One day, a Guru gave his disciple a big diamond, and told him to go to the town to get it appraised. Not being familiar with diamonds, and thinking it was just some kind of rock, the disciple went to town and showed it first to the vegetable seller and asked, "How much do you think this is worth?"

The vegetable seller said, "I'll give you two heads of cabbage and a pound of beans for it." The disciple replied, "That doesn't sound reasonable." Then he went to a cloth shop. The cloth merchant said, "This is very valuable. I'll give you 100 yards of silk cloth for it." "No, that doesn't sound right either," thought the disciple. Next, he went to the most reputable jewelry shop in town, and when they saw the diamond, they exclaimed, "This is invaluable!"

Similarly, due to Amma's simple language and our gross, impure and agitated minds, we sometimes fail to understand the greatness and depth of her words. In my first *'room darśhan,'*[15] Amma said four simple words in English to me. She repeated these four words twice. They were so simple that I did not attribute much importance to them.

Shortly after my darśhan, I mentioned these four words in a conversation with Swāmī Jñānāmṛitānandajī. The way Swāmījī repeated those words, and the way he inquired once more about them, almost as if to himself, was enough to make me realize that there had to be something very special about them. It was

[15] A room darśhan is when Amma gives darśhan to the āśhram residents in her room.

like the jeweler pointing out to the disciple, "This is invaluable." These four words have remained with me ever since, and my humble contemplation on them is the topic of this *satsang*.

The four words are: 'Why sad? No need.'

"Why sad?" — With this question Amma encouraged me to inquire into the cause of my sadness. And with her statement, "No need," Amma questioned the very validity of feeling sad, questioning the reality of my experience, confronting it with the ultimate truth that she is established in.

Let me tell you about a girl's life, first from an angle of darkness, and then from an angle which is full of light. From a gross perspective, the first angle will provide an answer to the question, "Why sad?" The second angle will provide an answer to Amma's statement, "No need."

"Why sad?"

There once was a girl who was born in Lebanon while civil war was raging in the country. She was born to a father who was the leader of a special group on one side of the fight. He was a baker by trade, but involved in arms dealings and other things she never asked about. He had physical scars from battle, and was missing a finger that had been shot off.

After a few years, her father became disillusioned with his party; he had become a political target. During the first three and a half years of her life, this girl, her mother, and older brother would repeatedly be forced to hide under the bed when special heavily-armed paramilitary units stormed their home in search of her father. This remained the theme of her recurring nightmares up to this day.

Her mother protected her from the grenades that were bursting all around by throwing herself on top of her daughter's stroller. Some of the larger pieces of shrapnel her mother received have been removed, but the smaller ones are still in her body today. Her maternal Jewish grandmother had been relocated to Lebanon from what had been Palestine against her will and lived there until she breathed her last in a Muslim refugee camp in Lebanon.

For their safety, her father realized they needed to leave Lebanon, but this girl's mother did not have papers, or a passport. Fleeing would be difficult and dangerous.

They eventually sought political asylum in Germany, and were resettled in a small village. A German family became attached to this little girl. They raised her alongside her biological parents, giving her tuition for school, and offering her a world of abundance and pleasure.

Yet, due to differences in culture and tradition, the two families started criticizing each other in front of her, each side claiming to be the better parents. Thus, the term 'home' lost its clarity and feeling of security.

When the girl had her first menstrual period at twelve-years old and therefore, according to her parents' culture, had reached the age for marriage, they decided she did not need to continue her education. Her parents locked her up in her room and prevented her from going to school. This led to intervention by the police and youth welfare services, and they put her in a foster home for some time.

At twenty-one, she acquired German citizenship. Despite having done her entire education in Germany, she realized at one point that she would never really fit in there, nor would she ever be considered part of the Lebanese community, as she hadn't learned Arabic, nor learned about Lebanese culture, history or customs. Therefore, the question haunting her was, "Where do I belong?"

She moved to Switzerland when she was thirty-two years old. She had a very well-paid job, a large flat overlooking Lake

Geneva, with a terrace from which she could see the sun setting behind the snow covered peaks of the French Alps. Yet, this high level of comfort, wealth, and social recognition was equally offset by a feeling of emptiness inside.

Her search for belonging and safety led her into several relationships that provided temporary shelter. It was as though a male companion was needed for a life which had never had a strong, stable, or secure foundation...but no relationship lasted. After a failed marriage, came the understanding that no external relationship would ever last; she was on her own.

***

For Amma's statement, "No need" (to be sad), we will now look at the same girl's life from the angle of light:

This girl was born to a father whose life had been spared by war, and who had the courage to take his whole family away from relatives, friends, and what he considered his home to a totally unknown future.

She was born to a mother who would rather sacrifice her life by using her body as a protective shield, rather than let her baby daughter get injured.

In Germany, not knowing the language or anything really about the country, her Muslim parents tried their best to adjust to smoothly integrate their family. They tried to find the balance between preserving the gems of their own culture and religion, letting go of old-fashioned aspects of it, and welcoming in the positive aspects of western culture.

Though not their own religion, her parents encouraged her to follow the community routine of attending Sunday Christian-church services. They carried a deep reverence for Allah in their hearts, and were grateful that Allah would enter her life in this way. They even attended her baptism when she was six-years old.

Jesus Christ became her first idol, the very first love of her life. She watched movies about Jesus, and drew pictures of Christ on the cross. At the tender age of seven, she sobbed, crouched on the floor, heart-broken over Jesus' crucifixion; that such a pure being had given his life for a humanity that is so cruel and hypocritical.

Even at that age she could clearly see the gap between the values shown by Jesus' life and the behavior of people around her. She wanted to be with Jesus and agonized over not having lived when he was alive. This longing became the dim, glowing ember waiting for the breeze of the Divine Mother to make it burn bright.

Though at the age of twelve, she could have become one of millions of girls who are deprived of a proper education, she found herself in a country whose laws make primary and secondary education compulsory. Thus, this girl was able to acquire not only a high school diploma but also a university degree.

Also, love won over tradition. Not wanting to lose their daughter's heart, her parents started reaching out to her in every possible way. Her father would cycle regularly the twenty kilometers to her boarding school just to bring her fruits, and maybe to get a glimpse of her, and then cycled the twenty kilometers back. They kept trying to regain her trust. This went on for ten years. Finally, with time she matured. Instead of clinging to the past, her parents taught her that only the present moment is in our hands. And that it is now that love can be withheld or expressed.

Disillusioned by the limitations of worldly accomplishments and pleasures, at the age of thirty-two, she started searching for vocational training in some kind of physical therapy. By divine grace, she was led to taking an Āyurvēdic massage course. It was time to get ready to meet her Guru, our Amma. It was time for the ember to begin burning bright.

***

At the āyurvēdic course, she saw a photo of Amma, and was immediately attracted to what so many have already said attracted them — Amma's radiant face, Amma's shining eyes, Amma's compassionate gaze.

She went to Amma's program in Winterthur. Seeing the tenderness and intimacy with which Amma received each and every person, her eyes welled up with tears. A deep conviction took root within her: "Oh Amma, all the virtues I cherished as a child, seeing them in my beloved Jesus Christ, are right in front of me, now in this female body in which you have chosen to take birth." The painful regret of the seven-year old girl who had wished to live in the presence of Jesus turned into overwhelming gratitude. To this day, words fail to express the depth of that recognition.

For thirty-three years, she hadn't been able to answer the questions, "Where is home?" "Where do I belong?" However, a year or two after meeting Amma, these haunting questions fully dissolved, never to resurface. She had reached her real home; she had reached where she belongs.

This girl's journey is neither special nor unique. The various satsangs we have listened to over this last year are proof of it. Looking back with gratitude, she sees that divine protection was already enveloping her in her mother's womb. Here is the truth: every single step of the way, we are being held and at times even carried by our Amma. How could *Jagadjananī* — the mother of this entire universe, ever abandon her beloved child?

***

Whether we allow our minds to turn away from the light and go towards darkness, or make the conscious choice to be happy and keep our windows wide open to the light, is up to each one of us. As Amma says, "Happiness is a decision." And this decision needs to be taken over and over and over again. We need to remind ourselves, "Why sad? No need." How to remind ourselves? Here are three things which have helped and continue to help me:

1. *Kīrtanam*: I would like to use this term in the sense of positive sound vibrations. Experiences get stored as memories. What are memories? Memories are thoughts. What are thoughts? Sound vibrations. Sound vibrations are very subtle. Even our intellect is too gross to reach these vibrations. That is why whatever reasoning we try is bound to fail if practiced exclusively. My experience is that just by chanting one *archana* (1000 names of the Divine Mother) a day is enough to keep the nightmares I mentioned earlier at bay. While chanting the *Bhagavad Gītā*, I experience an inner strength, as though being straightened up from within, a feeling of confidence and calm no external support could ever provide.

2. *Abhyāsa – vairāgya*: constant practice and detachment. Am "I" really sad? Isn't sadness just one of the various modifications of the mind that "I" can observe just like any external object? And isn't whatever "I" can observe, something different from me — the one who witnesses this feeling of sadness? Due to our identification with the mind, we befriend and identify with these changing emotions and are thus being tossed around by life's opposite experiences. Whoever has sincerely tried to master the mind, like Arjuna in the Gītā, has arrived at the same conclusion that, "This is

extremely difficult." In Chapter 6, verse 35 of the *Bhagavad Gītā*, Lord Kṛiṣhṇa says to his disciple Arjuna:

> *asaṁśhayaṁ mahā-bāhō manō durnigrahaṁ chalam*
> *abhyāsēna tu kauntēya vairāgyēṇa cha gṛihyatē*
> 'No doubt, O mighty-armed, the mind is difficult to control and wavering; but by practice and non-attachment it is held, O son of Kunti.'

The Lord mentions abhyāsa — constant practice, and vairāgya — detachment as a means to restrain the mind. To remain equanimous we need to gain the ability to detach and divert our focus from the object — here, the feeling of sadness — to the *sākṣhi*, the witness. For this, vairāgya is most essential.

Amma gives the example of a driver who needs to know how to apply the breaks. Only if we learn to apply the brakes of reflection and contemplation on the changing nature of emotions will we be able to slowly redirect the mind within, to the unaffected, unchanging substratum, to our true nature. This needs to be done not once, not twice, but constantly — abhyāsa, constant practice.

3. *Samarpaṇam* — surrender to the Guru: even if we put in our best efforts; are regular in our sādhanā, in sēva, and in scriptural studies; perform our actions with divine remembrance; and receive the fruits of our actions with *prasāda buddhi* (accepting all that comes as God's gift), we still might feel that deep impressions from the past keep surfacing and pulling us down. Why? There are many reasons, but I'd like to mention two:

> a. We are dealing with the Lord's illusory power — māyā, which is almost as powerful as the Lord.

> b. We do not only carry impressions from this birth but from countless births, and our efforts can be compared to wanting to empty an ocean using a blade of grass.

Therefore, let us take refuge in the one on whom even māyā depends for its existence; in the one who gives us the assurance that if we fix our minds on her, and exclusively depend on her alone, we will awaken to our true nature.

In short, better than focusing on the dark side is to focus on the bright side. Better than focusing on the bright side is to focus on the substratum of both which is our Amma, our true nature.

May we start from where we are, full of trust in our charioteer — our beloved Amma. Her light is showing us the path and the goal but it is we who need to be willing to tread the path.

Amma said four seemingly simple words, "Why sad? No need." But these four words contain the entire Gītā. The first chapter of the *Bhagavad Gītā* called *Arjuna Viṣhāda Yōga* (Yōga of Arjuna's Despondency) is inherent in the question, "Why sad?" and the Lord's teachings in the subsequent seventeen chapters is hidden in capsule form in the two words, "No need."

May we give reverence to Amma's words with the firm conviction, "I am listening to the wisdom that has descended down from time immemorial. I am listening to the indweller of the hearts of all — reaching out, uplifting us to her realm, to our true nature."

***

Let me conclude by sharing how my parents met Amma for the first time:

By the summer of 2010, my father was wheelchair bound. I touched his hand; it had become bony and fragile. I was heartbroken, still the little girl looking up to her invincible dad.

Later that year, my father became mostly bedridden. He didn't want homecare or nurses, so my mother had to do everything for him. Something triggered within me. I could see that time was running out.

My mother still ached with grief for her mother. And though their reunion wasn't possible, I knew that she could be held by Amma. After everything they both had been through and sacrificed for our family, I wanted them so much to meet Amma.

The German program was in Munich, and my parents lived ten hours to the north. However, I was determined to make the trip, to pick my parents up and bring them to meet Amma. When I arrived my mother said, "We can't go. He's in such bad condition right now, he's really not doing well." I begged, "Please, please, let us at least try."

In the Arabic tradition, when you meet someone special, you bring something special. My mother wondered what would be an appropriate gift. I told her, "What if you went to see your mom, what would you bring her?"

While on the road, every thirty minutes my dad would ask, "Where are we going?" and I would answer, "We're going to Munich, to meet an Indian woman." Then I would list one of Amma's many humanitarian initiatives, to which my father would answer, "So? There are very good people in Lebanon who have also done this, what's so special about her?" This went on every half an hour for about seven hours until finally I said, "We're going to Munich, to meet this Indian woman, and she is very special to me." At that moment he said, "Ok" and there were no more questions.

When going for darśhan, my mother gave Amma one of her most beloved items, a *Qur'an* (holy book of Islam) and a *Misbaha* — a muslim rosary, she had brought back from a pilgrimage to

Mecca. Amma kissed the gifts again and again, enveloping my mom in a very long, beautiful hug.

I felt such relief. After all these years, my mother was receiving the maternal loving embrace, she so desperately craved. There was a completion to it; the struggle, the pain, the regret. For me, it meant that for once she could experience total peace, relaxation and safety.

I'm not sure if my father could make sense of what was going on. He never actually looked at Amma. He got an apple, and piece of candy as *prasād* from Amma. She was so sweet with him. I was finally able to give back to my parents something most precious to me — a gift beyond what I could ever give as a daughter.

When the morning program ended, people lined up on either side of the pathway Amma used to exit the hall.

As my father was in a wheelchair, he was seated in the front row, with my mother sitting next to him, and me standing behind them.

Amma began to walk down the aisle. When she saw my parents, she turned towards them and stopped right in front of us. Amma gave my family an unexpected darśhan, and when she did, a photographer was there to take the picture. My father's face lit up, and I got the sense then that he understood what made Amma so special. As we left the program, he asked my mother, "Is she some kind of saint, or holy person?"

Two and a half months later, my father passed away. When I went to see my father's body, he had never looked so beautiful. He was at total peace; no frown, or hard lines in his face. Finally, after a long journey which had started in utter darkness, he was full of light. My mother keeps that picture of my father and her with Amma stored in her beloved Qur'an.

My prayer is that parents and children never give up on each other and always believe in the day when things change for the better, with our sincere efforts, prayers, and divine grace. Let us children remember when we notice the hurt or anger arising within, against our parents, that our parents had lives that greatly affected them before they became our dad and mom.

Let us remember how much our parents had to sacrifice to raise us. And may parents give their children time and space to heal and understand, while staying in touch with them.

As a daughter, my healing started with forgiveness based on love and understanding inspired by Amma's teachings and example. As for my mother and father, my prayer is that Amma's embrace may remain deeply imprinted in their hearts. As long as she is there, no darkness can dispel her light.

I pray that the love and compassion that developed in me through my family's journey together may grow and become more expansive. For that, I humbly pray to Amma to turn this child of yours into one of your beautiful white flowers of love and peace.

7

A Householder's Journey through Life with Amma

Anita Sreekumar – India

When Amma asked her householder children to come forward and share their experiences, I finally geared up for the task after months of uncertainty, for two reasons:

First, it is my duty to obey Amma, my Guru. Amma, you have often said that you are looking for ways to shower your grace on us, your children. Your love for us prompts you to devise easy, doable activities like having us drink rice water with meals; take daily morning walks; participate in giving *satsangs*; do *sādhanā*, etc. Performing these actions, combined with your grace helps us evolve towards our final goal. I bow down in gratitude before such unconditional love.

Second, I would also like to express my gratitude to all those who have shared their wealth of knowledge and experiences, all of which has helped me learn a lot. Compared to all of you, I am in no way qualified to talk about scriptures or Amma. Instead, I will share some of the experiences and lessons that I learned from Amma, and that I learned from being a householder in the āśhram.

Amma says, "Parents are the first gurus. Children express what is taught to them, and what they have experienced while growing up. Each word you utter, each deed you perform creates a deep impression in the child's mind, and goes deep into his or her heart because those are the first things the child sees and hears."

When I was a child, my parents balanced work and home beautifully. My mother not only held a job outside the home, but was a devout lady who participated in spiritual observances, and ran the household meticulously. Father maintained a home library with a collection of biographical books and teachings of various saints. I loved reading, and so I read these books with great interest. As a teenager, the impact of these books on my life led to spiritual discussions with my father. I asked, "Who is God?" "What is God?"

Though some of my relatives were already long-time devotees of Amma, I discovered her only when my uncle gave me Amma's biography as a wedding gift. Everything happens at its destined time and place.

I would read a few pages of Amma's biography every morning after my husband left for work, until an hour or so before he arrived home for lunch. The biography was so absorbing that it was difficult to tear myself away from it.

Every evening, upon my husband's return from work, I would share with him whatever I had read that day, so that he too could get introduced to Amma's life and teachings.

One day when picking up the mail, I saw a flier announcing Amma's visit to Washington, DC the following summer. I was astonished to see the flier, as there were no families in our neighborhood who were Amma devotees, nor was my husband involved with Amma in any way.

How could our names have been put on an Amma mailing list? The flier was clearly addressed to us. Who could have mailed this flier to us? We never found out, but now we understand who it must have been.

Amma had sensed the deep yearning and longing of this heart wanting to meet her, and so responded by sending the flier, calling us to her. It is said that when the student is ready, the teacher appears.

***

We attended the Washington, DC program where we met Amma physically for the first time. The swāmīs accompanying Amma all looked so calm and composed with a palpable serenity about them.

On meeting Amma, I felt like I was visiting one of my own family members. Amma has said that we have been with her in all our previous lives. She remembers, but we don't.

This reminds me of what Lord Kṛiṣhṇa (God incarnate) said to his devotee Arjuna in Chapter 4, verse 5, of the *Bhagavad Gītā*:

> *bahūni mē vyatītāni janmāni tava chārjuna*
> *tānyahaṁ vēda sarvāṇi na tvaṁ vēttha parantapa*
> 'Many births have passed for me and for you also Arjuna. I know them all but you know them not, O scorcher of foes.'

What attracted me most about Amma was her loving motherly embrace. When I was younger, our family visited a few *mahātmās* (great souls), but we could never touch them. Traditionally, a master is seen and not touched. But, I longed to touch them, as they were God-realized beings and touching them meant touching God.

This wish was fulfilled in receiving Amma's *darśhan*. I could not only touch her, but also got hugs, kisses, smiles, nuzzles on the cheek, sweet words whispered in my ear and *prasād* too. Truly, when God gives, She gives abundantly!

Something happened within us after meeting Amma. We thought of her all the time, and developed a distaste for worldly life. We stopped socializing, got in contact with satsang groups, and attended weekly *bhajan* gatherings that became our lifeline. Being with Amma devotees was now more enjoyable and meaningful than worldly relationships.

At home, we only watched Amma videos and played her bhajans all day long. We were mad with love for Amma! She became our goal and sole purpose for living.

During her next visit, we went up for darśhan and informed Amma of our inability to live without her anymore. With great kindness and mercy, she said we could move to the āśhram after her summer tour. Thus, with our six-year old daughter and two-month old son, we arrived at *Amritapuri* āśhram for the first time.

Before moving here, some people wondered if we had properly considered our decision to move into this totally new environment with two little children.

However, with Amma's hands on the steering wheel of our lives, the transition was not at all difficult. She made everything easy for us. We knew this was where we should be.

Amma says, "While moving towards the goal, we may encounter many obstacles. We should not lend an ear to words that may turn us away from the path to our goal."

I am reminded of a story Amma tells to illustrate this point:

There was a herd of goats who eyed green pastures on a high, steep mountain. Every one of them wanted to eat that grass, but was afraid of the steep climb. Among them was a little kid-goat who started climbing the mountain on its own.

Disconcerted by this, every goat in the herd except its mother, started discouraging and making fun of the little one. The kid ignored them and continued on, as his mother prayed for his safety. Eventually, the kid managed to reach the top of the mountain and enjoyed the lush grass. The other goats were astonished by this and asked the mother-goat, "How is it that your kid ignored our warnings, and did what none of us would even attempt?" The mother-goat replied, "My little one is deaf."

The moral of the story is that we should learn to focus on our goal in life, turning a deaf ear to all the unwanted and discouraging talk we may have to face on our journey.

Amma says, "Be steadfast in your commitment to the spiritual path."

We never regretted moving to Amritapuri. The children have effortlessly opened up to Amma and to the personal guidance she gives them in all matters. These interactions are rare blessings and cherished experiences.

Our initial days settling in were made easy and comfortable with the āśhram residents' help and support, and we are forever grateful for their selflessness.

***

Amma stresses prioritizing spiritual values in life saying, "If we stop giving moral values the place they deserve, our life will rot away like a termite-infested log. We will lack the courage to face problems in life."

This is why the ancient *ṛiṣhis* considered *dharma bodham* — awareness of proper action — as all important. We need to keep this awareness to ensure that all of our social interactions are as beneficial to others as to ourselves. This principle is reflected in the Amrita Vidyalayam schools founded by Amma. These schools provide a unique blend of modern education combined with cultural and spiritual values.

Amma's advice to householders is that family life should be used to bring us closer to God, not to take us away from him.

Amma says, "They have to stand in fire without getting burnt — that is the life of a householder. Without shoes, they have to walk over thorns without getting wounded; shoes being freedom from worldly ties. Householders don't have that freedom. It is a great thing to call out to God in the midst of all the family *prārabdha* (effects of past actions)."

She also points out that worrying about family robs us of our happiness, and that we should move forward in life considering everything as ordained by God.

Family life is busy and all-engrossing. Wherever we may be living, there is no escape from its obligations and duties, whether towards spouse, children, or parents-in-law, if they are living under the same roof. Generally, life for me pretty much revolves around the children — caring for them; being involved in their upbringing; their schooling; extra-curricular activities; homework; spending sleepless nights with them when they fall sick; and so on. I am sure these experiences strike a chord with most of the householders here who are walking the same path.

We weren't able to run at the ringing of the program bell like most āśhramites can, or to attend meditation or to see Amma. Nor could we participate in many of the other spiritual activities.

But Amma's words telling us to move forward in life considering everything as God's will has helped us accept our role in this lifetime. We find solace in the fact that everything is under her control.

The benefits of raising children in a spiritual atmosphere are, as Amma points out, the values they imbibe. These values help them to develop the culture of the heart from a very young age. Amma stresses inculcating spiritual values in children to help them grow into healthy adults who have the self-control and compassion necessary to always treat others with love and respect.

Amma sometimes uses the analogy of a plant that when transplanted, still has some soil clinging to its roots from the place where it had originally been, as a comparison to spiritually-raised children. No matter where those children go, they will always take some of their spiritual values with them. These values even help us adults to revamp our lifestyle, take stock of our priorities, and to live life in a proper way.

Amma is continually working on us, creating various situations in our lives that chisel out unwanted negativities, painful though that may be, to bring out our true nature.

I remember the times when Amma's gaze, and her interactions with me would bliss me out! Then there were times when though I was in front of Amma, I felt as if she did not see me. This is a common complaint from her children. In response, Amma has suggested that we remember the 283rd name from the *Lalitā Sahasranāma:*

> *ōm sahasrākṣhyai namaḥ*
> 'I bow down to her who has a thousand eyes.'

Amma says, "My children should try to see Amma inside. Amma is not limited to this physical body."

She also said that a shortcut to forgetting body consciousness is to remember the Guru's words, actions, face, smile, the way she has looked at us, etc.

Thus, Amma continues teaching me lessons on overcoming likes, dislikes, and accepting situations with *prasāda buddhi*, the attitude of accepting all that comes as God's blessing.

Sometimes, Amma works on my ego in the least expected situations, like when I am waiting in line for food and somebody cuts the line just in front of me. I feel mounting irritation at this unfairness, but with conscious effort, I am able to exercise patience so as not to lose my peace of mind. I try to recall Amma's words that it is up to us to decide to be happy or sad, cheerful or irritated, calm or agitated.

Through many such situations, Amma as Guru puts us through the cleaning process. It doesn't take her long to grab hold of us and give us a good scrubbing!

***

In all the years we've lived here, we have discovered rich treasures that are available to all. These treasures are: the *Gurukula*[16] way of living; *Gītā* class; scripture class; Vēdic chanting; dance and music classes; Sanskrit class; bhajans; meditation; various sēvā activities; spoken English class for householders; and giving satsangs.

Best of all, we are witnessing the incarnation of *Saraswatī* herself presiding over all these activities. During bhajans, Amma gives practical lessons in music, while nourishing our souls with doses of scriptural wisdom; a unique *līlā* that has no substitute!

When speaking on the importance of the Gurukula system of education, Amma said, "Modern education which ignores human values, and the development which neglects the environment is a threat to society. Earlier, there was the Gurukula system of education where students were taught to respect elders, teachers, and parents. However, the modern education system ignores all such social values thus resulting in a degraded society."

Regarding the need for a dramatic change in the existing system of education, the Dalai Lama said, "Serious discussions on how to include the ancient Indian traditions in the educational system should begin. India has the capability to combine modern education with its ancient traditions to help solve problems in the world."

---

[16] Literally, the clan (kula) of the preceptor (Guru); traditional school where students would stay with the Guru for the entire duration of their scriptural studies.

We are all witness to the truth of this statement, tangibly seen in all of Amma's schools and colleges, where a synthesis of technological innovation and traditional learning methods form their foundation. They are the reemergence of the *Nālanda* and *Takṣhaśhilā* Universities of ancient India, now renamed *Amrita Vishwa Vidyapeetham*, Amma's offering to the modern world.

Amma says that there are two kinds of education: education for life and education for livelihood. Amma is bringing the two together, creating professionals in all fields with the skills, the mental strength, and the heart to uplift the world.

Exposing young minds to mindfulness-meditation practices, and moral values builds good character, and they gain the mental strength and confidence to face life's challenges with an inner fortitude instead of succumbing to stress, depression, and suicide.

Such children are our hope for the future, and the world will look to them for solace from the scorching heat of degraded societies bereft of human values and spiritual principles. I shudder to think what all of our fates would have been if it were not for Amma.

When asked about the origin of the *Vēdas* Amma replied, "It is impossible to say when exactly the Vēdic culture began. They are *anādi* (without beginning). The Vēdas were there even before the human race. It is from India alone that the Vēdic culture took birth." We are so fortunate to have access to this ancient treasure of *Sanātana Dharma*, given directly through Amma's teachings, and through the scriptural classes being conducted here.

Regarding Sanskrit, Amma says, "If one is truly interested, one should learn Sanskrit as otherwise understanding the true import of *Vēdānta*[17] is not easy. In order to study the *Gītā* and the *upaniṣhads* it is very beneficial to understand Sanskrit."

In the *Lalitā Sahasranāma*, Dēvī is described in name 992 as:

> *ōm avyāja karuṇā mūrtayē namaḥ*
> 'I bow down to her who is pure compassion.'

This reminds me of an incident where Amma's boundless compassion worked nothing short of a miracle. One day, my son was outside playing during Amma's darśhan. He was young and very fond of riding bicycles. He had a *vāsanā* (mental inclination) for going fast, which Amma knew about but we did not. Hence per her advice, we did not buy him a bicycle, though he wanted one. That evening, he borrowed a friend's bicycle to ride.

While waiting for him in the dining hall, a student came up to me holding my son in her arms, saying that he had fallen off the bicycle and was hurt. She turned him over and I saw blood dripping down the back of his head.

Covering the injury with one hand, I held him and ran with him through the crowded hall to the hospital. I informed the nurse about the fall, but that I didn't know all the details. They quickly took him inside, sutured the cut and bandaged his head. They said that the cut was deep and very close to the skull.

We questioned him about the accident. He said that he was speeding towards the dining hall to join me when he saw an elderly lady ahead. To avert a collision, he braked hard which stopped the tires, resulting in him being thrown to the ground, and slamming his head against a concrete bench.

The hospital staff suggested that I take him up to Amma and inform her about the accident. Amma held him and said, "*Kṛipā*

---

[17] 'The end of the Vēdas.' It refers to the upaniṣhads, which deal with the subject of Brahman, the supreme truth, and the path to realize that truth.

rakṣhichu," meaning grace had saved him. These words which She uttered so simply, drove home the fact that Amma had actually protected and saved him from a worse fate, even before being informed of the incident.

This revealed to me how her ever-watchful eyes are always upon us, and that we are always under her protection and saving grace. To this great mother of all, before whose will-power even destiny bows down to, I offer my thankfulness and gratitude.

Amma has been a mother, in every sense of the word, to the children she has blessed me with, and I consider myself a foster mother just doing my duty to raise them. Amma's motherly love and compassion knows no bounds. Like a flowing river, its cooling touch gives relief to anyone who would care to take the plunge for solace from their miseries.

When asked about the special features of Hinduism, Amma replied, "Divinity lies latent in every human being. The Creator manifests as creation. To realize this non-dual truth is the ultimate goal of life. The Hindu religion is called Sanātana Dharma, the eternal principle, because it is appropriate for any country during any age.

This particular culture is the sum total of the experiences of many ṛiṣhis who lived during different ages, and experienced the ultimate truth directly. It is an all-encompassing philosophy of life. There is no such thing as eternal hell in Sanātana Dharma. It is believed that no matter how great a sin you have committed, you can still purify yourself through good thoughts and deeds and finally realize God. Any sin can be washed away with sincere repentance.

We may make mistakes as we proceed through life. But, Amma's children shouldn't be discouraged because of this. To make mistakes is natural, but we should make an attempt not to repeat them again. If you fall, think only that you have fallen in order to get up."

Amma, ignorant as I am, I have committed many mistakes. I know I have stumbled more than I have gotten up. Among all the rusted pieces of metal that you say you have gathered to turn into gold, I feel I am the most rusted, but please do not give up on me.

Amma, you have said, "Know that mother is always with you. My children, there is no need to be afraid. If you call mother with innocence and faith, she is always ready to help you."

I have placed my hand in yours as I need your help to reach the goal. Your infinite compassion and limitless patience are my only hope to reach your lotus feet where I wish to merge eternally.

I pray that every time we falter and fall, you hold our hands tight, lift us up and merge us in you. Offering my words and prayers as a garland of gratitude to adorn your lotus feet.

8

The Guru's Sandals

Sadānand - USA

Verse 1 of the *Guru Pādukā Stōtram* (Hymn to the Guru's Sandals) says:

> *ananta saṁsāra samudratāra*
> *naukāyitābhyāṁ gurubhaktidābhyām*
> *vairāgya sāmrājyada pūjanābhyām*
> *namō namaḥ śhrī gurupādukābhyām*
> 'My prostrations to the holy sandals of the Guru, which serve as the boat to cross this endless ocean of *saṁsāra*, which endow one with devotion to the Guru, and which by worshiping, grace one with renunciation — *vairāgya*.'

On Amma's international tours, I sometimes went to Amma late at night during *Dēvī Bhāva darśhan* with questions. Now, during the lockdown, it is Amma asking questions to the āśhram residents. Āśhramites raise their hand after *bhajans* and Amma calls on a few people. At first, I did not participate.

One day, the western devotees were called to come for darśhan. I went without any objective. After darśhan, Amma spoke to me. She said, "You should speak after bhajans." Before I could object, Amma added, "It would be good for you to reflect on the questions."

A few evenings later during a question and answer session, I raised my hand. Amma called on me to answer her question. My legs shook the entire time; three long minutes. Amma was tackling my fear. Amma took something overwhelming for me — a thirty-minute talk — and created small stepping stones towards it. Spirituality with a perfect master is just like that, step-by-step. We may not know where we are going, but the Guru does.

Recently on *Guru Pūrṇimā,*[18] Amma said the Guru's spiritual presence is more important than their physical form. Let's look at how the Guru's subtle presence guides us. This guidance began even before I met Amma.

As a child, I loved fantasy stories. One of my favorites was Star Wars. The main character is Luke: a young man who lives a normal life, but Fate brings him to meet a Jedi master, the Guru figure Yoda. Luke trains to learn the ways of 'the Force,' the subtle power flowing through the universe. Yoda, this ancient, tiny, wise Guru figure, teaches Luke:

"My ally is the Force... Its energy surrounds us and binds us. Luminous beings are we, not this crude matter. You must feel the Force around you... everywhere."

Many people are skeptical of spirituality. I was too. I became an atheist halfway through high school. I wanted God to be real but had no proof. I thought the scriptures and divine incarnations were myths to give meaning to life before modern science could explain things. Late at night I would contemplate, "One day I will die and cease to exist." The thought of no longer existing terrified me. During this period, I kept revisiting Star Wars. I wished that life was a fantasy. I enrolled in the University of Michigan, the next phase of a normal life.

I began holistic therapies to ease my anxiety. One day, during a mind-body healing session, I was feeling very peaceful. Suddenly, bubbles of joy welled up within me and beautiful colors flashed before my eyes. I burst out laughing. It felt so

---

[18] The full moon ('pūrṇimā') day in the Hindu month of Āṣhāḍha (June – July) in which disciples honor the Guru.

wonderful. I had never experienced anything like it before; those indescribable feelings of joy.

This made me wonder, "What is the peak of joy? How could I experience that again?"

While I wasn't sure if God existed, I remembered reading about bliss. I needed to find a way to bliss.

I developed an urgent need for someone to guide me. I called out to the universe with every cell of my being, "Help me! I need to meet a Jedi Knight! I need to meet Yoda!"

That was the language I used. I didn't know what a Guru was. In Star Wars, Yoda is the strongest Jedi in the universe. I wanted a mentor just like Yoda: wise, humble, and immensely powerful, yet funny, innocent, and hiding in plain sight. Yoda spoke in simple broken English with a deep, husky voice.

My call rang out.

A still voice within said, "You will meet who you need to in two weeks." For the next two weeks, I must have seemed strange. I walked around with my eyes wide open, looking for a Jedi...or ways to find one.

Two weeks later I met an Amma devotee, and I heard Amma's name for the first time. The devotee said, "Some people consider Amma to be an incarnation like Jesus Christ, Buddha or Lord Kṛiṣhṇa."

Today? Did incarnations really exist? I had to find out for myself. Amma's 2007 U.S. Summer Tour had just begun. I left for San Francisco immediately.

Two days later, I was in Amma's arms at MA Center, Amma's āśhram in San Ramon, California. The universal, loving energy was sitting before me, manifest on Earth. I took refuge at Amma's feet and received my *mantra*. Fate brought me from a normal life into the 'Legend of Amṛita.'

At first, I didn't understand many things in the Indian tradition. For example: the food! Why so spicy?

I also really wondered, "Why do people adore the feet of the master?" In the spirit of being open-minded, I asked around. Adoring the feet was not unique to Amma, but part of the general spiritual tradition of India. The totality of the *Satguru* (true Guru) is contained within their feet. The Guru's feet are the source of all knowledge. I was told knowledge naturally unfolds within for those who sit at the master's feet, just as flowers naturally bloom in the light of the sun.

While intellectual knowledge can be useful, direct experience penetrates the heart. I remember the first time I saw Amma's feet. It was in the summer of 2008 at Amma's Chicago program. I was sitting right near Amma. Amma's socks came off. And there they were — Amma's feet. Amma's feet were glowing; I felt deep peace.

By being with Amma, I experienced feelings of love and happiness that flowed outwards as gratitude and a desire to serve. Time with Amma increased an inner connection with the divine. As this connection increased, other interests fell away like dry leaves in Autumn.

The Guru Pādukā Stōtram says:

> *gurubhaktidābhyām, vairāgya sāmrājyada pūjanābhyām*
> 'The Guru's sandals endow one with devotion to the Guru, which by worshiping, grace one with *vairāgya* — renunciation.'

I first came to *Amritapuri* in August 2009 for one month. I was twenty-one, going to the most magical place on earth — a pink castle in a coconut forest. It felt like a fairy tale. I talked to Amma's photos as if they could answer me, and wrote in my journal as if the pages were alive, listening.

After that first visit, I graduated college early and went back to Amritapuri in January, 2010 on a one-way ticket, intent on becoming a renunciate.

***

I always felt Amma's *prasād* was special. I kept and saved *vibhūti* (sacred ash) packets; prasād candy wrappers; my first prasād apple core carefully dried in Michigan; Dēvī Bhāva petals; holy water; Amma's toothpick from a chai stop; a broken pin from Amma's sāri...boxes and bins full. All of it had been handled by Amma, the Divine Mother.

Across the world, in every tradition are stories of how items touched, used, or worn by saints, sages, and even more rare — incarnations, have miraculous healing properties. They increase the divine connection for humanity. People all around the world have been blessed with Amma's prasād to cherish in their homes. Touching Amma's prasād can transmit the same feelings we associate with darśhan. This reminds me of a special memory:

In November 2011, the Dēvī Bhāva in Detroit had just ended. I wouldn't see Amma again for six months as I was working to save money to move to India. My sweatshirt pocket was packed full of Dēvī Bhāva flower petals and Amma's prasād: two Hershey's-chocolate 'kisses.' I was very fortunate to see Amma off at the airport.

I then planned to visit my grandmother in Ohio the next day. She was dying — the last of her large, Christian Lebanese family. I never physically told Amma she was in hospice or showed Amma her photo, believing Amma's teaching that once you focus on spirituality, God will take care of everything else. When my parents picked me up, we received an urgent call, "Grandma isn't doing well. Don't wait until tomorrow. Come now." We drove to Ohio straight from the airport, straight from Dēvī Bhāva.

I walked into Grandma's room. She smiled very peacefully from her bed and said, "Oh, you've come to say goodbye. All my brothers are waiting for me." She was so content and peaceful, fully accepting her death.

I felt for the scent-free carnation flower petals in my pocket and scattered them across her body. She breathed in deeply and said, "Ahh, they smell so heavenly." My mother and brother also smelled Amma's rose-scent. A thick angelic presence filled the air. It felt so holy, like Amma was there. The next day, my grandmother became unconscious. A week later, she passed away in peace, surrounded by loved ones.

While life often pulls people apart, death brings people together. When all the relatives gathered, there was a cake on the table. I took the prasād chocolate-kisses I'd kept, chopped them into tiny pieces, and sprinkled them all over the cake.

Will my extended family ever meet Amma? I don't know. But, I knew they would eat cake. And even if they didn't manage to eat any of the prasād, God still takes care of the generations that come before and after a spiritual aspirant. Amma proved this to me.

The Guru Pādukā Stōtram says:

> *ananta saṁsāra samudratāra naukāyitābhyām*
> 'The holy sandals of the Guru serve as the boat to cross the endless ocean of saṁsāra.'

This has truly been my experience.

One day in Amritapuri, I passed the 'Amma prasād' table, which offers articles Amma has worn or used, or were given to Amma. The donations they receive go towards Amma's charities. A devotee called me over.

She showed me a bin filled with the most valuable treasure on Earth — Amma's sandals! Not just one pair, but over a dozen pairs of white sandals which had been given to Amma, and had come from Amma's room. For a moment I felt like I was in a dream — where am I? How can something so rare and valuable, the sandals of the Divine Mother — flow so abundantly?

I was in Amritapuri, the city — *puri*, of immortality — *amṛita*. Amritapuri: the City of Immortality; the land of fairytales. When I picked up the pair at the top of the bin, I felt an electric current and a deep cooling presence that reminded me of Amma. I received the most precious item in this universe — The Guru's *pādukās* (sandals).

One night, I lay in bed in the āśhram missing Amma. We were in Amritapuri together — I wasn't physically away. But I wanted to be even closer, secretly wishing I could attend to Amma physically. I placed Amma's sandals on my chest and fell asleep that way, hoping to offer myself at Amma's feet in total surrender.

That night I had an interesting dream — I flew with Amma across the ocean on a plane to three countries, foreign places I had never been to. I was on Amma's tour. As darśhan was ending, one of Amma's attendants tossed Amma's shoes at me and I caught them. I woke up feeling very peaceful, like I had been with Amma and received her darśhan.

Several months later I was on Amma's spring tour, traveling to Malaysia, Singapore, and Australia for the first time. I even got to fly on Amma's flight. At the first program, Prāṇā, one of Amma's darśhan attendants approached me and said, "I need to talk to you about Amma's shoes." I got chills.

She continued, "After Amma finishes darśhan, a local devotee assists Amma with putting her shoes on before she leaves the hall. We need someone to help by bringing Amma's shoes to the local devotee."

I was so surprised — everything was just like the dream with Amma. My prayers made in Amritapuri had been answered: I got to attend to Amma physically, and be nearby when Amma left the hall — a program highlight. When Amma walks to the exit, she stops and gives so much love and attention to her children lining the path. This outpour of love is reflected back by hundreds of smiling faces, giggling and laughing, blissed out with divine love.

It is a miracle to spend so much time with Amma; Jesus' disciples only had three years.

But sometimes I take prasād and Amma for granted. I don't put in the extra effort to savor my experiences or note down what happened.

Each prasād item transmits Amma's śhakti (divine energy) and consciousness. With it, Amma may provide a *saṅkalpa* or divine resolve. If prasād is approached with reverence and respect, it can teach us. That attitude will influence our relationship with other objects, people, and the natural world.

Prasād is a gift to help us climb the ladder of seeing the divine in everything, to recognize that creator and creation are not two, but one. For example, most people see candy wrappers and think of waste. But when devotees see candy wrappers, we think of Amma and her positive vibrations.

Amma asks us to approach everything with reverence, to even bow before using a pen. This attitude of respect towards all of creation allows us to grow and see everything as prasād, as sacred. By doing this, the vibrations around those objects change. They get permeated with a distinct, positive śhakti coming from our attitude, our mantras, and our visualizations.

***

As we age memory can fade, so capture the moments with the Guru. They are an ongoing puzzle and mystery to be studied with love. Some only make sense years later. Others continue to reveal new meaning.

One time at a beach meditation, a devotee got on the mic during the open mic time, and started praising Amma out of love. Amma interrupted and said, "Ehhh? Screws loose, me!" indicating she was crazy. I laughed so hard. She reminded me of Yoda! I remembered my original prayer to meet a Jedi. Amma really is like Yoda, speaking plain, simple English, yet secretly all-powerful. I have received so much more than I could ever have dreamed of — the mother of all.

Two years into my honeymoon with Amma, during the 2009 U.S. Summer Tour, Amma named me *Sadānand* — eternal bliss. She had me carefully practice the pronunciation three times, which I butchered with my Michigan accent.

"SAAdanand," I repeated.

"No, SadAAnand," replied Amma.

"SadAAnand," I corrected myself.

The *brahmachārī* translating explained that my name consists of two words, *sadā* — always and ānand — bliss. Sadānand can be translated as 'always happy,' or 'eternal bliss.'

An Indian devotee told me that '*Sādanand*' actually means depressed and without any bliss! So the pronunciation really makes a huge difference. Only years later did I remember how eternal bliss was my initial spiritual goal. Amma was at the beginning and will be at the end. Amma is there every step of the way.

Despite the name, I don't always feel joyful. Sometimes I feel very low and identify as Sādanand. I joked with my friend that while traveling on Amma's world tours, I learned that I can be depressed on tropical islands, in ancient Indian cities, in Paris, in the desert — anywhere! But why? In Amma's pure, divine presence, I constantly face the contrast of my shortcomings and selfishness. There is no escape.

I have experienced a very sobering inability to change through self-effort. Despite this, I have often felt too ashamed to come to Amma about my *vāsanās*[19]. In Dallas, I asked Amma about this. She smiled so sweetly, touched my face, and said, "Don't worry. Everyone is like this. There is a bhajan, 'I give you my shame and my pride.' Think of yourself as an onion and offer everything to Amma, stripping away all of the layers."

I felt inspired to give Amma my negativity but didn't know how. I thought about making an origami onion with my vāsanās written on it but couldn't manage it. Slowly the concept slipped from my mind.

The tour concluded that year in Tokyo with the celebration of Guru Pūrṇimā followed by Dēvī Bhāva. There I was, flying with Amma around the world, my deepest wish, yet still tortured by my mind and desires. I couldn't fully enjoy these special events. At the end of Dēvī Bhāva, something in the trash caught my eye. It was a box that had contained prasād offered to Amma. It was the most beautiful box, made with love and care. Suddenly everything clicked. That was going to become my vāsanā box. I would fill it with my mental trash, offer it to Amma, and ask her to take the garbage out. It would be my Guru Pūrṇimā offering.

I wrote out my vāsanās in Malayalam on different scraps of clean trash so that Amma could read them one by one and I wouldn't need a translator. This way it would also be very discreet, just the two of us. I wrote a different vāsanā on various pieces of garbage — plastic, cardboard, paper, foil, and cloth,

---

[19] Latent tendency or subtle desire that manifests as thought, motive and action; subconscious impression gained from experience. Here, the author specifically refers to the negative tendencies of the mind.

placed them inside a clear garbage bag, and put that bag in the vāsanā box.

If you offer your shame to the Guru, be prepared. Amma took the box and slowly read out the vāsanās in front of everyone, one by one, again and again. *Krōdham*, *kāmam*, *duḥkham*, and so on — anger, desire, depression, lust, laziness, greed, rivalry, jealousy, hatred, shame and pride.

Amma said, "You forgot competitiveness!" Then she added lust a second time. Amma took my shame and pride, and began her work making the whole thing as public as possible. She looked at me with so much supernatural love. As Amma held the vāsanā box, the vāsanās became prasād.

Back in Amritapuri, whenever Amma saw me she would say, "That boy gave me a vāsanā box. It was full of anger, lust, depression and so on." She told everyone about the vāsanā box. It was an incredible outpouring of love and attention.

Amma even brought the box from her room to evening bhajans and showed it to the entire āśhram, just like a kid doing 'show and tell' at school.

The next spring in Australia, Amma told me, "You are famous now, because of the vāsanā box. It's on Facebook, it's in the āśhram's *Matruvani* magazine, it's on the āśhram website too. It's in Swāminī Amma's (Swāminī Kṛiṣhṇāmṛita Prāṇā's) book." It even became an English bhajan.

I wish I could share a happy ending — that I gave Amma all of my vāsanās and that they are now all gone! However, it's a long process. Amma calls me "vāsanā box," especially when I've behaved badly, reminding me of her all-knowing nature. Let's just say, Amma still often calls me "vāsanā box."

I had one victory though. By even trying to give Amma my shortcomings, Amma rewarded me with her love, unconditional and limitless. Amma's love is the saving grace and inspiration for us to get up and keep trying, no matter how many times we may fail or fall.

Amma's attendant, Swāminī Śhrī Lakṣhmī Prāṇājī recently told me the vāsanā box is still in Amma's room.

This shows Amma is not disgusted by our weaknesses. We are like babies with dirty diapers. A baby cannot change its own diaper. The mother patiently addresses the need of the hour with sincere love. I am like such a baby, stuck in a dirty, filthy diaper, totally helpless and in need of saving grace.

There is a prayer in Amma's *Mānasa Pūjā* (mental worship) to the Divine Mother:

'O Mother, You are pure love. I am too impure to deserve your grace. Still, bear with me. Mother, please be with me. You are the holiest river. I am a stagnant, dirty pond. You flow to me and purify me, overlooking my shortcomings and forgiving my mistakes.'

May we all cross the ocean of saṁsāra under the infinite care and compassion of our most beloved Amma. Our patient and ever-caring mother, teacher, and friend who comes down to our level without losing enthusiasm. We have all won the universal lottery to have Amma.

We will all surely progress, as long as we are patient and just stay on the boat. If we do fall off the boat and start to drown, we must keep reaching for the life-preserver of Amma's sandals, the most sacred wonder of wonders — and hold on tight. Surely, Amma is nearby ready to save us, never forsaking us.

9

Satsang and Sēvā in my Life

Nihsima M Sandhu - USA

Let me start by sharing a few words about my past and how I arrived at *Amritapuri* — Amma's holy abode.

I'm most grateful to you Amma for my human birth and that too, for being born into a spiritual and loving Sikh family. During my childhood, we were most fortunate as you gave us Bābājī, a living saint from Punjab as our family Guru and guide. We often went to his āśhram to do *sēvā*, for *satsang* and to receive his spiritual guidance. Through Amma's grace, we also received the blessings of other saints and sages including a visit by Sathya Sai Baba to our home in Delhi.

Atithi dēvō bhava — the culture of treating a guest as god — was also given much importance in our home. Guests could drop in anytime for a meal or for overnight stays; some stayed for months.

Our happy, loving world came crashing down when my mother and grandmother were taken from us suddenly in a tragic car accident. I was fifteen at the time. This was my first real lesson in the impermanence of human life. It was our worst nightmare, and a real test of our faith. My brother encouraged us to be strong, and to remember the sacrifices our Sikh Gurus had made to inspire us and instill us with faith and courage.

Thus our spiritual foundation gave us added courage to not fall victim to our circumstances, but to gallop forward like true spiritual warriors with full faith in the Lord.

Upon successfully finishing high school in Delhi with high marks, I was blessed with the opportunity to further my studies in the U.S.. Upon arriving in the U.S., I was disappointed to find out that a close relative had cheated us out of a large sum of money, most of which had been earmarked for my education and stay in America.

Without losing hope, and to avoid unnecessary financial strain on my father, I decided to work and pay for my education. Divine grace helped me transition easily from a luxurious life-style to a very simple one. Full time work and full time college also taught me to be very focused and disciplined with my time.

The Lord was kind and rewarded my sincere efforts. I graduated at the top of my business school, and was placed on the national dean's list that ranked me in the top 2% of graduates in the U.S. for that year. This coupled with good work experience gave me a very good start in my career, and I quickly climbed the corporate ladder.

I was blessed with a high salary, an unlimited expense account, a fancy car, a luxurious home in San Francisco, many friends and five-star vacations around the world. My career also brought me in touch with some very successful people including celebrities, high profile politicians, and presidents of multi-billion dollar companies. However, I soon realized that none of these people seemed to share the freedom found in the joyful presence of the simple sages that I had come into contact with in my past.

I was grateful that the lord had fulfilled most of my worldly desires, but I also began to recognize that *apāra prakṛiti* or the external world of the senses brought with it much suffering.

I started to read spiritual books and became introspective, as my hunger to discover the Divine within myself deepened. I wanted *samatvam* or equanimity of mind, that would help me wade through the waters of the many sorrows in life.

I prayed to the lord to show me the way, and within six months my sincere prayers were answered in an unimaginable way. The Divine Mother herself, manifested in my life.

The 742nd name of the *Lalitā Sahasranāma* is:

> *ōm bhava dāva sudhā vṛiṣhtyai namaḥ*
> 'I bow to Her, who is the rain of nectar falling on the forest fire of worldly existence.'

My first meeting with Amma happened when my sister Guramrit saw an article in the local newspaper about Amma, "the hugging saint," who was holding a program only two miles from her home in Marin County, California. Guramrit invited me to join her the next day on November 19th, 2000 so that we could receive Amma's *darśhan* together.

We excitedly arrived at the venue at 9:00 the next morning. To our dismay, we were denied entry as we were told, it was the last day of a closed retreat. Not knowing what to do, we were on the verge of tears, because we didn't want to have to wait until the next year for our darśhan. Just then, a long-time devotee magically showed up, and helped us get permission to register late for the retreat. We are eternally grateful for his assistance, and felt it to be divine intervention.

We hastily registered, were given darśhan tokens, and got seated. The atmosphere seemed magical and surreal. Soon, we heard the celestial sound of a conch shell being blown, and the most beautiful divine being dressed in a white sāri arrived.

With a beaming smile, she made her way to the *pīṭham* (a platform-like seat) after a heartwarming *pāda pūjā* welcoming ceremony. As meditation started, I found myself slipping into deep meditation, and had a vision of Lord Gaṇēśha and Lord Kṛiṣhṇa standing to the right of Gaṇēśha. Gradually, I opened my eyes after meditation, and my gaze fell directly on the *'Immortal Bliss'* magazine sitting in front of me.

I randomly opened the magazine and froze. There was a picture of Lord Gaṇēśha on the left page, and on his right was Lord Kṛiṣhṇa. Amazed at this coincidence, I took it as a good omen that the divine had brought me to the right place.

When our token numbers were called, we both excitedly joined the darśhan line. As Amma embraced us for a joint darśhan together, strong emotions gripped me. First I sensed the deep joy of returning home and being reunited with my beloved, followed by a deep pain caused by years of separation, which made me cry uncontrollably as I lay in Amma's arms. Upon lifting out of her divine embrace, I felt so much lighter, like a huge weight had just been taken off my shoulders...

The 631st name of the *Lalitā Sahasranāma* is:

> *ōm divya gandhāḍhyāyai namaḥ*
> 'I bow to the one who is richly endowed with divine fragrance.'

Over the next few days following our darśhan, I often strangely smelled a rose fragrance in my flat, and heard the soft whisper of a voice saying in Hindi, *"Āo merī beṭī āo"* which means, "Come my daughter, come."

A few weeks later, my inner Amma guided me to read the book *On the Road to Freedom,* written by one of Amma's senior disciples, Swāmī Paramātmānandajī.

In one of the chapters, he mentioned his deep sadness upon leaving Amma, and how he missed being in her presence and his experience of smelling a rose fragrance in the train compartment throughout his journey. Amma later told him that she never left him and was with him all along his journey and in the train compartment too.

In her special way, Amma was also letting me know of her omniscience and her daily presence in my life through her voice and her rose perfume, and was calling me to her.

Sant Kabir, in one of his *bhajans* sings about the glory of the Guru, without whose help one cannot cross this ocean of transmigration:

> *guru gōvind dōnō khaḍe kākē lāgū pāy*
> *balihārī guru āpnē gōvind diyō batāy*
> 'If both God in the form of Gōvind and the Guru were to appear at the door, whose feet would I worship first?'

He answers himself, saying, "It has to be the Guru's feet first, because without him, how would I have known God?"

In the *Bhagavad Gītā* Chapter 4, verse 34, Lord Kṛiṣhṇa says:

> *tad viddhi praṇipātēna pariprashnēna sēvayā*
> *upadēkṣhyanti tē jñānaṁ jñāninas tattva darshinaḥ*
> 'Know that the wise who have experienced the truth will teach you the knowledge through long prostration, repeated enquiry and service.'

My *Satguru* had arrived on my doorstep and had saved me, thus starting a new chapter in my life. With Amma's grace, I started visiting MA Center in San Ramon on Saturdays for satsang and sēvā.

***

In 2001, I was thrilled to receive a *mantra* from Amma. The word 'mantra' consists of two words: 'mananāt,' (by constant repetition) and 'tra' or 'trāyate' (one is saved). So mantra means 'By constant repetition one is saved.'

The *Guru Granth Sahib,* which is the sacred book of the Sikhs, says that *mantra japa* (mantra repetition) is the way that we can conquer the five evils of ego, greed, attachment, anger and lust, thus transforming the impure mind into a pure, contemplative and strong mind.

Recognizing that I was well endowed with *vāsanās*, and eager to purify my mind, and also to keep a constant connection with Amma, I started chanting my mantra so obsessively that I almost answered my office phone with it. I'd start with Ōm...then would quickly add good morning, catching myself just in time.

Amma, the all-knowing, also knew my deep rooted connection to music and dance. In my early years with Amma, as part of the music that is always played during darśhan, a recording of a Punjabi bhajan would miraculously be playing whenever I joined the darśhan line, and much to Amma's delight, I would find myself shaking my shoulders playfully, lost in a Punjabi *bhangra* dance move as I fell into her arms for darśhan.

During other darśhans, I would find myself crying and asking for true love, or to help fulfill my deep-rooted desire to serve the poor.

When crying or laughing, Amma would lovingly rock this grown daughter like a baby from side to side, showering me with kisses and immense love.

In another bhajan, Sant Kabirji sings:

> *sabai rasāyan mai kiyā prēm samān na kōī*
> *rati ek tan mē sancharai sab tan kanchan hōī*
> 'I've tested all sorts of medicines but nothing is comparable to pure love. You just take one drop of it, and your whole being is transformed into pure gold.'

The flower bud of my new life was carefully opening one petal at a time; nothing was being forced. Friendships that weren't in sync with my path, very naturally dissolved. I started to enjoy solitude. A small pocket booklet of the *Gītā* became my new friend, in fact I got extra copies to hand out to any interested seekers.

Saturday satsang and sēvā at the San Ramon āśhram, Sundays at the *Gurdwara* (Sikh temple), and Monday satsang in San Francisco became a regular family practice for my father, my sister, and me. In addition to my daily *sādhanā* of *archana*, mantra japa and meditation, I switched to a healthy vegetarian diet, and began to practice daily *Sūrya Namaskār* or 'Sun Salutation' yōga postures.

***

My sister and I started to follow and serve Amma on her U.S. tours, as well as through helping with numerous Amma events and fundraisers. Later we were both blessed by Amma to become satsang coordinators, and were most fortunate to host satsangs in our homes as well.

Amma's unconditional love and service to humanity really inspired me. I was now craving to do something more meaningful than just working a corporate job in financial services. Therefore, at the June 2003 San Ramon program, I asked Amma if I could resign from my job to come to India to serve her in time for her fiftieth birthday celebrations.

Amma hesitated and asked me to wait until summer, which left me confused as it was already summer. To my surprise, a couple of months later in August, I got a letter from my company saying that they were closing their West Coast offices, and offered me a very comfortable severance package.

My joy knew no bounds; Amma had saved me! Had I resigned, I would have lost the whole compensation package.

I joyfully attended Amma's fiftieth birthday celebration in Amritapuri. While serving with the 'Women's Sēvā Team,' I witnessed this most amazing spiritual event. At the same time, it provided me with many lessons in humility and surrender.

During the 2004 U.S. Summer Tour, Amma gave me the name '*Nihsīma*' — Limitless. I legalized it, and per Amma's wish, that same year I started a new career as a jewelry designer.

Amma had inspired me to think beyond my selfish needs. I now wanted my work to be part of my sādhanā, and as a means of giving back to humanity, especially to women's and children's charities. I prayed that while performing my *svadharma* (one's own duty), I would be able to feel Amma's presence wherever I went.

Amma had rekindled the artist in me, and jewelry design became a form of meditation for me. My jewelry became one of Amma's instruments helping to promote her in the world.

Each piece in the collection that was created was named after a universal goddess. Each 'Thank you' card accompanying the jewelry gave the divine properties of each goddess for the wearer to embrace, and thus connected them to their own divinity. Beautiful pouches intended for holding the jewelry were made with love by children in an orphanage in Jaipur, and every card ended with the *Vēdic* chant, '*lokāḥ samastāḥ sukhinō bhavantu*' — May all beings in all the worlds be happy.

By Amma's grace, I was blessed with an amazing team to work with, and was able to share my Amma story with thousands of amazing women while supporting their causes at various fundraisers across the U.S.. Thus many people became aware of Amma and her humanitarian efforts. I was happy to see some of them come for Amma's darśhan too.

During the 2009 U.S. Summer Tour, Amma asked me to create a new jewelry department for all the western tours. I was overjoyed and felt tremendous gratitude to be her tiny instrument in this new sēvā.

With just two and a half months to prepare for the upcoming Europe Tour, I happily put my own business on hold, tied up any loose ends, and a few weeks later boarded a flight to Jaipur. After placing my jewelry orders in Jaipur, I arrived in Amritapuri a couple of weeks later to show Amma the new jewelry samples.

***

Upon enquiring about the upcoming tour, I was informed that the Europe Tour was known to be the most physically demanding, due to very cold weather, very long bus rides, and long sēvā hours.

Injuries caused by a couple of earlier car accidents had left me with a very fragile back. I was unsure if my back would survive the twenty-hour long bus rides without it going into spasm, and I wondered if that would hinder me in performing my sēvā with maximum efficiency and *śhraddhā*.

In the *Bhagavad Gītā*, Chapter 2 verse 7, Arjuna says:

> *kārpaṇya dōṣhōpahata svabhāvaḥ*
> *pṛichchhāmi tvāṁ dharmasammūḍha chētāḥ*
> *yachchhrēyaḥ syān niśhchitaṁ brūhi tanmē*
> *śhiṣhyaste'haṁ śhādhi māṁ tvāṁ prapannam*
> 'My nature is affected by inner weakness, my mind confused about my duty. I ask you, tell me decisively what is best for me. I am your disciple; teach me for I have taken refuge in You.'

In a state of '*Kārpaṇya dōṣham*' — inner weakness — my mind in turmoil, frustrated and struggling with indecision for days, with the tour only a couple of weeks away, I finally decided to seek Amma's advice, hoping that I would be relieved of my fears and anxiety through her reassuring words of wisdom.

During darśhan, as I shared my plight with Amma, she quickly responded with, "You think about it and come back." Disappointed, and with no solution at hand, I went back to my room with a heavy heart.

That same night, my sister offered me a book to read. It was the biography of a Punjabi saint called Tapasvijī Mahārāj. I felt a strong urge to start reading the book that night, and couldn't put it down... It was about this saint who was born as Prince Kṛiṣhṇa Siṅgh into the royal family of Punjab.

Fed up with the political unrest in his father's kingdom which kept it in a state of perpetual war with neighboring kings, the young prince rode to Delhi to request the help of the emperor in a final effort to bring peace to his kingdom, and to his own state of mind.

When the young prince met Emperor Bahādur Shāh, he found him repeating the Lord's name, doing japa on his *mālā* (rosary). Hearing the young prince's plight, the Emperor said, "Prince Kṛiṣhṇa Siṅgh, neither you nor I have any peace of mind. I now feel that devotion to God brings more happiness to man than the possession of an empire, and that a saint's life is preferable to that of a king. I now bid you farewell — Peace be with you."

These words had a profound effect on the prince. Instead of returning to his kingdom he changed directions, and rode towards Haridwar instead. The spirit of renunciation started burning within him. He removed all his costly jewels, clothing, and his sword.

Tying it all in a bundle and putting it on his horse's back, he wrote a note and tied it around his horse's neck asking anyone who found the jewels to take care of his horse too. With that, Kṛiṣhṇa Siṅgh gave up the world in pursuit of *mōkṣha*.

He practiced severe austerities: He spent twenty-seven years standing with one arm raised while sleeping or meditating, and another five years sitting continuously next to a blazing fire, even under the scorching sun of the Indian summer. He performed all that penance just to receive a vision of Lord Kṛishṇa.

This story touched me deeply and made me realize how lucky we are that Lord Kṛishṇa and the Divine Mother herself have descended to our plane of existence in the singular form of Amma, and that I had been offered this most amazing opportunity to be of service.

Above all, having the opportunity to receive her darśhan through touch, sight, sound, word, and thought was enough to make even the *dēvas* and *dēvīs,* the gods and goddesses, in all the worlds jealous.

I finally got it. I just needed to take the final leap of faith and surrender all my fears at her lotus feet. I realized my body was never mine, it was the Lord's; and only the Lord knew what was the best way to use it.

It's often mentioned that our faith in the divine should be akin to a baby monkey holding onto its mother. The little one totally surrenders without any doubt that its mother won't let it fall. The mother monkey leaps from tree to tree, yet the baby grips tightly with immense faith. This is the kind of faith humans are expected to repose in the Lord.

In my next darśhan, with joined palms and tears profusely rolling down my cheeks, I begged Amma for her forgiveness for my lack of śhraddhā and trust. I added that I no longer had any confusion, and felt blessed to serve her on all the western tours starting with the Europe Tour. Happy with my response, Amma hugged me and showered me with many kisses, and had me sit next to her for hours.

With Amma's grace, I managed to sleep very comfortably without pain through all the long bus rides, and was thus able to serve with much enthusiasm and vigor even after long hours of sēvā through the entire Europe Tour.

By Amma's grace, since 2009, our department has really grown, and Amma has blessed me as her tiny instrument in many other sēvās in India as well as overseas.

Thank you so much Amma for your grace and infinite love. My humble prayer to you is that we live each day according to your teachings, and as the bhajan says:

> *śhyām śhyām kūkadī maiṅ āpē śhyām hō ga yī*
> 'Calling your name over and over again, O Śhyām
> (another name for Kṛiṣhṇa), I become one with you.'

Amma, please bless us all with *parābhakti* — supreme devotion — so that we can all ultimately merge into your lotus feet while chanting your holy name.

10

The Center of My Spiritual World — Amma's Divine Embrace

Susi - Germany

The 92nd name in the *108 names of Amma* is:

> *ōm śhiṣhya saṅkrāmita svīya projjvalad brahma varchasē namaḥ*
> 'I bow down to Amma, who has transmitted her divine brilliance to her disciples.'

To start with, I would like to thank Amma for inspiring so many of her darling children to come up with brilliant talks that have brightened up our days during this dreadful lockdown. From now on we will not just see unknown faces around us, but will be able to connect stories to them, and in this way feel like a true Amma family.

Something happened in the mid-1990s which showed that even back then, Amma foresaw that difficult times would be coming upon us. During one of the Europe tours, in Munich, I informed Amma that my father had invited her to visit his garden on Sunday morning so that she could take rest there.

Amma knew exactly how much my father struggled to understand who Amma was. A conservative businessman, he felt uneasy about this holy woman from India that his daughter was so attracted to. Amma agreed to come to the garden, and my heart began racing at the thought of these two worlds — Amma and my father — coming together for the first time.

Sunday morning came, and Amma left for my father's garden. My flat was just around the corner from my parents' house, not even a two-minute walk away, so I had just enough time to run ahead, and alert them that Amma was about to arrive.

My parents were sunbathing in the garden in shorts and tee-shirts, not very appropriate attire to receive Amma in, but it was too late for them to change, as Amma and the *swāmīs* had already arrived.

Amma walked straight up to him and gave him a hug. Can you imagine? Amma looking like a beautiful white cloud, embracing a man even taller and heavier than I, standing there in his Sunday morning garden shorts...

In no time, Amma made my father feel at ease by starting a conversation about our family business. Suddenly, the bells from a nearby church rang out. My parents' house was just across the street from a big Catholic church, so the sound was deafening. My father told Amma that the neighbors felt so disturbed by the bells that they filed a complaint with the city authority to try to prevent the church from ringing them.

Amma looked very pensive and said, "Now they feel disturbed by the sound of the bells, but in the future, times will become so hard that people will long to hear the sound of the bells just to feel some hope."

We wondered then to which time in the future Amma may be referring, but now with the isolation people are facing during this pandemic, many feel depressed and jailed in their own homes, missing social contact and the freedom to move about as they please. Today the sound of those bells most probably gives people hope that this pandemic will pass, and that good days are soon to come.

***

Amma's *darśhan* is the center of my spiritual world. For me, all questions get answered through that one profound gesture of compassion. Watching Amma giving darśhan for hours and hours has made me come to understand the nature of divinity — it is a constant flow of love between God and his creation.

In front of our eyes, the underlying principle of creation unfolds during Amma's darśhan. She is definitely the most powerful, sacred warrior of all time, defending this principle of love and compassion with every breath of her life — not teaching it through mere words, but by enacting it, and creating concrete examples, such as her vast charitable network for all to see, experience, and take part in.

Once we have taken in a good amount of Amma's sweet selfless love, we come to the point where the question arises, how do I make this stream of love a constant experience in my life? How do I transform my sadness, my anger, my negativities, and my fears so I can stay in that state of experiencing the divine at all times?

Coming from a Catholic background where we live in constant fear of falling prey to sin, the picture that Amma creates of divinity lies in stark contrast. Experiencing God-as-mother, pouring love upon you no matter what you do, was one of the biggest revelations for me. It was so healing and reassuring and gave me a solid emotional foundation to build my life on. Amma picks us up and teaches us patiently how to lead a decent life.

Another quality that we can learn by witnessing Amma's darśhan is accepting both good and bad with equanimity. Once, Amma was taking a walk with us in the neighborhood in Munich where I grew up. We reached a little park and Amma sat down on a bench. All of us sat around her on the ground. After a while a man passed by, stopped, and stared at Amma — he could not believe his eyes that Amma was sitting there. Overjoyed he asked, “Amma what are you doing here?”

Amma humbly answered that she was just taking a walk to catch some fresh air after a long journey. The man folded his hands in reverence and told Amma that he could never have dreamt of meeting Amma outside in a park, in such an intimate setting. He felt deeply blessed and thanked Amma for taking a minute to speak with him.

After a few minutes, another man came by and stopped. He too looked at Amma and those around her, but his reaction was the opposite. The man apparently found the exotic-looking people he had come across during his evening walk disturbing.

He shouted something like, “Why don’t you go back to where you came from?” then left. I felt so upset about his rudeness but Amma calmly said, “This is the nature of the world – within not more than fifteen minutes, both good and bad experiences have occurred. We should learn to accept both with the same attitude of even-mindedness.”

Without perfect even-mindedness, how could Amma run her vast, global charitable network? Endless challenges and problems must arise, but I have never seen Amma despondent or in a state of defeat. She puts forth endless enthusiasm, coping calmly with each situation, and inspires her children to do the same.

Another divine quality we see in Amma is infinite patience. I once asked Swāmījī, “What are the most frequent questions that devotees ask Amma?” He replied that it’s the same all over the world: questions about relationships, health, career, and money. How has Amma been so patiently able to listen to and answer these same questions over and over for the past thirty years?

***

Before I met Amma, I sought help through psychotherapy to overcome the trauma I had experienced when I was eight-years old. My mother had already suffered through many years of depression and psychosis when she decided to end her life. For me, the hidden message in this act of desperation was that I was not good enough to make her want to live. I developed a strong sense of self-rejection which followed me like a shadow for many years.

When I had my first darśhan, I experienced the unconditional love that I had been longing for, for so many years. The sadness that had manifested in my throat like a lump of iron lifted the moment Amma hugged me, and never returned.

What psychotherapy could not heal after many sessions, Amma's darśhan transformed with one hug. However, without the experience of extreme pain caused by that trauma, I would not have been able to gauge the magnitude of the blessing that lies in Amma's embrace. I felt unburdened like I never had before in my life.

In the summer of 1990, I discovered Amma's biography in a bookstore. The young Indian woman in the black and white photo on the cover was radiating a pure love that captured my heart instantly. I purchased the book, read it in one day, and told everybody that I was determined to find this saintly woman no matter what. Who would have guessed that meeting Amma was just around the corner for me, without having to travel anywhere.

In July of the same year, I married a brahmin man from Bangalore. Some of my friends whom I had invited to my wedding turned down the invitation, as Amma was holding her program in Munich on the very same day. Oh lord...was I torn between two conflicting desires!

I also wanted to meet Amma right away. Though it seemed unlikely, I carried a little hope in my heart that perhaps after the marriage festivities were over, I could sneak away, and see Amma before we left for India, where a traditional Hindu wedding ceremony awaited us.

My wish came true! The evening before we were supposed to leave for India, my husband, my mother-in-law, and I drove to Amma's program in downtown Munich.

As we moved up in the darśhan line, closer and closer to Amma, she saw us from a distance and gave me a glance that made my heart leap with joy. It was as if I had plunged into an ocean of love. Memories of my life raced through my mind at high speed, and by the time it was our turn for darśhan, I was sure something profound was about to happen.

When Amma opened her arms, she said, "Finally you have come, my children." I was more than surprised to hear this, though everything felt perfectly right. Amma talked to my mother-in-law for a long time as she sobbed, unloading all her anxiety about her only son getting married to a Christian girl, and how this marriage would be the end of their brahmin lineage.

Amma lovingly scolded her, saying couldn't she see that my husband and I were meant for each other? Then she added, "They are my children, don't worry, Amma will take care of everything."

From that night of July 28, 1990 on, Amma took it upon herself to make our marriage work in all aspects. The two families from different cultures grew together in a beautiful way. Everything unfolded like in a dream and looking back, it was Amma's blessings and grace alone that brought everything in life.

***

After returning from India, I contacted the main organizer of Amma's Munich program, and signed up to do *sēvā* for the local *satsang* group. When my husband invited Amma and the swāmīs to stay in our house, Amma graciously agreed.

Since 1992 until now, we have been blessed to host Amma when she holds programs in Munich. Whenever Amma arrived, her divine vibration would take over the whole house. It was as if the entire neighborhood was soaked in a deep stillness and peace.

Over the years, we have felt that our family has been healed, and that people can always feel Amma's presence in our house. On one occasion, Amma told me to never sell the house. Since she had stayed there so many times, it had become a temple. When I eventually moved to Amritapuri, the house was transferred to Amma, and it is now part of M.A. Foundation, Germany.

While many things in my life have changed, only Amma has stayed by my side as the unchanging support.

At some point, it became clear that I was unable to conceive; a fact that I was never unhappy about.

In my prayers I promised Amma, "If you don't make me go through the experience of having children of my own, I will try my best to follow your example of universal motherhood." This became the first spiritual exercise I attempted to put into practice: take the time to listen to people, and try as best I could to help them solve their problems.

In 1994 I got a *mantra* from Amma. I practiced focusing on repeating the mantra no matter what I was doing, and it became my foundation in life. What was happening on the outside was no longer so important, as through repetition of the mantra, I felt connected to Amma.

Although I wasn't able to spend much time in Amma's physical presence when I was married, I felt a strong inner bond with her. My *sādhanā* was very simple: attend the weekly Munich Amma satsang program, and try to think of Amma in all situations.

I had also lived a life surrounded by material abundance. Before meeting Amma, I felt that all that wealth was meaningless and empty. Once I met Amma however, I learned that money was a blessing from God, and should be used to help other people.

After ten years of marriage, it became obvious that the plans my husband had for his future and mine were different. From the day we met Amma, I thought that our lives would become more and more devoted to her service, and I always thought that if I waited long enough, my husband would share my dreams.

He was very active when Amma visited Munich, helping to get everything ready for the program. Beyond this, he didn't share my desire to live with Amma. The years went by, and slowly our lives drifted apart.

Amma described what I was going through when she said, "Human love is binding love, divine love is liberating love — a constant flow of bliss, a never-ending honeymoon."

There were times when I was so drunk with love for Amma, that everybody else felt like a stranger to me, including my husband. My mind was struggling with the question of whether it was my *dharma* (life duty) to stay married, or to break away and follow Amma.

In 2005, I was diagnosed with ovarian cancer and had to go through surgery and chemotherapy. I realized that I needed to experience the possibility of death to have the strength to stand up for what I wanted, and to not compromise anymore. After being released from the hospital, I moved to the horse farm near Frankfurt, which has become the German āśhram.

When it became clear that my husband would not join me in my new home, I told Amma adamantly that I would not go back to him. In this way, my marriage came to an end.

By Amma's grace, I recovered very quickly from cancer and was ready for the next step. In December 2008, I moved to Amritapuri. I did not make any resolve other than to always remain in Amma's physical presence. Every one of Amma's children has their own individual path to follow. And no one except our Divine Mother can properly guide the paths tread by her millions of children.

One of my sēvās is to beautify the corridors and waiting areas at AIMS (Amrita Institute of Medical Sciences, Kochi). I told Amma during one darśhan that I felt that the look of the hospital did not reflect the high standard of medical services that AIMS provides.

Without hesitation, Amma called the administrator at AIMS. She told him that I had a university degree in art, and that I would be coming to beautify AIMS.

My task was to put up nature photos that would provide a soothing effect on people while they waited to see their doctor. I tried to imagine what patients would be interested in seeing, so I put up different themes like 'Historic Monuments of Kerala,' 'The Sacred River Ganges,' and 'Animals of Africa.'

What makes AIMS so unique is that the moment you enter the building, you sense a feeling of family spirit — a spirit that wants to facilitate the best possible treatment using the highest standards, combined with the best loving care from all levels of the hospital staff.

***

I would like to end this satsang with a story about something that happened in 2006. Sometimes it is necessary for Amma to straighten us out a little when our egos go out of control. Amma's lessons give a moment of pain for the ego, while simultaneously providing the soothing remedy — her love that shakes us out of our *tamasic* (inert, dull) state, and makes us more aware and cautious.

I will never forget a first-hand experience I had of being put through the spin cycle of Amma's ego-washing machine. Sometimes, when Amma flew back to India after her U.S. Tour, she would make a short stopover in Germany.

So that Amma could have a few hours of rest, no one was supposed to know about her going there. When Amma landed at the airport, I picked her up at the gate, and let Amma know with a little touch of pride in my voice, that absolutely nobody knew about her stopping in Munich.

Amma laughed, and I thought it was in appreciation of her visit being kept secret. But the opposite was true! Amma was not at all pleased, and said that she wanted to give *prasād* (food blessed by Amma) to the main organizers of the Munich program that evening on her way back to the airport. At this point I still thought, "Everything is under control, the mission to make sure that Amma gets a few hours of rest can still be accomplished..."

However, everything turned out far differently than I could ever have imagined. Anyone who has hosted Amma knows that once Amma and the group reach the house, there is a constant flow of little chores that have to be attended to — from serving food; to helping with laundry; to setting up the Wi-Fi etc.

I got so busy that I just didn't have time to call the eight main Munich program organizers. I only made one call, and asked that organizer to call the other seven people.

In addition, in the heat of the moment, I must have forgotten to tell the organizer that apart from these eight people, nobody else was supposed to know that Amma was in town. I never found out who spread the word, but just after Amma had settled down to rest in her room, the doorbell rang, and the first group of devotees entered the garden, and sat waiting on the grass to see their beloved Amma.

I watched from the window as more and more people came streaming into the compound — I was in total distress. The first thing I did was to disconnect the doorbell so that Amma would not be disturbed by the sound. Then I disconnected the phone to stop people from calling and inquiring as to when the evening program with Amma would be starting.

I went around the entire house pulling curtains down to prevent the devotees from looking inside, hoping to protect the last bit of privacy for Amma's group. Then I went to the kitchen and cooked the *pāyasam* (sweet rice pudding) for the prasād, trying to add as much love as I had left in my heart — the rest was pure guilt!

Amma must have been informed of what was happening, because she came out to the garden a few hours after her arrival. To my surprise, she asked for a chair, sat down, and looked at all her children with a beaming smile — she seemed delighted to see each one of them.

Making a bigger fool of myself than I already had, I jumped up and announced, "Amma is not giving darśhan, only prasād!" I was trying to 'save' Amma from the physical strain of giving darśhan...

Amma looked at me as if I had gone mad, and started affectionately waving the devotees over to her to give them darśhan one by one.

Setting aside her own comfort, Amma turned the afternoon into a festival of love for her children — a blessed memory — an unexpected shower of grace that the devotees remember vividly to this day.

On the way back to the airport, I apologized to Amma for my inability to protect what little time she had had in Germany, so that she could rest. Amma's answer still rings in my ears today. She said, "What do you expect? You cannot stop the flow of love from a mother to her children."

May we all be worthy of this divine love that shines on us now, and that will shine on generations yet to come.

11
Form and Formless Worship

Sugata Duygu Akartuna - Türkiye

Bhakti and the worship of two different aspects of the divine are elaborated by Lord Kṛiṣhṇa in Chapter 12 of the *Bhagavad Gītā*. I will attempt to relate this kind of worship to my own experiences with our beloved Amma.

The two aspects are called *saguṇa* and *nirguṇa* in Sanskrit, and come from the root word *guṇa*, meaning quality, attribute, shape or form. Saguṇa signifies with attributes — in this context with form, and nirguṇa signifies without attributes — in this context without form. Sage Nārada in verse 2 of his *Bhakti Sūtras* defines *bhakti* as:

> *sā tu asmin paramaprēmarūpā*
> 'Bhakti is the form of supreme love towards God.'

During a question-answer session with Amma, I wanted to ask Amma a question related to this topic: how to present the insights of the *Bhagavad Gītā* to people who follow different faiths, many of whom believe only in a formless God, the nirguṇa aspect of the divine? This question arose as a result of the challenges I was encountering in my PhD research.

Amma glanced at me and nodded her beautiful head, signifying I should ask my question. However, before I could stand up, they passed the mic on to someone on the men's side. He started to speak without looking at Amma, leaving me silently standing there. It was a funny moment; Amma made a sweet gesture of 'what to do?'

I was a little sad because I was leaving the next day. However, it got back to me that Amma had asked for me at the following Tuesday question-answer session. How priceless it is to be in our mother's heart and mind. May we be worthy of her infinite love.

Let me explain how I became interested in the topic of saguṇa versus nirguṇa bhakti.

My parents both come from Türkiye. My father is someone firmly opposed to organized religion, and although my mother comes from a Sufi saint lineage, she also is not very interested in religion or spirituality.

I was born and grew up in a small beautiful German town, where I mostly spent my time in nature. When I was seven, our neighbors' niece came over one day and informed me she was going to take a course learning to read the Koran and write in Arabic. I was thrilled by the idea and asked my father if I could join the class. He refused.

Nevertheless, God is not limited to any religion. My classmates were mostly Germans who were also Christians. A lady in our neighborhood held a Bible-study group where we listened to Bible stories, sang devotional songs, and did arts-and-crafts activities. I attended those gatherings and really appreciated the satsang.

Looking back at those years, I feel that the *saṁskāra*[20] of seeking God that we carry over from previous births, brings us closer to God; nothing and no one can hinder our search.

After graduating from college, I was successful in the corporate world, lived in the best area of Istanbul, had a car, and lived life to the fullest. I discovered yōga in 2003, and following

---

[20] Saṁskāras are imprints or impressions left on the mind as a result of past experiences, actions, and thoughts. These imprints shape an individual's character, tendencies, and reactions in future situations. For this reason, traditional rites in *Sanātana Dharma* are also called saṁskāras.

the death of my ex-fiancée in 2007, I immersed myself in yōga. It completely altered my way of living. I became more introverted and devoted.

Although Türkiye is a secular country with no official religion, Islam is the religion followed by most. In Islam, God is worshiped as the one who is beyond attributes. No paintings, pictures or idols are allowed. In Turkish, the word '*Put*,' meaning 'idol' is derived from Lord *Buddha*. Islam was aggressively propagated amongst Turkish clans that had previously practiced *Tengrisim*, *Buddhism* and *Shamanism*. As I was born with an inquiring mind, philosophy, religion, and spirituality were and continue to be areas where I feel I'm in my element.

***

The 12th chapter of the *Bhagavad Gītā* begins with Arjuna (warrior-disciple of Kṛiṣhṇa, and my personal hero) inquiring into who the best knower of yōga is. This question arose in his mind after seeing the Lord's *viśhvarūpa* (universal form). He asks the Lord:

> *ēvam satatayuktā yē bhaktāstvām paryupāsatē*
> *yē chāpyakṣharam avyaktam tēṣhām kē yōgavittamāh*
> 'Which yogi is the best? The one who worships you or the one who worships the imperishable unmanifested *Brahman* (the Absolute)?' (12.1)

In commenting on this verse, our teacher mentioned during a class in the āśhram that, "Those devotees who make consistent effort fall into two categories: those who worship the Lord's form (saguṇa), and those who adore the Lord as formless (nirguṇa)."

Which type of devotion is higher?

In the next verse, Lord Kṛiṣhṇa talks about saguṇa bhakti:

> *mayyāvēśhya manō yē māṁ nitya-yuktā upāsatē*
> *śhraddhayā parayopētās tē mē yukta-tamā matāḥ*
> 'I consider them the best yogis, who, fixing their mind on me, worship me, ever-steadfast, and are endowed with supreme *śhraddhā* or faith.' (12.2)

Kṛiṣhṇa follows this in the next few verses by emphasizing the difficulties presented by nirguṇa bhakti:

'But those also, who worship the imperishable, the indefinable, the unmanifested, the omnipresent, the unthinkable, the unchangeable, the immovable, and eternal — having controlled all their senses, even-minded towards all and engaged in the welfare of all beings — verily they reach only me. (12.3 – 4)

The striving is greater for those whose minds are set on the unmanifested, for the goal of the unmanifested is very hard for the embodied to reach.' (12.5)

Kṛiṣhṇa glorifies saguṇa bhakti because it is easier for us. Why? Is it possible to think about the unthinkable? Or the unmanifested...the uncreated? We can only think about those things which are manifested or observable. We are continuously drawn into the world of duality as we identify ourselves with the body, mind, and intellect. Consequently, the path of *avyakta* (the unmanifested) becomes challenging.

Most of us are slaves to our thoughts and emotions. However, through *sēva* and *sādhanā*, we can observe certain emotions and control them.

Emotions are subtle entities; hence they are difficult to handle. There are certain evidence-based practices for dealing with emotions such as pounding a pillow when we are angry at someone; crying our heart out to a plant or a tree; talking to our pets when we are sad; going for a walk when we've had a fight; or watching a funny movie when we are frustrated.

There is one specific aspect of emotions that can be used for saguṇa bhakti: just as focusing on a perceivable gross object leads to apprehending its subtle elements. Focusing on a perceivable object of faith elicits strong emotions directed towards the divine.

In Chapter 12, verses 6 – 7 of the *Bhagavad Gītā*, Lord Kṛiṣhṇa says,

'But those who worship me, giving up all their activities unto me and being devoted to me without deviation, engaged in devotional service and always meditating upon me, having fixed their minds upon me, O Pārtha (Arjuna) — for them, I am the swift deliverer from the ocean of birth and death.'

As limited human beings, we have difficulties imagining the formless divinity. Don't we mostly fail to see Amma in everyone and everything, especially when we receive unfair criticism from others?

Therefore, Kṛiṣhṇa gives a three-step instruction that if followed, ensures he will catch hold of us and take us across *saṁsāra,* the cycle of birth and death:

1. Fixation of senses and mind only on the Lord
2. Surrendering all actions to him
3. Meditating on his form

First Kṛiṣhṇa says, "Fix your senses and mind on me." Since the mind is naturally extroverted, it would be pretty troublesome to focus the senses on something that cannot be perceived. The mind and senses are like children. We always have to keep an eye on and engage them. Otherwise, they may create chaos.
In *Sanātana Dharma,* we have the option of performing worship with objects:

- We have idols and pictures for our sense of sight and touch.
- We have incense, flame, and *prasādam* for our sense of smell and taste.

- We have the bell and *bhajans* for our sense of sound.

Thus, all our senses are involved in worship without allowing any of our senses to escape.

Those supporting elements, however, are not employed in nirguṇa bhakti. A person who has controlled their senses; balanced their emotions; who has a calm and steady mind; and an alert intellect, is considered fit to seek God without attributes.

However, it can be challenging to keep one's attention on God if one lacks control of one's thoughts. The seeker needs discernment and detachment to be one-pointed, which comes only when the mind and intellect are purified through *karma yōga* (the path of selfless action) and scriptural studies. How many individuals in the world partake in such practices nowadays?

***

In the 7th Chapter of the *Bhagavad Gītā,* Kṛiṣhṇa describes the four types of devotees:

Ārta: a devotee who only calls out to God when she is suffering
Arthārthī: a devotee who calls out to God when she has a desire to be fulfilled
Jijñāsu: the seeker of knowledge
Jñānī: the one who is established in knowledge

I grew up with an ārta and arthārthī devotional attitude. If my family or I had a desire or was in need, we would go to the *'türbe'* — where a saint's tomb is located, and pray. My mother would distribute sugar or Turkish bagels if our wish came true. Isn't this a perfect example of what Amma frequently calls having a business-mind relationship with God?

Observing these acts performed without an understanding of the higher worship principle, and done in the name of faith or religion makes me contemplate deeply, but without judging any religion.

The mind and senses naturally seek something to latch onto. As our beloved Amma mentions, in Buddhism, the theory of śhūnyata (emptiness) is propagated, yet we find Lord Buddha's idol in their temples. In Islam, God is perceived as attributeless and omnipresent, yet for prayer, they turn their faces towards the *Kiblah,* the direction of the sacred cube-monument Ka'aba in Mecca.

However, it is risky to point out such matters in society. One day, the famous Sufi saint from the 10th century, Mansoor Al-Hallaj was in a divinely intoxicated state, and as he walked the streets of Baghdad, he was found constantly chanting 'Ana'l Haq — I Am the Truth.' This was interpreted as blasphemy by orthodox Muslims, who believed Mansoor was claiming to be God. Finally, they cut off all of his limbs and executed him. It is said, after the execution, each limb and each drop of blood continued to chant 'An-al Haq.'

I am also from a saint's lineage on my mother's side, dating back to the 16th century. *Gülbaba*, my great-great-grandfather, hailed from Ankara. Gülbaba is a Turkish word meaning 'father of roses.'

I visited Gülbaba's tomb only after I heard in a scripture class in *Amritapuri* about the significance of having a *sannyāsi* (monk) or saint in the family.

To my surprise, I saw a quote from Gülbaba that is in line with our beloved Amma's teachings:

> 'Don't stop praying
> Be modest
> Don't love the world too much
> Earn honestly
> Compete in charity and good deeds

Be kind-hearted'

When I first met Amma, I thought I was a fantastic yōga instructor — talk about modesty! I was already in India, working in a yōga school in Goa. Following a dispute with my yōga teacher, I left town, absolutely devastated at losing my direction in life. Not knowing what to do, I finally decided to go to Tiruvannamalai, Ramana Maharshi's āśhram, even though I had only heard about him.

However, I missed my train connection and found myself in Mangalore. I had to stay there since no trains were going to Tiruvannamalai that night. It was my first time in India outside of Goa, and I was not familiar with the area. When I reached the hotel, I looked at a map. I saw that Mangalore was close to the border with Kerala, and that made me think of Amma. I had read about Amma before, and definitely wanted to see her.

Suddenly, with fireworks going off in my head like in the movies, I realized that Amma was my Guru, and that I must go to her. The next day, some friends contacted me to say that they were in Kochi, and had thought of me as they planned a trip to Amritapuri. They had already booked a taxi and invited me to join them. I literally didn't have to make any arrangements; the path was unfolding by itself through Amma's grace. I arrived in Amritapuri in January 2011.

Since then, Amma has been holding my hand, accompanying me on the spiritual escalator to the goal. Although I might be childish and throw a tantrum when I want to go backwards on that forward-moving escalator, Amma lovingly navigates me back to the forward path.

With Amma's guidance and boundless grace, I completed my Masters in Philosophy at Amrita University. Those two years were, without a doubt, the most difficult of my life. Every other day, I wanted to quit. I used to cry on my way back from college to the āśhram.

I was a complete zero in my knowledge of Indian scriptures, and had no background knowledge of Kṛiṣhṇa or Dēvī, the Divine Mother, whereas all of my Indian classmates had grown up with this knowledge, leaving me far behind.

One day I went to the *Kaḷari,* the original small temple in the āśhram, and tried to create a connection with Lord Kṛiṣhṇa. I told him, "It seems you are a kind and sweet god, but I don't know you. Would you please help me to know you and love you?" Amma in the form of our dear Kṛiṣhṇa bestowed her grace on me and assisted me in finishing my masters with a first-class with distinction.

Can you guess the topic of my thesis?

'*Bhagavad Gītā* — A Storehouse of Psychological Capital.'

What a privilege it is to extol the glories of Lord Kṛiṣhṇa!

We cannot love someone we don't know. Devotion gives beauty and sweet fragrance to knowledge. That was the case in my experience with Lord Kṛiṣhṇa. Knowledge provides depth to devotion. The more I learned about him, the more my love grew. Knowledge without devotion is intellectual, while devotion without knowledge is wavering and easily shaken. It is indeed a virtuous cycle — the more bhakti we have, the more jnāna we want. The more jnāna we receive, the more our love for the divine.

***

God will hold our hand if we trust her completely. In connection with this, I once had a lucid dream about Amma:

We were in the āśhram and Amma was playing hide and seek with us. My dream Amma was the younger version of herself. Amma started climbing some stairs while giving me a mischievous smile. I followed right behind her, laughing and giggling.

Then Amma continued climbing higher up. The staircase was a pile of chairs and tables. It was not stable; it was shaky and scary. However, I wasn't concerned about the situation as I wanted to catch Amma. We climbed higher and higher but I lost sight of her. I reached a table that was piled on top of a chair. As I pulled myself onto the table, I noticed a *brahmachāri* without arms looking after a blind baby. I was shocked. "How can you take care of that baby?" I asked, "'It might fall from such a height. You can't hold it."

The brahmachāri replied, "Don't worry, Amma is taking care of it."

At that moment, I lost my balance and fell while calling out to Amma. When I awoke (still in the dream), I was lying on soft grass. My eyes welled up with tears. I asked a sister who was next to me how I had gotten here. She said, "Amma carried you here."

I awoke crying from my dream, moved by Amma's compassion. No matter what we do, Amma is always there for us. We should never deviate from our faith in Amma.

When the āśhram closed its doors due to Covid, I was in Türkiye with my family. We lost one uncle to the virus, and then my mother became ill with it. I had to witness my family's anguish and suffering as she was admitted to the intensive-care unit. Nobody had any idea what this disease was, and we were all feeling lost.

Amma's satsangs were little candles illuminating the dense darkness. Amma saved my mom from Lord Yama's (the god of death's) clutches. I bow down over and over for the presence of our dear Amma in my life.

These events taught me valuable lessons, showing me how much suffering there is in the world. It re-ignited a love in me to serve humanity while spreading the glory of our Divine Mother.

When we follow Amma's instructions, we are always guided by her within. We only need to be aware and not fall for the whispers of our personal desires, as that is the voice of our ego.

Although lecturing about spirituality may not have much influence, walking the talk has a huge impact on people. If we can inspire our family and friends by our actions, it can set off a chain reaction, with one candle lighting another, spreading from individual to family, from family to society, and from society to the whole world.

We have a small satsang group in Türkiye, where we gathered every Thursday online during the pandemic to do Amma's white flower meditation for world peace. We also supported an orphanage in Istanbul and a school in Kaṣ, buying electronic tablets for students who needed to follow their classes on-line. As part of our duty to Mother Nature, we also gave financial and physical help when Türkiye experienced destructive wildfires.

I want to thank Amma for her grace and thank everyone who kept those satsangs going each week. We pray that Amma may sanctify Türkiye by the touch of her holy feet, establishing dharma back in our land.

***

Amma's miracles are inexplicable. Those who criticized me harshly for following Amma's words became devotees themselves. In 2019 during the last Europe Tour, my mother and youngest cousin came to the German āśhram program. My aunt had lamented to me that my cousin had become an atheist. However, she fell in love with Amma after meeting her.

It's the same with my mom. I witnessed how my mother changed from being envious and critical of Amma, to becoming a child who yearned to have an Amma doll. When we all went for a family darśhan, Amma called us *Gülkizlarim* — meaning 'my daughters of roses.' This left us wonderstruck, because I had never told Amma about our grandfather-saint Gülbaba.

How does Amma know all this?

Amma says, "The Guru is the embodied form of the formless absolute. He or she is none other than God himself because God is a name attributed to the supreme Self when it chooses to assume a name and form."

Amma is not different from us. Amma knows our every thought and prayer, because we are one with her. Amma is the supreme truth that we are searching for in God with form or in the formless. May we comprehend and always remember this great truth.

I'd like to conclude with a story about how Amma hears our prayers and answers them instantly.

Once, Amma was giving darśhan in the *Kāḷī Temple* in Amritapuri. While waiting in the queue, I kept praying to Amma, "Amma please give me bhakti." When I was only one or two people away from getting darśhan, I glanced to the side and saw Bhakti, Amma's dog on stage. "Bhakti!" I called out. Bhakti came running over to me, wagging her tail and giving me dog kisses. When Amma saw this, She said, "Ohhh Bhakti!" And gave a perfect Kāḷī-like laugh. Our Lalitāmbikā — the ever-playful mother answers our prayers in delightful ways so that we never forget them!

12

Ahaṅkāra — The Ego

Dr. Sriram Ananthanarayanan - India

One day, a man saw a cute little kitten on the corner of his street and brought it home. He took the kitten to his Guru and requested him to name it. The Guru named the kitten 'Ego.' Soon Ego grew up and became a nuisance. He knocked over the milk kept in the kitchen, and dragged dead rats into the house. Fed up, the man's wife told him, "Ego must go!"

The man dropped Ego back on the street corner where he'd found him. A minute later, Ego reappeared in the house. The man then took Ego a few streets away and left him there. But Ego soon returned. He then decided to abandon Ego someplace far away. After walking a long time, taking many twists and turns, he let Ego go in a far-off location, then turned towards home. On the way, he got lost, so he called his wife and asked, "Is Ego there?" The wife replied, "Yes, Ego came back half an hour ago." The man said, "Can you please give the phone to Ego? I'm lost and need directions!"

This story shows how difficult it is to get rid of the ego. Amma says, "The ego is the greatest obstacle on your path towards the truth." How can we overcome this obstacle and realize the supreme truth?

Once during darśhan, a man asked Amma for a simple definition of spirituality. Amma said, "Compassionately considering others is spirituality." Amma then told the following story:

"Once a man was sleeping with his mouth wide open. A fly flew into his mouth and woke him up. The man became worried. He thought he could feel it buzzing around inside him.

He consulted several doctors but they all told him there was nothing there. The man remained unconvinced. One day, he went to a *mahātmā* — a great soul. The mahātmā heard the man's problem and then said, 'Yes, you are right. I can see a fly living inside you.' The man was elated. At last, someone understood his problem and agreed with him.

The mahātmā told him to lie down, covered him with a blanket, and told him to close his eyes and be still. Then the mahātmā went into another room, caught a fly alive, and brought it back in a bottle. Then the mahātmā pretended to catch the fly inside the man. Soon the mahātmā exclaimed, 'Ah yes, I caught it!' He asked the man to open his eyes and showed him the fly in the bottle. The man was overjoyed, and his worry and suffering came to an end."

Amma explained, "In reality, there never was a fly inside the man. Yet, he suffered. Only the mahātmā came down to the level of the man's understanding and helped him. The others remained in their level of understanding and did not consider the patient." Amma continued, "Son, this is the whole process of spiritual realization. The master considers the disciple's fly of ignorance — the ego, as true and then helps the disciple to awaken to reality."

Due to Amma's boundless compassion, she comes down to our level. For us, the ego appears to be very real. We feel we are a separate individual, separate from the rest of the world. This feeling of separateness is the ego. The ego restricts us to our petty personal desires and fears; likes and dislikes! We experience stress and anxiety. The ego is like a prison. Amma says that this ego is our own creation, our own imagination. It is the root cause of our suffering. For Amma, there is no feeling of separateness — no ego. Where there is no ego, there is no fear. Where there is no ego, there is only oneness; only pure love.

Just as darkness vanishes in the presence of light, the Guru bestows Self-knowledge and the ego vanishes. The ego is the knot that binds us to our past actions. When the ego disappears, so too, the bondage of all past actions.

***

About ten years ago, when Amma had just returned from one of her tours, she called all the āśhram residents to the *Kāḷī Temple* for *darśhan*. Just as I approached, Amma came from the other direction.

I was standing there between two other men. Amma looked at the person on my left and smiled at him. Then Amma looked at the person on my right and gave him a sweet smile. Ignoring me completely, she moved on. What a blow to my ego! Amma then started giving darśhan in the temple.

I sat on the floor to Amma's right and a little behind her. I didn't go for darśhan, and Amma took no notice of me. I sat there observing Amma. Four or five hours passed. I watched as the administrator of Amma's university approached Amma from one side. On the other side, little children were showing Amma their drawings, and in front the darśhan queue was moving along.

The thought came to me that though I'd never see Lord Kṛiṣhṇa playfully hold aloft the *Gōvardhana* mountain, I got to witness Amma holding aloft her institutions while simultaneously admiring the children's drawings, and giving darśhan with that same ease and playfulness!

I mentally said, "Amma, you are Kṛiṣhṇa!" The next moment, Amma turned all the way around, looked at me, and waved her arm indicating that I should come for darśhan. I was stunned! It seemed she had just responded to my thoughts. Even so, I hesitated to go for darśhan.

After a couple of minutes, my wife who had been sitting elsewhere came up to me and said, "Let's go for darśhan!" How could I refuse? I got up and we went for darśhan. After giving me darśhan, Amma held my hand and did not let go of it even as she embraced the next person.

It was clear to me that Amma wanted me to say something. I said, "Amma, you are Kṛiṣhṇa!" Amma gave me a radiant look, beaming with love and compassion. I then requested Amma to teach me the *Bhagavad Gītā*, and Amma smiled.

Amma teaches us through experience. Her teachings continue to this day, sometimes in unexpected ways. Through this particular experience, I realized that Amma is aware of all our thoughts. How is this possible? It is because Amma is the pure ātmā — the supreme Self, the essence of our own being — that consciousness which illumines the mind.

In Chapter 10, verse 20 of the *Bhagavad Gītā*, Lord Kṛiṣhṇa says to his devotee Arjuna:

> *aham ātmā guḍākēśha sarva-bhūtāśhaya-sthitaḥ*
> *aham ādiśh cha madhyaṁ cha bhūtānām anta ēva cha*
> 'I am the Self, O Arjuna, seated in the heart of all beings; I am the beginning, the middle and also the end of all beings.'

Amma often gives the example of the sun reflected in many pots filled with water. Though the reflections are many, the real sun is only one. Similarly, consciousness is reflected in every mind as 'I.' In reality, there is only one consciousness, only one 'I.' Amma says that this consciousness, which has no birth or death, is our true nature.

***

One evening here in *Amritapuri*, we had all gathered in the courtyard in front of the Kāḷī Temple. It was a beautiful setting, sitting in Amma's divine presence, the sun going down, a gentle breeze with trees all around. After Amma had led us in the white flower visualization meditation, a white substance landed on my lap. The bird sitting on the branch above me not only liked to meditate, but also liked dropping a white substance during meditation.

The next day, though I sat in a different location, another bird had the same idea. This time, its timing was perfect. Just as Swāmī said, "Visualize white flowers gently falling from the sky," the white substance landed on my head and clothes!

Perhaps the bird was trying to teach me something. I looked up. The bird appeared to start speaking. The bird said, "*Sarvam Brahmamayam.* — All this is *Brahman* (the absolute)." "My droppings are Brahman. You too are Brahman. From Brahman, emerged Brahman and landed on Brahman, so what's the problem?" I said, "I have not fully imbibed the teachings of *Vedānta*." The bird said, "Well then, continue doing śhravaṇam (listening) and *mananam* (contemplation)."

The bird continued, "Listen to the teachings of the scriptures and contemplate their meaning. Only then can you do *nididhyāsana* — assimilation of the Vēdāntic teachings, and apply them to every life situation. From a more devotional perspective, have you heard the prayer: 'God, grant me the serenity to accept the things I cannot change, the courage to change the things I can, and the wisdom to know the difference?'"

I replied, "Yes, I have."

The bird said, "As far as the droppings on your head and clothes are concerned, you can't leave in the middle of meditation, so just accept what is. Amma says that acceptance is surrender. Isn't surrender the goal of devotion?"

"Yes, it is!" I replied. "You have taught me how to face this situation with *jñāna* (knowledge) and *bhakti* (devotion). Please also teach me the path of *karma yōga* (path of selfless action)."

The bird said, "Sure. You came and sat for meditation. You visualized the white flowers of peace falling everywhere. All that was selfless action that you did with a worshipful attitude — *pūjā manō bhāva*. I have dropped white substance on you as *prasād*. When you perform actions with pūjā manō bhāva and *prasāda buddhi* — accepting all that comes as God's gift — it is karma yōga. *Samatvam yōga uchyatē* — equanimity is yōga."

I prostrated mentally to the bird for this unexpected *Bhagavad Gītā* lesson. Amma says that karma yōga and bhakti yōga are like the two wings of a bird, and jñāna yōga is like the bird's tail. I pray to Amma that I imbibe these teachings so that the bird does not have to repeat this lesson!

Amma says, "There is no problem with the world. The problem is with the human mind — the ego." The fundamental problem is that we identify ourselves with the body-mind and not the real Self. This false identification with the body-mind is a very deep-rooted conditioning. The ego feeling arises due to ignorance, and the ego creates egocentric desires.

All the negative tendencies of the mind such as lust, anger, greed, pride, attachment and jealousy emerge from the ego. All conflicts and wars, whether between individuals or between nations, occur only due to the ego.

***

Before I met Amma the ego slayer, I graduated from IIT Bombay with a BS in Engineering, then moved to California for graduate studies at UC Irvine. After my studies, I got a good job at a software technology company in Sunnyvale, California and got married. My wife, Padmamālā, was spiritually inclined and loved to sing *bhajans.*

However, my innocent childhood faith in God disappeared during my college days, and I had many questions that went unanswered. I had no knowledge of the scriptures, and wondered whether God truly existed, or if people believed in God for some kind of solace and comfort. My prayer at that time was "God, if you exist, please reveal yourself to me."

It was with this attitude that I received my first darśhan from Amma at Amma's āśhram in San Ramon, California in 1996.

I was quite surprised by Amma. It was a *Dēvī Bhāva* night. Looking at the radiant form of Amma dressed as a goddess wearing a sāri and crown, I thought "How strange!" I got a token and received Amma's darśhan. A little later, several people started dancing to the bhajans. I wondered if they were getting high on the bhajans. On the way home I thought, "All this is very strange!"

As Swāmī Amṛitaswarūpānandajī said, "When you cannot grasp something, understand something, you stamp it as strange." That's exactly what I did. I didn't think I'd go again, but Amma had other plans. Amma had planted a seed of transformation in me.

Later, the question, "What is the purpose of life?" arose in my mind. The question simply wouldn't go away. Then, in stillness, the answer was revealed. I started realizing that Amma is God's love in human form, and that the purpose of life is to merge into that state of oneness; that state of pure love.

Amma says that the spiritual journey begins and ends with compassion. I feel that the spiritual journey begins with, sustains, and culminates in the Guru's compassion.

With a single touch or glance, Amma awakens in us the quest for the true purpose of life. Therefore, Amma is Brahmā — the creator. However, the spiritual journey is full of pitfalls. In the scripture called the *Kathōpaniṣhad*, Lord Yama, the god of death says, "Sharp as a razor's edge is the [spiritual] path." It is only our *Guru* Amma, who sustains and protects us on the spiritual journey. Therefore, Amma is Viṣhṇu — the protector.

Without her guidance and grace, I would have forsaken this path a long time ago. We can be confident that ultimately, Amma will uproot our ignorance and liberate us from the cycle of birth and death. Therefore, Amma is Śhiva, the destroyer of the ego; the destroyer of ignorance. And Amma does all this with motherly compassion.

The next time we went for darśhan in San Ramon, Amma made me and my wife sit close to her on the stage. Then Amma asked us, "What do you want?" I felt that she was ready to grant us any desire, but that we shouldn't squander this opportunity. I prayed to her mentally, "Amma, if we ask you for something, no doubt it will give happiness. But that happiness will soon fade. So please give that happiness which does not go away."

When darśhan ended, Amma stood up, but before leaving, she said something about us to Swāmī Ramakṛiṣhṇānandajī. Swāmījī told us that Amma had made a *saṅkalpa* — a divine resolve — for us. At that time, I did not know its meaning or significance, but guessed that it was a blessing, as Swāmījī looked very happy about it.

No doubt, it is Amma's divine resolve that has given us shelter at her divine feet. We became residents of the Amritapuri āśhram a few years later.

Going for darśhan the next year in San Ramon, I felt that the only way my life would be of value was if I were near Amma and could serve her. I told Amma that I would like to move back to India to be with her. Amma asked me what I had studied. I felt like a tiny candle in front of the sun, and remained silent.

Then Amma added, "You can come right away [to India] or you can come later. If you want to come now, then come here again tomorrow." After going home, I thought about leaving the U.S. and heading off to live in Amma's āśhram which I had never visited. It did not seem practical, though my heart was with Amma.

The next morning, I decided to just go to my office and not to the San Ramon āśhram. On the way to work, I felt like I had chickened out. Though I went to my office, my thoughts were on Amma. That day I happened to read one of Amma's parables:

'A baby eagle happened to hatch along with some chickens and was raised by a hen. It learned to scratch for worms and behave like other chickens. One day, another eagle flying high in the sky noticed the baby eagle below acting like a chicken. The eagle swooped down and approached the baby eagle. The young one was afraid and tried to escape along with the other chickens. Finally the older eagle led the young one to a water pond where it could see that its own reflection was similar to the majestic eagle whom it had feared at first. On learning its true identity, it soon was soaring through the sky just like the other eagle!'

Reading this story on that day was not a mere coincidence. It gave me hope that Amma would call me at a later time. By Amma's grace, a couple of years later we moved to India, and became faculty members at Amma's college in Bangalore.

***

Amma's visits to Bangalore were always memorable events. On one of those visits, Amma suddenly announced that she planned to visit our college campus. A few of us rushed from the program venue to the campus to prepare for Amma's visit.

We also informed the students that Amma would be coming, and to gather in the assembly hall.

As soon as Amma arrived, she asked the faculty members to leave the hall. She wanted the students to feel free to speak openly. One of the students complained about the quality of the chapatis served at meals in a very rude manner to Amma, without any respect at all.

Anyone else would have felt insulted and reacted angrily; not Amma! Full of motherly love, with nothing but compassion and concern for the students, Amma brainstormed with them about possible solutions, like purchasing a chapati-making machine.

Amma has been honored all over the world, yet remains absolutely humble, and comes down to the level of each person who interacts with her. Only Amma can do this. The *Bhagavad Gītā* talks about the enlightened person who treats praise and insult, honor and dishonor just the same. I saw this in action. Amma does not merely teach Vēdānta, Amma lives Vēdānta.

During another one of Amma's visits to Bangalore, Swāmī Amṛitagītānandajī gave me and my wife the opportunity to welcome Amma by garlanding her on the first day of programs. We had the most beautiful darśhan! I am thankful to Swāmījī for giving us this precious opportunity.

Amma's life is compassion in action. With help from Swāmī Abhayāmritānandajī, and being the engineering college student's *sēvā* coordinator, I took thirty students from our Bangalore campus to Nagapattinam in Tamil Nadu to help with the āśhram's tsunami relief efforts there. The student volunteers participated in building houses for those who had lost their homes.

I was impressed by how well the houses had been planned and built despite many challenges. We met some local fishermen.

One of them told us, "I have not seen God. But in Amma, I see God!"

In September 2008, I came to Amritapuri and asked Amma if I could purchase a flat in the āśhram. Amma took a good look at me and said, "Will you move here?" Then she added, "You can buy a flat." I was delighted. I went back to Bangalore with Amma's words echoing in my heart. I told my wife about it. She too was eager to move to Amma's divine abode at Amritapuri. Four months later, I again visited Amritapuri accompanied by my wife and six-year old daughter.

We went for Amma's darśhan, and I asked, "Amma, shall we move here?" Amma leaned back and burst out laughing. I was puzzled. Had I told a really funny joke? But then Amma compassionately said, "Amma is happy." I realized I had misunderstood.

Amma then gave all the instructions that we needed and by Amma's grace, we moved to the āśhram in May 2009.

I'll conclude with a story about something that happened after we moved to the āśhram:

Amma says, "Do not see Amma only as this body. Sorrow will be the result if you children think that Amma is limited to this body. Always know that Amma is all-pervading."

When Amma was on the North India Tour, my wife and daughter went to Bangalore to attend Amma's program there. Missing Amma intensely, I sat down and wrote her a letter. I started with "Dear Amma," but then the letter took the form of a poem, expressing my heartfelt feelings, and praying for her guidance and grace.

I folded the letter and placed it in front of Amma's picture in my room. That night, Amma came to me in a dream and blessed me in a most compassionate way. When Amma returned to Amritapuri after the tour, she called all āśhram residents for darśhan. As I approached, Amma asked me if I had written a letter to her.

It took a few seconds for me to recall the poem-letter I'd written a few weeks before. I had told no one about it. Amazed at Amma's omniscience, I said, "Yes Amma, but how did you know?" Amma just smiled at me, and compassionately gave me darśhan!

Amma, please forgive my ignorance even after you have given me so many glimpses of your divinity. May I never forget that you have incarnated on this earth only to rescue us from the cycle of birth and death.

Amma, please shower your grace upon all of your children so that we may attain the true purpose of life.

13

Selflessness

Sahaja - Australia

We are all so fortunate that Amma's infinite compassion has created *'Amritapuri'*— a spiritual oasis for her children. Amma is like a divine shepherd who for years has traveled all over the world, gathering her flock. Amma is always guiding and watching over her children whether we are with her physically or not. Her body is like a moving temple that purifies and graces everywhere she goes.

Amma's life is a wonderful example of the ideal integration of *jñāna* (knowledge), *bhakti* (devotion), and *karma* (selfless action), and will be a model for humanity to emulate for all eternity. In this way, Amma shows us that the head, heart, and hand all lead us along the path to Self-realization.

I once read an interesting story in a Buddhist journal: Once there were two men from the same village; one of them was miserly while the other one was generous. They both happened to pass away at around the same time. In death, they appeared before Lord Yama (the god of death), who was about to pass judgement on their past actions.

He told the two men, "I'm going to let both of you be reborn into the world. One of you will always be giving, while the other will always be receiving. Which would you rather be?" The miserly man immediately spoke up and said, "I want to be the one that will always be receiving." The other man did not mind being the one who would be continually giving, and so he nodded in agreement.

As they stood waiting for the final judgement, Lord Yama picked up his staff and pounded it on the ground. He turned to the miserly man and decreed, "Since you choose to be receiving from others, you will be reborn as a beggar. This will give you plenty of opportunities to be on the receiving end." He then turned to the other man and said, "You will be reborn into great wealth. Share that wealth with those who are less fortunate and give alms." The moral of the story, of course, is that the experience of giving is far more fulfilling than that of receiving.

This story introduces the theme of my *satsang* — 'selflessness,' and I will share some teachings and experiences from my years with Amma in this regard.

Amma says that we need to be ever watchful of our minds, because the mind doesn't want us to do anything selfless. Its one and only aim is to drive us along the path of selfishness, as that is its nature.

The Ganges river gives cool, pure water and does not expect anything in return. The sun sheds its light on all without anticipating any reward. Amma is like the living embodiment of nature. Her entire existence is one of giving. We have all heard her say how she yearns to serve her children, and she never seeks any appreciation or recognition for anything she does.

Lord Kṛiṣhṇa says in Chapter 2, verse 47 of the *Bhagavad Gītā*:

> 'You have control over action alone, never over its fruit. Live not for the fruit of action nor attach yourself to inaction.'

The following incident shows how my ego got a nice little slam from being attached to the fruit of action:

During one Gold Coast retreat in Australia, my roommate's back went out on the first night. She had to spend the entire retreat lying down on the hard surface of the floor. She didn't want to leave the retreat, as she wanted to be near Amma no matter how much pain she was in.

I was helping her, and got her meals for her throughout this period. I told Amma during *darśhan* about my roommate's condition, and without a second thought Amma pulled a hot-water bottle out from behind her back and gave it to me, telling me to go and apply it to her back.

I was thrilled at Amma's gesture of compassion, and went back to the room to do this. My roommate was also delighted that Amma had done this for her. I was feeling quite smug with myself thinking I had done something nice for her, but it wasn't long before that all changed. Within minutes there was frantic knocking at the door. When I opened it a woman whom I had never met before was standing there demanding that I give the hot-water bottle back immediately!

To my horror, I realized that this woman thought I had just run off with it, so I explained the situation and what Amma said to me but she kept insisting that I return it. I started to feel very embarrassed, and just thought it best to give it to her and go down and sort it out. The misunderstanding was quickly worked out. We ended up getting another hot-water bottle, however I couldn't shake off this uneasy feeling within me from what had happened, thinking that my actions may have only ended up causing my roommate more distress.

The next day to our surprise, the all-knowing and compassionate Amma came to our room after *Dēvī Bhāva* to personally check on my roommate and give her darśhan, showing her that Amma was well aware of everything she had been going through.

Life gives us opportunities everyday to practice the art of giving, and we don't need to be wealthy to do this. Amma says that it is through giving that we progress on the spiritual path.

Small actions such as showing concern for others' wellbeing, helping someone who is ill, and expressing gratitude are all acts of kindness that do not cost anything, but make huge differences in people's lives.

They are like small seeds that grow into enormous trees that grace our communities with pleasant, cool shade. When we use the flame of one candle to light other candles, all the candles merge into a unified glow making the room that much brighter. The act of giving is much like the candle flame.

Amma says that she worships every being in creation as a manifestation of God, and that at a particular stage of meditation, we will acquire knowledge about the essential principles of any object in nature.

As mentioned in the book *The Untethered Soul* our inner growth is dependent upon the realization that the only way to find peace and contentment is to stop thinking about ourselves. Before our current problems came into our lives, there were different ones. This is a never-ending cycle. When can we honestly say there was a time when something wasn't bothering us? Like Amma says, our minds are like the pendulum of a clock, constantly swinging back and forth from happiness to unhappiness.

Amma shared the following Kṛiṣhṇa story with me once when I spoke with her during darśhan:

One day Kṛiṣhṇa sent a messenger back to *Vṛindāvan,* the village where Kṛiṣhṇa lived as a child, with many gifts for all the *gōpis* who lived there. The gopis were thrilled upon seeing the messenger's arrival. Each gōpi was given her special gift from Kṛiṣhṇa, and cries of delight could be heard from each of them as they opened their presents.

After the messenger finished handing out all the gifts, he realized that Kṛiṣhṇa had sent nothing for Rādhā[21]. He looked around, and saw Rādhā sitting by herself under a tree. He approached and asked her if she was sad that she hadn't received a gift from Kṛiṣhṇa. Rādhā's face lit up and she said, "Oh no! Watching my sisters receive their gifts from my beloved fills me with so much happiness."

From this story, I understood that Amma was hinting at the value of selflessness above all, and to try and feel a connection to everyone around me. I have often reflected on this story to help redirect my mind from getting so caught up in itself when things don't go my way.

Great souls such as Amma generally hide their greatness as they have no need to prove anything to anyone. They are willing to take whatever comes their way, and are naturally very humble.

The following incident shows how Amma beautifully handled a very challenging situation:

Some years ago, the meditation and Q&A session at the Gold Coast Retreat was held outside in a tennis court area that was closely bordered by hotel rooms. During the Q&A, a man who was staying in one of the hotel rooms came out onto his balcony and started to yell over to us to turn the sound down as it was too loud. He then went back into his room.

Those of us sitting in the back heard him say this, but chose to ignore his request and continued listening to the Q&A. Not long after, he came out again onto his balcony, and this time made sure everyone heard him. In a much louder and aggressive tone, and using foul language to get his point across yelled at us to turn the sound down.

---

[21] The gōpī who exemplifies the highest form of devotion also revered as eternal companion of Lord Kṛiṣhṇa.

We all sat there completely stunned and mortified that this man had spoken like this in Amma's presence. Amma's response was an immediate reflection of her divine nature. She started defending the man's actions saying that we were the ones at fault, as he had tried to politely request us to turn the sound down, but since no one listened to him, it resulted in him getting very angry. In a matter of seconds Amma managed to transform this unpleasant situation into a teaching for us all, and also made this man happy too by supporting his request to lower the sound.

Amma says, "Love is Amma's nature. She cannot be otherwise. Just as egotism is our present nature, egolessness is the nature of a *mahātmā*. For this reason, Amma cannot return our anger, hatred, or abuse. She can only bestow boundless love and compassion."

***

Once during an Australian tour, Amma showed me that when we do make sacrifices, she will definitely be there for us. As I come from the Brisbane area, the local coordinator invited me to come to her house when Amma came to do a 'house *pūjā*' [22] to bless the house. This was going to happen around noon, just before Amma left for the Gold Coast. That morning, I went to the program hall to see how the after-program clean up was going.

To my surprise, I saw that there was still a huge amount of cleaning to do. I decided not to go to the coordinator's house, but instead stayed at the hall to help with all the cleaning up. Suddenly, I got a phone call from the coordinator saying that Amma had requested one of the Amrita TV camera people to come and film the house pūjā.

---

[22] Pūjā is ritualistic or ceremonial worship.

I went and informed the cameraman, and arranged for some devotees to take him there. An agreed-upon time was arranged for everyone to meet. The cameraman told me that he wanted to go for a walk around the venue to take some pictures, but that he would return in time. I said okay, and continued cleaning. At the agreed-upon time to meet, the other devotees came and told me he hadn't shown up. I had no way of contacting him.

I told them not to worry, but to please wait. After some time there was still no sight of him, and the devotees informed me they could wait no longer and left. I was very upset as I had tried to do what Amma requested but it hadn't worked out. I went back to cleaning, but kept an eye out for the cameraman, mentally preparing the verbal blasting I was going to give him. Finally he came back.

I stormed up to him and asked why he hadn't shown up? He completely disarmed me by his utter surprise and innocence, saying he had completely forgotten the time. I realized there was no point getting angry at him, but in an irritated manner said, "Well, I guess I'll have to take you there myself!"

I had no idea if we would arrive in time. It was about a half hour drive to the house where Amma was, and with grace, traffic was light. When we got there, I breathed a sigh of relief that the pūjā hadn't happened yet. Moments later, Amma walked down the stairs like a radiant flower, and proceeded to do the house pūjā.

Afterwards she came up to me and asked how the tour staff were doing, and then walked around the garden to look at all the plants before leaving. Through all the little dramas that had happened, Amma's infinite mercy ended up giving me the opportunity to be there with her after all.

Śhrī Nārāyaṇa Guru[23] once said that hardships in life can end up being blessings in disguise. They have the potential to help turn our minds towards spirituality and break the chain of delusion. That was certainly the case for me.

I had a very privileged and happy childhood until I was twelve years old, when life completely changed. The carefree, happy days were gone, replaced by a lot of turmoil within the family that caused a lot of suffering for me for many years. I now see that all the hardships and difficulties in life are there just to help us grow and become more understanding and compassionate, provided we choose to see them in a positive light.

I had wanted to come to India since I was fifteen. I couldn't accept that life was just about family and work, and felt there had to be something deeper. I wasn't a conventionally-religious type of person at all. My connection to God was through nature and animals.

When I was in college, I was in a terrible car accident, and sustained some serious injuries. This accident proved to be a major turning point in my life, as I received monetary compensation from it. I was suddenly financially independent, and could buy a ticket to India.

The year was 1994 and I was nineteen-years old. In the grip of youthful arrogance, it didn't even occur to me that I needed to make preparations for arriving in India. I remember looking out the plane's window when it was descending and was shocked, seeing this vast city below, suddenly realizing I knew nothing about it.

It felt like I was landing on another world. However, my internal cries of helplessness were heard, and everything fell into place. The most amazing journey then unfolded, ending

[23] Social reformer, philosopher, and spiritual leader (1856 – 1928) from Kerala.

up with the divine leading me seven months later to the lotus feet of our beloved Amma in Amritapuri.

I arrived at night, and Dēvī Bhāva was going on. The *Kāḷī Temple* where the program was being held, seemed to be pulsating, alive with an otherworldly energy from the soul-stirring *bhajans* being sung within it.

I had never heard of the concept of meeting the divine in a human form before, and was quite surprised to see Amma wearing a lovely sāri and crown, a living goddess. The closer I got to Amma's form in the darśhan queue, the more overwhelmed I became. Suddenly Amma glanced over in my direction with the most beautiful expression of love, compassion, and understanding, and all my anxiety dropped away.

Soon I was kneeling before her, and she was giving me a big beautiful bear hug! Her divine love was so overwhelming, tears welled up in my eyes. I realized that Amma knew everything about me and had only love and acceptance for me.

She felt very familiar to me, like reconnecting with a loved one after not seeing them for a long time. I was completely mesmerized by her. Amma knew my hopeless state of mind, and pointed for me to sit next to her. It was dazzling to watch Amma give darśhan, and at the same time, I enjoyed receiving her side glances.

I stayed for a period of time in the huts with the *brahmachāriṇīs*, and I remember having to use the 'washing stones,' to do my laundry. I stood there in front of a waist-high concrete slab, feeling at a complete loss as to what to do. The brahmachāriṇīs around me were all washing their clothes with expert proficiency, and I felt too silly to ask them.

Just then, a western woman was passing by. She had a big smile and a lot of light about her. She seemed well liked by all the brahmachāriṇīs there, so I thought to ask her for help. She cheerfully told me what to do, and gave me her top tips on how to wash clothes.

Later somebody told me that the person I was speaking to was Lakṣhmī (now known as Swāminī Śhrī Lakṣhmī Prāṇā), and that her sēvā is in Amma's room. I was surprised to hear this, as she must have been so busy, however she showed no impatience.

These small acts of kindness that we may think nothing of, can often mean a lot to the person receiving them. The greatest people in the world are also the humblest. Amma of course, is a shining example of this in all her actions. Amma has said that she does not see any greatness in only showing her respect. What she looks for is whether her children are selfless, have humility, and respect each other.

***

Soon it was time for the North India Tour which was like being on a divine camping trip. It was a thrill to see Amma's fun-loving side with all the swimming, and chai and meal stops. Sometimes she would even jump on the bus and ride along with us.

I remember an incident during that 1995 North India Tour that made me see how being in Amma's presence helps us go beyond what we think we are physically and mentally capable of.

When we arrived in Delhi we had just gone through an extremely difficult nightlong bus journey. Many of us, myself included, had suddenly become very ill after the dinner stop on the road. The bus had to continually pull over due to the desperate calls of people having relentless stomach issues. There was also an intense traffic jam going into Delhi that made the journey even longer.

It was quite late in the morning when we finally arrived at the Delhi āśhram. When the bus finally got there, we pretty much walked straight into a construction site. The inauguration of the Delhi *Brahmasthānam* temple was going to be held the next day and there was still a lot of building work that needed to be done before it was ready.

The next thing I knew I was standing in a line, passing buckets of sand from one person to the next. Soon Amma herself came to inspect the work. I remember her smiling at us as we passed the buckets of sand.

All feelings of sickness and fatigue suddenly disappeared, and were now replaced with the joy of being in Amma's presence. Amma is not one to stand idle, so she began to help us with the work. Amma's beautiful and radiant form completely uplifted and energized us all, and now I realize how truly special it was to help build the Brahmasthānam Temple alongside the Divine Mother herself.

I started to understand that Amma is showing us through these experiences that when we stop identifying with our mind/body limitations, we are really capable of so much more than what we think we can do.

While in Delhi, Amma suddenly canceled the next stop on the tour which was to Rishikesh. Some of the westerners on the tour were very upset about this, and decided they would leave and go there themselves. After we left Delhi, the bus stopped in the evening for a dinner/swim stop with Amma. Amma said how sad she was that some of her children had left the tour to go to Rishikesh. She then said that wherever we are with Amma – we are in the *Gaṅgā* with her.

That statement had a deep effect on my mind. At this very moment we are all in the Ganges river with Amma, being purified by her divine love and presence. Distance is no barrier, and selflessness in our actions always draws Amma's grace to us.

14

From Banking World to Amma's World — A Devotee's Journey

Daya Chandrahas - India

During my childhood in Vijayawādā, Andhra Pradesh, my family celebrated all the Hindu festivals like Gaṇēśh Chaturthī, Kṛiṣhṇa Jayantī, Hōlī, Śhivarātrī, and many others. However, not having any spiritual background, these celebrations did not have much spiritual impact on me.

Still, when I was around twelve years old, I had the good fortune of receiving *vibhūti* — sacred ash — from Sathya Sai Baba when he visited my aunt's house in Chennai. By his blessings, I attended the *bhajans* at the Sathya Sai Samithi near our home. Once when Baba came to Vijayawādā, I was allowed to sing bhajans for him sitting in the front row with the other kids.

I moved to Mumbai to attend college. The part of Mumbai where Baba visited was too far for me as a teenager to travel to by myself, so I had to give up visiting Baba and his programs.

Instead, I not only attended to my studies but also started working. My hands were full and I didn't think much about spirituality. I had good jobs working for banks. Life continued. I got married and had a daughter. Suddenly, I received a terrible blow — my husband was killed in a car accident. It was a rude shock, to say the least. It wasn't just the financial difficulties it created that bothered me so much, but my ego was terribly hurt; I felt abandoned. I also worried about my daughter never being able to experience her father's love.

Anyway, we managed. My mother came to live with us and looked after my daughter while I worked. In fact, throughout my career which spanned about 40 years, I regularly worked twelve-hour days. There was a silver lining to all of this — I loved my work. The work-environment at the bank was very congenial. I got timely promotions, and the job provided plenty of international travel.

In June 1998, I received a second blow — my mother was diagnosed with a malignant brain tumor. The doctors gave her six to seven months to live. After surgery and radiation (chemotherapy wasn't recommended), she seemed to recover and was pain free.

However, she continued to weaken, and slowed down a lot. A few months after her operation, she fell in the bathroom and became bedridden. It was only then that I began to understand the seriousness of the situation.

I prayed for the first time. An astrologer had suggested that I pray to Durgā Mātā. I started negotiating with the Divine Mother for my mother's life. I prayed that if she saved my mother, in return I would do whatever she asks.

Without a *mantra* from any Guru, my spontaneous mantra was *'Jai mātā ki'* — victory to the Divine Mother. I chanted this mantra almost non-stop throughout the day, and slept very little. I was extremely worried.

I knew that without my mother, I wouldn't be able to continue working those long twelve-hour days, as my daughter was only thirteen years old at the time. She refused to go to a day-care center, and I didn't want her staying home alone after school for many hours until I finally got back from work. I prepared myself to take a much less desirable job nearby, at a greatly reduced salary and with much lower job satisfaction.

My mother passed away in January 1999. A month later, a neighbor who had helped me during my mother's illness, suggested that I come with her to see Amma. I point-blank refused asking her, "Will she bring my mother back?" However, my neighbor kept insisting. I figured I had to do her this 'favor' as she had helped me during my mother's illness.

Amma says that in *Kali Yuga* (the current age where unrighteousness is predominant), it's not the disciple who goes in search of the Guru, but the Guru who goes in search of the disciple.

So it was in my case.

When I saw Amma for the first time at her āśhram in Mumbai, I couldn't believe how she had the energy to hug so many people for hours together! When I received my *darśhan*, Amma said in clear Hindi, "*Mērī bēti, chintā mat karō*" meaning, "My daughter, do not worry." I didn't understand then why she said that, as she 'didn't know me.'

Tears flowed from my eyes and even from my neighbor's eyes. I asked her why she was crying. She said tears flow from everyone's eyes when they meet Amma.

I forgot about that darśhan and went about my life as usual. I was planning to quit my job in a couple of months, coinciding with the start of school vacation. To my utter surprise, a week after my darśhan with Amma, I received a promotion that I clearly didn't deserve, as I'd hardly gone to work in the past three months. I was also transferred to the Pune office.

The great thing about this office was that the office and the residential quarters were located in the same plot. I went from a three-and-a-half hour commute, to a three-and-a-half minute one! It was like getting an additional three and a half hours of life every day. My daughter got admission into a good school, and life became much happier than before for us, as for the first time, we had time to spend with each other. Our school and work schedules fit together like a jigsaw puzzle. I realized that this truly was due to Amma's infinite grace!

I started chanting the *archana* of the 1000 names of the Divine Mother everyday as suggested by Swāmī Vidyāmṛitajī of the Pune āśhram. In February 2000, Amma visited the Pune āśhram. During a bhajan session during the program days, I was sitting in the front row and as Amma was singing, tears kept flowing incessantly down my cheeks.

At one point I remember telling Amma mentally that there was an open position at my bank's Singapore branch, and could she please bless me to get the position? With Amma's grace, everyone in the office including myself, was surprised that I was chosen for the post of Regional Manager of the Singapore branch. I had tried for the position for the last four years but was considered unsuitable as I was single.

When Amma visited Singapore in 2001, I was on a high. I couldn't eat or drink on the program days. During *Dēvī Bhāva* Amma looked at me while showering flower petals on everyone, and I was completely smitten. I saw beautiful, colorful rays of radiant light flowing from her eyes which came towards my eyes and then disappeared. This happened continuously for sometime, and I kept saying through tears, "Oh Amma, you are not just Amma; you are Dēvī, you are Durgā Mātā!"

My faith in Amma increased as I was now convinced that Amma was no ordinary person. But the question was, who was Amma? I had read several books about the lives of various saints but I didn't think that I could ever meet a Self-realized master, particularly in these times when people are so selfish.

Another day, when I was sitting in prayer in front of a picture of Durgā Mātā hanging over the altar in my Singapore home, I opened my eyes and saw the crown in the picture shining with beautiful lights emanating from it, making it sparkle in a manner I'd never seen before. Thus, Amma made me understand that she alone is Durgā Mātā.

When I returned to India from Singapore, I would visit *Amritapuri* at the drop of a hat, as they say. Amma had become my wish fulfilling tree. All other outings with friends gave way to visits to Amritapuri.

Amma, the Divine Mother who is also Lord Dhanvantari — the god of medicine — has showered her immense blessings on me. In 2003 during *AmṛitaVarṣham50,* Amma's fiftieth birthday celebration, I was having severe gynecological problems. On one of the program days, I managed to reach the stage just as Amma was about to give darśhan.

Amma moved to the center of the stage where her *pīṭham* was positioned, and I quietly moved next to her on her right side. No one asked me to move, so I sat next to Amma chanting my mantra. Amma started giving darśhan and after each hug, Amma showed me her palm, clearly indicating that I needed to put something in it. I found an apple, picked it up and put it in Amma's hand. This happened a second time, a third time, and on and on.

I was thrilled. I asked the stage volunteers to refill the baskets of apples. Somehow everyone must have thought I'd been designated to do this *sēvā*, so no one asked me to leave. I continued to sit next to our beloved Amma for the next three hours. I was so delighted, and was the envy of all my Singapore friends who were watching online! Amma had showered her immense grace on me. From that day forth, my gynecological problem diminished, and later completely vanished.

In 2007 during an annual check up, a lump in my breast was detected. I conferred with a couple of leading oncologists in Mumbai, and they both confirmed that it needed to be removed.

However, they weren't sure whether it was malignant or not. The lump could be felt by touching the outer skin. I was devastated. I went to Amma and just said, "Amma I am not well."

Amma replied, "Go to AIMS" (Amma's super-specialty hospital in Kochi). I went to AIMS and was checked by the doctors there.They said that only the senior surgeon could make a determination, but as he was in surgery, they weren't sure if he'd be available later.

***

I returned to Amritapuri. When Amma was on her way to her room after darśhan, I told her that I was leaving for Mumbai the next day. She again said, "Go to AIMS." I wondered why Amma was asking me to go to AIMS again. I stopped by AIMS, planning to leave for the airport from there.

This time I was able to meet with the senior surgeon. He did a needle biopsy, looked at the scans and said, "I don't think we should do anything right now; I don't think you need to worry. Come back if there's a problem. Otherwise, let's wait and see for three months."

I felt relieved and returned to Mumbai. To my surprise, a few days after my visit to AIMS, the lump disappeared. I touched the area again and again but couldn't feel it. I had another scan done shortly thereafter, and nothing showed up. I couldn't believe it! What grace from our beloved Amma! The lump never returned.

It's no wonder that name number 326 in the *Lalitā Sahasranāma* is:

> *ōm karuṇā rasa sāgarāyai namaḥ*
> 'She who is the ocean of compassion.'

Did I deserve it? Of course not. But can the Divine Mother do otherwise?

***

Finding Amma is like finding a gold mine; one should never let it out of one's sight. I still feel that way about Amma — that I should never let her out of my sight, but alas that is not always possible. Therefore, I'm trying to tune into the inner Amma, as Amma tells us to do.

After retiring in June 2016, I asked Amma for further guidance. She quickly replied, "Come here, come here!" as if she couldn't wait for me to move here. I was overjoyed, for earlier, I wasn't sure if Amma would allow me to stay here permanently. I've been living in the āśhram now for the past four and a half years.

My life in the āśhram has consisted primarily of going on tours — both the Indian and overseas tours. When I'm in Amritapuri, I do sēvā at *Matruvani* (Amma's monthly spiritual magazine), and also hand out darśhan tokens.

By Amma's grace, I have gone on almost all of her tours for the last three years. I've been told that the tours are the fastest way to grow spiritually. For me, everything done on the Indian tours was a first-time experience: traveling long distances by non-a/c buses; peeing in fields; having lunch stops next to the highway; sleeping on mats in newly-built or unused classrooms at Amma's schools; bathing in a room that doubled as the toilet; washing clothes on a stone on the terrace; eating hot food in a hot kitchen with no fans; and the list goes on.

I had many first-time experiences on the international tours too: sleeping on cold floors in sleeping bags in various countries throughout Europe; veggie chopping in tents outside in the cold; traveling by bus for eighteen or nineteen hours continuously to reach our next destination etc.

We enthusiastically accept these challenges inspired by Amma's immense, unconditional love. Her abundant love, her tender face, her all-giving nature, her compassion for everyone, doesn't allow my mind any room for excuses not to go on tour. I am simply carried away by the river of love, and there is no stopping!

***

Living in the āśhram has had a deep impact on me. I would like to share how much clarity I have gotten about certain things by living in the āśhram versus when I was just visiting in the early years. I thank Amma from the bottom of my heart for permitting me to stay in this holy place:

Sēvā: For householder devotees who are immersed in their own household responsibilities, participation in sēvā activities definitely requires a lot of extra effort and opportunities are fewer. Amma's āśhrams provide plenty of sēvā opportunities to householders, which can bring about a positive transformation in one's life.

Gītā discourses: Although I had read the *Bhagavad Gītā* in the past, the impact it had on me after I attended the scripture classes in the āśhram was profound. I'm sure this is true for many other householders. Because Amma speaks on the same issues as the Gītā such as renunciation, knowledge, devotion, faith, surrender etc., we can understand Amma's words at a deeper level by studying the Gītā.

Not only does Amma give *satsangs* on these topics, she walks the talk. Having Amma as a role model and knowledge of both the Gītā and Amma's satsangs makes it easier to grasp these principles and to try to put them into practice.

Satsang: the spiritual discourses given by the āśhram residents have been a complete eye opener for me. Instead of knowing just what I've learned about Amma from my own experiences and those shared by friends, I get to hear about experiences with Amma from a multitude of sources: stories of crisis and joy; stories of Amma giving spiritual guidance; even stories of Amma saving or extending lives. We need to remember all these stories and try to deepen our faith and devotion with complete surrender to Amma, and do exactly as she advises us to do.

Knowledge of the upaniṣhads: there is a big gap between upaniṣhadic knowledge and the worldly knowledge that I'd learned in life. Some have learned to chant these scriptures by rote, but that's not enough. We need to do *śhravaṇam* (listening), *mananam* (reflecting), and *nididhyāsanam* (assimilating) on these teachings. This is a life-long task.

Amma helps us as her satsangs provide much more clarity on these scriptural teachings. In my own case, I previously had no knowledge of the scriptures. The most profound thing I've learned from the scriptures, and which I try to repeat every day is that I am not the body, mind or intellect; I am the eternal, immortal, Self. Just to intellectually know this creates a paradigm shift in one's thinking.

Although Self-realization has yet to dawn in me, with Amma's grace, just to conceive even the possibility of it has given me immense self-confidence and a change in attitude. However, constant effort is required.

That we are not the body, mind or intellect but the eternal Self is the crux of all upaniṣhadic teachings. Our desires and fears are the cause of all our problems and sorrows. These desires and sorrows are inherent in the idea 'I am the body and mind.' 'Needs' by nature are necessary, and so do not cause the same suffering.

Amma says the purpose of this human birth is to realize that we are God or the Self, but we are so muddled up with the happenings in and around our lives that we do not know how to proceed. This agitated state of mind coupled with our latent tendencies accumulated over several lifetimes creates a lot of upheaval in our lives.

To overcome such a mind is not an easy task. Silencing the mind is the only way, but this is easier said than done. Amma is showing us the way, each according to his or her tendencies.

Amma's divine tools such as *archana, mantra japa, sēvā, Vēdic* chanting, *Gītā* study, and meditation are all aimed at taming our mind. In addition, I have personally found the practice of *nēti, nēti* — 'not this, not this' — helps us to experience the peace that lies beyond the transitory agitations of our mind that are the root cause of all our sufferings.

Amma is not affected by the ups and downs in life because she is ever established in that bliss. Out of her overflowing compassion she is tirelessly working to help the world come out of sorrow.

The task before us is an adventure of the highest order. It may seem arduous, but above all, we have our beloved Amma holding our hands and taking us forward.

Amma says that money lost can always be earned again; but time wasted is lost forever. Time is precious and Amma has created the right environment to dive into *sādhanā* and sēvā. We have to arise and awaken, and make use of this unparalleled opportunity to progress on our spiritual path.

I pray to our beloved Amma to please shower her abundant grace on all her children, that we may attain Self-realization in this lifetime.

I would like to conclude with a passage from a bhajan:

dar dar mē bhaṭaktā rahā
manzil kahā nahī thā patā
arth milā is jīvan kō
jab mā tērē charaṇa āyā

koṭi praṇām, koṭi praṇām, śhata koṭi praṇām, amma.

kitna kuch hai diyā tū nē
tujhe dēnē kō mā kuch bhī nahī
hai arpit ye mērā jīvan
śhrī charaṇō mē mā amṛitēśhvarī

'I was wandering from door to door
I did not know my destination
My life got a sense of purpose when I touched your lotus feet

A million salutations, million salutations, million salutations, Amma.

You have given me so much
I have nothing to offer you back
I offer my very life at your radiant lotus feet
My auspicious support, Mother Amṛitēśhwarī'

15

This Precious Life

Tejasvini – USA

A partial translation of Amma's *bhajan*, *'Ini Oru Janmam'* is as follows:

> *'O Kṛiṣhṇa, give me not another birth lest I fall into the deep quagmire of delusion. If thou givest, then bestow the boon of taking birth as the servant of thy servants forever.'*
>
> *If I should get another birth, let it be beneficial to the world by giving the imperishable joy to others as well. If thou allowest me that, then please give me any number of births as a human being.'*

Seeing as Amma's bhajans are, in and of themselves, a kind of musical scripture, and seeing as I am not versed in the śhāstras (scriptures), and can only do my best to fumble behind Amma's words like a child, I'd like to mold my talk today loosely around this and two other bhajans. I pray to Amma that I don't make too many errors in this bold endeavor, and kindly ask your patience with me as I untangle some of my questions along this path to the goal.

About a year ago, I found myself grappling with a sudden fear, not so much of death, but of rebirth. One day it hit me hard... that someday I will be subjected, once again, to the traumatic events of entry into this world.

My response to this began on a superficial level, with all of my best faces of sarcasm rearing their heads to cover up the grim truth before me. Inwardly I commented wryly to myself, "Woah

woah, hold on a second; you mean I have to do that again? All alone? Crying and screaming into this harsh world, subject to the culture, the society, the — family!

Oh God have mercy, the family! The mother! The father! Thrust again into this never ending pit of despair, at the mercy of two people and their pains and traumas from their own lives... I mean, c'mon! Am I really so powerless to my *prārabdha karma* — the effects of my past actions — that I'll be whisked back into a family and have to wade through so much pain, again?"

The pain. As the days passed, I realized that this was at the root of my fear. The pain of being born into this world. The pain of being so innocent and at the mercy of others who are also in pain. The pain of trying to find yourself in this world. The pain of losing yourself in this world. The pain of, well, this world.

Soon enough, the sarcastic façade melted into genuinely somber contemplation. I couldn't bear the idea of again shouldering the kind of sadness I had experienced as a child. Childhood meant many things to my impressionable mind: to be unstable...to be unsafe...to be lost in a sea of heartache. Then to say nothing of growing up with those pains imprinted on your psyche, and trying to prevent them from making a total mess of your adult life!

I really began to feel a weight. A weight that burdened my mind and heart while I grappled with this sobering reminder that, indeed, we just keep doing this thing called life again and again.

Of course, this is exactly what we are being told in our śhāstras; that the cycle of life continues, human suffering goes on and on, until each one of us makes the change within to strive to merge with the eternal *Brahman*.

Nevertheless, even though I knew this intellectually, I was surprised to see my inner intolerance toward this idea of suffering; it took so long and so much pain to get to where I am today, cradled in Amma's divine lap. The thought of experiencing all of that again was becoming too much. "Please dear God," I found myself praying, "Don't make me struggle like this any more!"

But...aren't those exactly the rules of this game of life? There are beautiful gifts and there are heartbreaking losses. There are moments of beauty and magic, and there are piercing pains that shake us to the core. Who among us does not walk around with their own painful memories of the past?

Often it is our pain that acts as a catalyst in our search for the Divine and ultimately brings us to take refuge in Amma.

Eventually, a thought appeared in my mind that for some reason calmed me, "Even *mahātmās* experience this pain that you're trying to avoid."

Huh. This simple thought, albeit a bit of a sad one, indeed changed something in me, as I remembered that yes; Kṛiṣhṇa was born in a prison cell, Rāma (another incarnation of God) was exiled to live in an unruly forest for fourteen years. The human lives led by these mahātmās were no less wrought with suffering than the lives we see played out before us. If they could brave the pains of human life, couldn't I?

The first verse of Amma's bhajan *'Tapta Mānasam'* translates as:

'Within this heart lies a vast ocean of sorrow. O Queen of vast and unconditional love, lord of the whole world, please do not tell me that you are not my mother.'

Perhaps this transient, dream-like state is simply my destiny! Could it also be that this sadness within — this vast ocean of sorrow in my heart — is really just an expression of the true pain of separation between my wandering soul and God? Is there anything more beautiful, in that case, than living?

A brave statement to make, that 'Life is Beautiful;' what with such unthinkable horrors of war and immense worldwide unrest happening all around us. And indeed, would I have thought so much about the beauties of life in my early years, as I was stumbling aimlessly through the world?

Let me revisit this life I began with. Most of my hardest childhood years that I mentioned before were intricately linked to my mother. I know better now than to say my traumas were because of her, but much of my fear of being born again stems from those years, and much of my efforts on this path to the goal have involved trying my level best to accept the events of the past and forgive them.

The details are not so important, but my mother also entered into this world wrought with her own inner turmoil. She was plagued by anger, distrust of those around her, and an inability to find that stable inner compass of peace. She fell into postpartum depression after giving birth to me and had no helping hand to climb out of it. Early life with her was full of emotional strain, and it took me many years to untangle the pain and move on.

But my story is not so unique. I'm not the only one here with a hard start to life, so how do I reconcile such a past and awaken to acceptance about it? Thanks to Amma's immeasurable grace, she has shown me that these challenges of life are not to be shunned or erased from memory. They come with the territory and you know what? The forgiveness of my mother, and even gratitude toward her, has flourished from one simple thought:

My mother gave me the single greatest gift of all — The gift of life.

This gift, in and of itself, is cause to erase a whole lifetime of resentment. Everything that I have right now, is thanks to being given life. There is literally no greater gift than to be born at this unprecedented time when the mother of the universe has also taken birth. Each and every one of us here has been given this most precious gift, and we have our mothers to thank for it.

***

Amma's omniscience of my birth goes back to my very first days in *Amritapuri*, nearly ten years ago.

I had justified my trip on the basis that I wanted to spend my birthday with Amma. And since my birthday was at the end of August, the only way to do so was to come to India. I bid farewell to my friends and family, "I'm going to spend my birthday with Amma! I'll be home by Christmas!" and packed my bags.

As I was on the plane, however, a doubt crept into my mind: "Does Amma even know who I am? Will she remember me? I'm just one girl out of millions. She hasn't seen me in many months." Oh, what the mind can do with a few idle hours!

Despite my fears, I joyfully arrived at the āśhram, and felt an indescribable feeling of returning home. I soon found out that August 28th was not only my birthday that year, but Lord Kṛiṣhṇa's as well! With what little time I had, I prepared for my first *Kṛiṣhṇa Jayanthi* celebration in Amritapuri.

I had asked for a party — and Amma threw a party! The air of celebration and joy rang out from the break of dawn, and I heard the precious mooing of cows and tambourines below as, with my friend Shashi's help, I desperately tried to wrap myself in a *sāri*.

Everything felt like it glimmered with an invisible sweetness. Friends were welcoming and kind, festivities rang through the air, *Ammamars* (grandmothers) dragged me to the side of the temple to fix my terribly-wrapped sāri...and I got my long-awaited token for *darśhan*.

In the darśhan line, my insidious mind still wondered "Yeah but...does Amma really know who I am?"

I arrived at her *pīṭham* (seat) for darśhan. The moment I had been waiting for. They told Amma it was my birthday and she burst into a radiant smile. She showered me with every *prasād* one could hope for and then paused for a moment, gazing at me with the most loving and knowing smile. "*Mōlē*," She sighed. "Daughter."

Oh, she knew me, alright! More than I knew myself.

As I walked down the ramp after darśhan, the *pūjārī* (temple priest) came up to me and kindly asked, "Do you want to hold Amma's *pādukās*?" Of course I said yes.

He told me to run to the *Kaḷari*[24] in five minutes. I ran after him joyfully. At the Kaḷari, he handed me Amma's silver pādukās resting on a beautiful plate. A friend who had come along was given a large, festive umbrella to hold over Amma's sandals and therefore, me as well...

I never imagined the upcoming scene in my wildest dreams... I saw Lakṣhmī the elephant standing in full festive garb, surrounded by drummers, kids dressed as Rādhā, Kṛiṣhṇa, *gōpīs* and *gōpās*, with tambourines, bells et cetera... and I was at the front, leading the procession with Amma's pādukās!

We went to the hall to get Amma's blessings, then walked through the āśhram, and the seaside village! Amma's sandals... Lakṣhmī the elephant...forty drummers, eighty āśhramites, the kids... we all took a left outside the north gate and it felt like we never came back!

The parade finally circled back in time to see the *Uriyaḍi* pot-breaking festivities and Amma's bhajans on the *Kāḷī Temple* steps, and by the end of the day, after evening bhajans and dinner, when Amma returned at midnight to sing and distribute

---

[24] Original small temple in the āśhram where Amma used to hold Kṛiṣhṇa Bhāva and Dēvī Bhāva darśhans.

prasād full of energy, I realized that I cannot keep up with Amma when it comes to celebrating.

I've often looked back on this story and wondered if this was what one gets when you ask the goddess of the universe to throw you a birthday party...

Such precious stories we all have with Amma...and thanks to this precious life, we can tell them and share them with one another. Thanks to my mother, I could meet my Mother. Thanks to this body, these feet, I could parade Amma's pādukās through town. This life, and its preciousness, is what we have to live for.

The first verse from the bhajan *'Aridu Aridu'* translates as:

'To be born as a human being is very rare. It is rarer still to have an interest in liberation. And extremely rare to have a relationship with God in the form of the Guru. If we waste our life even after gaining these three, it is like a pitch dark night.'

***

Allow me to elaborate a bit more on my limitations when it comes to making the most out of this precious gift of life. Despite the existential fear of rebirth that I felt last year, I don't exactly have a strong drive to attain salvation because I feel, in some ways, what's the rush?

Now, I don't mean this as it may sound. I don't mean to say we should while away the days and forget God, but I have never been able to reconcile in my mind one thing: if we race to some kind of 'finish line' called 'liberation' (and by some miracle someday attain it!), then what? What happens after we have stepped off the wheel of *saṁsāra — the cycle of* birth and death; are we racing there to melt into everythingness for all eternity?

Is liberation something that I am searching for, for myself so that I don't suffer any more? "Phew! I made it out of that horrible place! Too bad for the rest who haven't made it yet."

Or, am I walking toward this state for another purpose? When I look at our most divine being sitting here, I observe her pointing towards a higher purpose that is not so much for ourselves, but for selfless service toward others.

After all, what good is my own individual liberation if others are stuck in the mire of worldly suffering? Where does the hand of the clock go after it reaches twelve? Back to one.

Let me pose this final question in this long series of hypotheses: if Amma were to return to Earth in human form, and we had already attained salvation, would we not want to come back to be with her?

Won't Amma continue to come, again and again to this world, to bring each one of us back into her oneness? No matter how much I hear that salvation is the goal, I can't help but think that I would instead want to follow Amma wherever she goes — to whatever planet, whatever *lōka* or world, I would long to follow and serve in any small way I could.

Years ago, driving in Los Angeles, I found myself thinking, "The mother of the universe has incarnated in a human body. She is alive right now. Would I not follow her, wherever she may be, even if it means to the ends of the Earth?" Sitting here today, I expand that thought, "Would I not follow her, across lifetimes if I could?"

So I continue to think, "What's the rush on this seemingly eternal, never-ending journey? I suppose all I can ask is that, if thou allowest me another birth Amma, that is beneficial to the world, then please — give me any number of births as a human being."

For someone like me, with a relatively bad track record of spiritual discipline, I struggle with what it means to be 'beneficial to the world.' I always interpreted it to mean 'beneficial to the whole world,' as if we are supposed to personally touch the lives of millions of people — the job that literally only Amma can do. Instead, in the years when all I can seem to do is live life one day at a time, I see that Amma has given me enough inner strength and subtlety to (sometimes!) be present for those around me.

The experience of becoming a mother, for example, extricated me out of my self-will, and placed my focus on being of service to another being. Perhaps, just being of service to those around me, can be a type of *sādhana* in and of itself, and even a type of mysterious alchemy that benefits one's whole family lineage.

No need to affect the entire world, just doing good to a few people can be enough to start, to see how Amma's infinite grace touches every being on earth, sometimes working through us.

When I returned to the United States last year in October, for example, I had a pressing priority in my mind: to see my mother. I had a feeling that I really needed to check in on her in person. When I finally saw her, she confided in me that she had lost the only small job that she had, and that she was down to her last ten dollars in her bank account. She was also facing some challenges with her apartment, and it seemed that it was time to look for a new place for her to live.

This seemed like a task that surely wouldn't be completed in the short time that I was there, but I had a distinct feeling and inner confidence that Amma was taking care of her.

Imagine my surprise when the first apartment I saw online was a mere few blocks away from where she currently lived. I applied, simply thinking of it as a 'test run.' Within a few days, however, I had received this message one morning: "Your mother is the kind of tenant I'm looking for. I've got seventy-five other emails here but I would rather rent it to her so I don't have to deal with them. When can you come to see the apartment?"

The following day, she signed the lease.

There were so many infinite details for this miracle of timing to occur, but the part of this experience that touched me the most — that reflects Amma's boundless, all-knowing compassion for all beings — was what my mom said to me in the car as we drove away from the new place:

"Oh, thank you so much, Lani. I'm just so happy by how warm the apartment is."

"Warm, mom?"

"Yeah, my current place is cold in the winter."

I was struck without anything to say in response. Here is a woman, living in the modern, western world, sleeping in a cold apartment during the wintertime in Pennsylvania!

Most of her family has been unable to forgive her for her limitations and for the past...but not the mother of the universe, whose immense, boundless compassion and love stretches to every corner of the Earth...not by the *Prēma Sāgara Rājñī* — the Queen of the Ocean of Love — who knew that one of her daughters was cold at night.

Only the true mother of the universe could create such healing between broken hearts. Like a subtle, wafting breeze of fresh flowers, Amma's presence purifies even the most painful memories of our past. She heals each one of our vast oceans of sorrow, one by one, and shows us that Her love can truly carry us across even the most impenetrable waters of saṁsāra.

So, perhaps it is true, 'Life is Beautiful.' To walk through this transient, dream-like mystery of life as her *nimitta-mātram* — her instrument, allowing her to heal the generations of pain in our families and lives is beautiful. And if Amma can bear the weight of literally every family lineage on earth, I think I could handle being born into one of them again in order to serve her.

Some years ago I was sitting within earshot of Amma's pīṭham. She was consoling someone about their troubles and said that oftentimes, even when our worldly prayers are answered, God might still make it so hard that we won't want those things anymore. She laughed lovingly and then said, "And sometimes, Amma ties the rope right through the cow's nose, so that it doesn't wander too far away from her."

Dearest Amma, please string your rope tight through this little calf's nose, and keep me close, no matter what pastures you roam, or what lifetimes you take.

16

Overcoming Suffering with Amma's Love

Purnima - Germany

Amma sacrifices every second of her life, continuously giving everyone the precious chance to attain the goal of life.

Amma's love moves the unmovable.

Amma sees the unseen.

Amma knows the unknown.

Amma's love is able to instantly cure the incurable, and makes the impossible possible — blessing our lives.

The topic of my *satsang* is — Only with Amma's love and our own limited efforts can we overcome suffering...even such as the suffering created by being wheelchair-bound.

Amma, Your grace can transform any disability into wholeness. Amma is always aware that we are neither the mind nor the body. We are the indestructible, unchanging ātmān — the eternal Self.

Allow Amma to awaken your true inner Self with her eternal wisdom; with her selfless, pure actions; with her blissful *bhajans* and peaceful meditations; her dances; her surprises; her blissful smile; and through her uplifting, embracing love.

Wherever we may be suffering in this world, Amma will find us...our cry will be heard. Amma, our Divine Mother and no other will help us when we feel alone...

I was twenty-four years old when I was diagnosed with an incurable, very painful bone disease. The disease worsened dramatically. I was bedridden, unable to move or to even lift a cup, and was confined to a wheelchair.

My deepest longing was to live by the ocean under the sun. Helpless and lonely, I cried out and begged the heavens, "Please! I want to heal and live again!"

Amma Your grace appears undeserved,
unearned, gloriously
You come radiant as light, spontaneously
Amma, You reach out from nowhere, at any time,
from whatever place
You take our misery, You bathe us deeply in Your grace

During the time I was bedridden, my mother tried to find a *yōga* teacher to improve my health. In addition, I required and therefore searched for two caregivers.

In 2004, after years of isolation, Amma's mercy brought three new people to me. They all came to me in the same month, and all three knew Amma. One was a German yōga teacher, and the other two were caregivers studying in Germany, but who originally came not only from Kerala in India, but from *Vallikavu*, Amma's birthplace!

When I heard about an Indian, hugging saint — a flash of white light appeared within, at the third eye.

My thirty-seventh birthday became a divine birthday, because even without knowing Amma, my yōga teacher gave me Amma's biography, *'Mother of Immortal Bliss,'* which I read in one night. I cried for hours over *Sudhāmani's* (Amma's birth name) difficult childhood. Upon seeing Amma's photo for the first time, I was overjoyed. I felt like flipping backwards out of my wheelchair! I kissed Amma's photo again and again.

Then Amma's next miracle occurred...

I received a flier about Amma's 2004 visit to Germany. Happily, my Indian caregivers offered to take me to see Amma.

Amma Your compassion removes all obstacles in the way,
You reveal to us the sacred path to serve and pray

The Divine Mother made my wish to meet her stronger than any pain in my body. She gave me the courage to travel by train for the first time in a wheelchair. A ramp and a wheelchair-capable taxi assisted me in getting to my first *darśhan.*

Amma stroked my knees over and over, caressed my feet carefully, tenderly kissed each of my hands, caressed my back, and kissed my head repeatedly. I merged with Amma's eyes — stars of compassion, that looked into my inner being beyond the body. Amma blessed me with an apple, a chocolate, and her *mantra.*

Amma Your radiance awakens each life,
to find the true self is our goal — we have to strive

After my first darśhan, I longed with all my soul to be with Amma. The only thing I could do to make this happen was to post in the local online satsang group:

'Woman in wheelchair needs assistance to go on the 2005 Amma Europe Tour.'

I prayed deeply for someone to come. Amma hears everyone's prayers, and her grace will always respond. A devotee who I had never met before, offered to be my caregiver for the 2005 Europe Tour. I cried tears of gratitude.

Keep busy with self effort to do good things,
always Amma will carry us on her wings

Amma for any pain, You are the cure
Amma, I realize now, I am not the doer

Amma is the greatest healer in the universe. She brought a caregiver, and took me away from being bedridden in Germany. I was carried by four men while seated on a blanket, so that I could board a plane. I traveled for thirty hours in severe pain, all the way to California. After the 9,000 km flight, I arrived happily into Amma's loving embrace.

Strive forward with optimism, courage, and faith,
this will transform Your life in Amma's embrace

During my darśhan in Amma's āśhram in San Ramon California, I accepted Amma as my mother, my everything. Amma kissed me over and over. She held me tightly in her arms.

Amma's compassion even allowed me to come to *Amritapuri* without an assistant.

Amma asked me, "Amritapuri?"

"Yes please Amma," I replied.

Amma responded with, "Amritapuri OK!"

With Amma's *saṅkalpa* — her divine resolve — I flew the 7,000 km to India and arrived in Amritapuri. My body felt like a truck had driven over it. Tired and in pain, I had to ask for all kinds of help from unknown people.

Amma Only You. The soul of our souls is always aware,
Motherly You respond with fulfilling love and care

With Amma, I never feel that I'm in a wheelchair, or that I am different from others. Amma takes care of me as if I were a newborn baby. Many times in darśhan Amma loudly said in English to my caregivers, "Careful, careful! Pain."

Even though I experienced pain all throughout my body, my *sēvā* filled my heart with joy. My sēvā was in the cowshed where I bathed the little, jumping calves with a garden hose. None of the years I spent at university could give me this peace of mind and contentment.

***

In 2009, I found myself back in Germany. I missed Amma a lot. On Good Friday, I watched a movie about the life of Jesus. When he was crucified, I cried the whole night until the morning hours. I realized that this most precious gift to the world was killed by selfishness.

I imagined how much pain Mother Mary must have felt losing her son. I cried and cried and thought of Amma; that she is the most precious to me; that I never ever want to lose her.

The next day, the day before Easter, I woke up and discovered I was totally free from pain for the first time in sixteen years. I felt like I was swimming in white light. For the next two months, I kept my painkillers nearby, expecting the pain to come back. It never did.

Amma cured this incurable, all-destroying disease in one single night. This is Amma's indescribable miracle performed for the benefit of me and my doctors.

Amma You move everything in this Universe,
but we humans have to surrender and bow down on earth

With gratitude, I often sit in front of Amma, and chant the *archana*[25] and Amma's 108 names, over and over while gazing at her as she gives darśhan. Each glance from Amma, showers me with the mental strength needed to overcome many challenges, to find solutions to my problems, and to be able to move forward.

One day after darśhan, Amma came up to me, hugged me, and whispered a most beautiful truth in my ear. Amma said, "I

[25] Chanting of the names of God, e.g. the Lalitā Sahasranāma, the 1,000 names of the Divine Mother.

heard your archana." To explain, at the same time Amma was giving darśhan that day in the main hall, I was far away in the *Kāḷī Temple* chanting the archana. Everything happens inside of Amma.

Some devotees offered to help me after they saw me sitting all day in front of Amma, right up until the end of darśhan when Amma left.

Amma says, "We have to see God in each person we meet." Many sincere caregivers reveal Amma's purest love through their selfless service. Their help feels like Amma's darśhan to me.

Amma, the conqueror of the mind, who has infinite divine qualities, has taught me how to deal with being in a wheelchair, while remaining focused on the goal of life.

Amma has helped me to develop, if only to a very small degree, the qualities of gratitude, humility, patience, flexibility, and detachment. Also, to be practical; to adjust to each situation; to use time for a higher purpose; to be clear in communication; and to have forgiveness with myself and others' mistakes; to organize each step of my daily routine in advance with alertness and awareness; and to freely share everything with my caregivers.

I only keep faith in Amma. I see Amma as the cause of everything. Through Amma, I became free of shame. I smile and laugh mostly, and I am able to keep awareness when teaching my new caregivers.

Amma our dearest best friend, our Divine Mother,
You are the most precious treasure in this Universe
Mātā Amritānandamayī Dēvī,

You are the greatest servant for humanity and Mother Earth
You uplift the whole cosmos with Your own serving hands,

to remind us how to become and live as human beings in our gracelands

For the last fifteen years, I have gracefully lived in Amritapuri, a paradise of Mother Nature and Amma's unconditional love.

Amma herself serves us *prasād*, and uplifts all her children in her eternal overflowing love — this is beyond heaven.

Her amazing, selfless children come three times daily to lift me onto my bed, give me a bath in a loving and respectful way, and assist with each detail I need for my daily life. My deepest, endless thanks to all these amazing caregivers. In this age of *Kali Yuga* where there is a dearth of values and faith, not even our own family members will help us as much as Amma's children.

Amma, You upgrade everyone to be a winner
You give endless love, there is no sinner

All of us will reach the goal with Your compassion,
hand in hand a victory with dispassion

On the day of the full pandemic lockdown here in October 2020, I prayed for help. Amma's motherly grace embraced me deeply by immediately sending three caregivers, who were extremely careful about not catching the virus. In darśhan Amma told me, "Only grace protected You from catching Covid." Amma protects all of us at these times. All we have to do is to obey her words.

Amma, with You we can overcome any law of karma,
we have to help others,
this is our precious dharma

Amma wants her children to give more than take. In 2010, Amma blessed me with the sēvā of handing out the tokens for her divine darśhan. Seeing that Amma never rejects anyone fills my heart with compassion.

By opening our hearts, Amma's love carries us over any limitations
Amma's love is beyond any logic
Amma is the absolute power behind everything
Amma alone arranges our lives for us
Amma is the giver of absolute perfect faith

***

In 2014, a group of us booked flights to travel as a group for Amma's U.S. Tour, and then to return together back to Amritapuri.

However, before leaving, one of the tour coordinators told me that the bus company hired to take us to the airport would not take people in wheelchairs. Then another test presented itself; none of the caregivers I contacted could come with me. Finding a needle in the ocean seemed more possible than going on tour.

Ten days before the tour, I went for Amma's darśhan. I handed her the following letter:

'Dearest Amma, I booked all my flights so that I could travel with you from Cochin to Seattle, San Francisco, Toronto, then back to Cochin.

I couldn't find a caregiver, accommodation, or local transportation. Shall I come on the U.S. Tour, or stay back this year in Amritapuri? I surrender to your holy lotus feet.'

People near Amma's *pīṭham* (seat) were surprised by this question. I felt so stupid asking this, helpless in a wheelchair in front of the Divine Mother. I felt smaller than a worm.

Amma pulled my wheelchair closer to her, and stroked my arms again and again, looking deep into my eyes, bathing me in her waterfall of life strength, sending me oceans of motherly confidence and love.

Amma spoke to me in the sweetest way. All I understood was, "Help, help." Then the swāmī assisting during darśhan translated her answer, "You should try, you should come, Amma will help you."

That night I switched on the computer, and opened my email. The first message that popped out at me was from a devotee who wrote, "I will meet you in Seattle to assist you during the tour." Then other devotees offered both help, and to share accommodation for the whole tour.

With Amma's help in this way, I flew with her to Seattle. In the Seattle airport, everyone ran to catch the tour bus traveling with Amma. I couldn't get on the bus because my electric wheelchair had broken — unable to move an inch. By Amma's grace, a devotee took me in his car, as we were staying in the same hotel. However, once we arrived at the hotel parking lot, he received a phone call and needed to rush off urgently.

I sat in the parking lot under the midday sun after a fourteen-hour long flight with Amma. I had luggage for six weeks, and a totally damaged wheelchair.

I prayed, "Amma, please, I really need your help now!" A moment later, a car pulled up to me with a woman wearing a red tee-shirt that had 'I am a caregiver' written on it. She asked me, "What do you need?" My jaw dropped in shock. She rendered me assistance, and in return I told her stories of Amma.

This proved that Amma had been with me the whole time and I never felt closer to her. Since then, I always speak to Amma internally, letting her know the exact situations that I find myself in.

My main caregiver's flight was delayed. Again I asked Amma, the all-pervading, all-knowing consciousness for help. Immediately Amma sent another woman, who I'd never met before to help me. The fact that I needed help made this new caregiver happily decide to assist me for the whole U.S. Tour.

The woman with the caregiver tee-shirt was deeply impressed that we were going to do the whole tour together. She offered to be my third tour caregiver. Amma's grace has become my dearest, all protective, ever helpful companion, closer than my own thought, closer than my own heartbeat. Amma alone is my unfailing, invisible best friend who is always with me.

By the fourth day of the tour, Amma completed my amazing caregiver team by encouraging yet another devotee to travel with us for the entire tour.

During this tour, I wrote *The Book of Amma's Grace,* and did many hours of sēvā, handing out darśhan tokens every day.

Find only the true self in You
The truth of oneness will shine, not two
Dissolve Your mind, heart and breath in Amma's overflowing love
Your body, mind, and soul will heal and rise like a white dove

Amma's heart became the shining sun and the ever-flowing ocean I longed for my whole life. Amma's love transformed my life from being bedridden, into an exciting, dharmic life filled with joyful celebrations in Amma's enchanting presence.

Amma's radiant smile, her emphatic "Yes! Tour, Tour!" when I ask if I can join, and the endless love she showers on me, has empowered me to join more than fifty tours over the past thirteen years. I have joined all of Amma's world tours, and all of the South and North India tours. Traveling by bus on the bumpy roads feels like I am being rocked like a child on Amma's lap.

I feel blessed to have had the sēvā to hand out darśhan tokens to thousands of people around the world. Because of Amma's strong saṅkalpa, I have been able to sleep on the floor, and travel by plane or bus for over 800,000 km and counting...pain free!

With Amma's constant protection, I made it through many close-call accidents without receiving even a scratch, and I have never lost a single item on any of the tours.

By being determined to travel with Amma, she has completely removed the effects of my painful past, and has saved my life multiple times.

Circling the globe with Amma so many times, and visiting so many places makes me feel such gratitude for Mother Earth and Mother Nature.

Respect Mother Earth, correct Your mistake,
Give love to Mother Nature, finally awake

I would like to pray for Mother Earth with a song that I wrote:

Oh Dēvī, Bhumi Dēvī, Pacha Mama, Mother Gaṅgā
Amma take our selfishness. This is our illness
Praying to You with folded hands, oh Amma
Praying to You with folded hands
Heal our mother lands

In the book *Amma's Pearls of Wisdom*, Amma says, "Look at the optimism of nature. Nothing can stop it. Every aspect of nature tirelessly contributes its share to life."

Once on the Australia Tour, all of the buses transporting the tour staff drove through the lush Australian landscape, finally reaching the sea. The buses stopped there for a lunch break with Amma. Amma stood alone in the soft sand. The waves gently kissed her holy feet.

Standing there in her white sāri, Amma looked as soft as a cloud under the blue sky. Amma asked us, "Who wants to be a rainbow?"

Then Amma told a story of a little girl who was wheel-chair-bound. She had no friends and was very sad. One day, the girl saw a beautiful rainbow. She became so happy seeing all those beautiful colors. After a short while the rainbow disappeared, and the girl was very sad again.

On the next rainy day, the girl's mother drove the little girl to the top of a mountain. After the rain stopped, a beautiful, bright shining rainbow appeared.

"How have you become so beautiful and happy?" The girl asked the rainbow.

"Look at me closer. I was once just a raindrop with a very short lifespan, which always made me sad. Then I decided to make other people happy, and all of the colors inside of me started to bloom." Saying this, the rainbow disappeared.

After telling this story, Amma added, "Once we have the goal of making other people happy, then the full light of God can shine through us. In worldly life everyone is so selfish, and strives only to fulfill one's own desires. Their mantra is: 'I and mine.' But Amma's children are not like this, they try to make others happy." A few seconds after saying this, a big colorful rainbow graced the sky.

When Amma pointed at it, two even bigger rainbows, brighter in color appeared on the horizon. The colorful rainbows, the sky, the reflection of the water, the waves, the sand and Amma's indescribable beauty merged us all in the purest, magical, colorful, peaceful unity of God's creation.

Drops of rain started to sprinkle like peace on the ocean, on the sand, on us, and on Amma. Amma sang the bhajan *'Sṛiṣhṭium Nīyē'* — 'Oh Dēvī, You are creation!' — and became absorbed in it. We all sang with Amma. Amma's white sāri was fully drenched, yet she never stopped singing.

We were so happy to be with Amma in the heavy rain, however she didn't want her children to catch colds, so she sent us to the buses. Laughingly, we asked each other, "Did Amma create these rainbows from her fingertip?" Amma is our real rainbow, the miracle that is transforming our lives.

My deepest prayer is that I continue to be able to go everywhere Amma goes. May all our hearts swim in the joy of Amma's blissful love.

O Dēvī without You there is no life,
Bhumi Dēvī without You nothing can survive

Ōm Lokāḥ Samastāḥ Sukhinō Bhavantu –
May All Beings in All the Worlds Be Happy

17

Creation and Creator are not Two, but One

Prasadini - Germany

I would like to reflect on Amma's teaching: creation and creator are not two, but one. I am meditating on this, because if applied properly, it can be a cure for the illness of feeling separate from the divine, from nature, and from other people.

I've only had a few opportunities to study the scriptures. I am very inspired by them, and feel they are as vast as the ocean, and include all of creation. While experiencing creation, we should remember the creator. As humans, most of us tend to forget God, who is the changeless essence of all that exists.

In the *Bhagavad Gītā* Chapter 15, verses 12 and 13, Lord Kṛiṣhṇa says to his disciple Arjuna:

> *yad āditya-gataṁ tējō jagad bhāsayatē'khilam*
> *yachchandramasi yachchāgnau tat tējō viddhi māmakam*
> 'The light of the sun which illumines the whole universe, which is present in the moon and in fire – know that splendor to be mine.'
>
> *gām āviśhya ca bhūtāni dhārayāmyaham ōjasā*
> *puṣhṇāmi chauṣadhīḥ sarvāḥ sōmō bhūtvā rasātmakah*
> 'Entering the earth by my spiritual energy, I sustain all beings residing in it. As the moon, I nourish all herbs with the juice of life.'

In these two verses, Kṛiṣhṇa says that the entire creation is the manifestation of his energy.

When I was a child, my mother used to sing devotional songs to me. One song was about Kṛiṣhṇa and Rādhā, who represent the supreme self and primordial nature dancing together. If we had the eyes to see this, we would not only see the material form of nature, but also its divinity. We could see the whole of creation as a beautiful play of consciousness.

When Amma gives *darśhan*, we can witness this truth. Amma is the silent center of consciousness in the midst of all movement. She is like a rock in the wild ocean, unmoving, ever patient, constantly giving attention and love to those who come to her — she is ever abiding in that presence. Amma has time for every person telling them, "You are my darling child, you are divine."

Seeing others as Amma's children can help us to feel connected to the divine. All our negative tendencies such as hatred, jealousy, and anger come from the feeling of separation.

Amma tells a story which showed me how useless it is to see a problem outside of oneself. The story goes like this:

One day, a sailor was sailing his boat down a river. From a distance, he saw another boat approaching. As a precaution, he flashed signals to the crew of the other boat to move aside, but the other boat did not change direction.

The two boats almost collided, and only by taking evasive action did the sailor prevent an accident. Now he was furious. He jumped onto the other boat to teach the other sailor a lesson. However, he soon discovered that there was no one there. The other boat was empty and adrift, and so his anger immediately subsided.

When we realize that there is no one but ourselves, who is there to get angry with? If we can see our dearest sister or brother in the person who is getting so much attention from Amma at that moment, how can we be jealous? When we see

Amma in the person who is causing us trouble, how can we feel hatred?

***

I'd like to share how I came to be in Amma's divine presence, and what I've learned about the oneness of nature, God and Amma's devotees. I will also give some examples of what was helpful for me to overcome the feeling of separation, and to connect to the divine.

I was fortunate to grow up in a family with parents who were on a spiritual quest. My mother had a life-changing experience when she heard about Paramahansa Yogananda. As an eighteen-year old girl, she had tried to find the deeper meaning of life by taking drugs. One day, a young man approached my mom and her friends, and started talking to them about Yogananda.

He gave her a small book, *Meditations for Self-Realization,* which greatly inspired her to learn meditation. Within a week, she was able to leave behind her bad habits, and the bad company she was keeping, and start a spiritual life. The fact that the Guru reached her in the form of his teachings even in the midst of drug users, shows the unconditional compassion of a true master. We can also see the master as a mother who comes at the right moment to prevent her child from following a path that leads to destruction.

My parents always tried to live in harmony with nature as much as possible. We lived in the countryside and shared a garden with another family. I remember climbing a tree with my friends and telling them stories about Kṛiṣhṇa. I felt a subtle joy while sitting under the protective leaves of the tree. My elder sister built a small house between the branches of another tree. Climbing high up, I enjoyed looking down from that perspective, observing everything that happened down below without getting involved in it.

We lived in a village and never had a lot of money, but my parents had ideals that they implemented in our lives. They sent us to a Waldorf school where we received a value-oriented education, and learned a lot about handicrafts, art and music. The founder of the Waldorf schools, Rudolf Steiner, was deeply inspired by the divine 'Song of God' — the teachings of Lord Kṛiṣhṇa to Arjuna.

We never had a television, and the only film I was allowed to watch as a child was the life story of Saint Francis. St. Francis of Assisi is a well-known saint in Europe. As someone who saw God reflected in nature, St. Francis was a great lover of God's creation. He addressed the sun, the moon, all the elements of nature, and even death as his own brothers and sisters. This showed his experience of oneness with all creation. He was very humble, and spoke with a lot of reverence about God, the creator.

Amma says, "When you recognize God in everything, your mind is constantly filled with devotion. When there are no feelings of otherness, your whole life becomes an act of worship, a prayer and a song of praise."

I was seven-years old when I met Amma for the first time. My mother spent the summer holidays with me and my younger brother in a place called 'Schweibenalp,' high up in the Swiss Alps. This place, founded by devotees of Haidakhan Babaji, was meant to bring people from different cultures together. They used to worship Śhiva and the Divine Mother daily.

One day, Amma arrived and the people there said, "The Divine Mother is here!" To welcome her, Amma was seated on a beautiful chair and worshiped with many flowers. This was Amma's First World Tour in 1987.

The following year, when I saw Amma and her followers arrive in their pure white clothes, I ran up to them, feeling welcomed by their friendly faces, and their radiance of love and light. Once, one of them called me, took me by the hand, and together we walked to the darśhan hall. On *Dēvī Bhāva* nights, I would often sit near the musicians, totally forgetting about my family.

On the last day of the Schweibenalp programs, I decided on my own to receive a *mantra* from Amma. I was only eight-years old, so my mom tried to dissuade me. She thought mantras were only for grown-up people. Without listening to her objections, I remained steadfast. Finally my mom gave up, and Amma gave me a mantra. It was my heartfelt wish to receive a Kṛiṣhṇa mantra, and I still remember my joy when later at home, my mom placed a beautiful picture of Kṛiṣhṇa next to my bed, and told me stories about the great devotee Mīrabai and Kṛiṣhṇa. With loving devotion, I would sit every morning and evening for a few minutes, repeating my mantra in meditation.

It is said that the mantra is like a rope that saves us. It creates a bond with the master. Perhaps it's because of the mantra that Amma later called me back to her.

***

When Amma came for her Third Europe Tour, my mother decided to travel alone to see Amma. During that visit, Amma told her that she was a devotee of Sai Baba. At first, we didn't understand what Amma meant by this *līlā* or divine play. How could my mom be the devotee of someone whom she had never met?

However, after some time Amma's words came true and my mother became a Sai devotee. The local Sai group met regularly at our home. My mother fulfilled her *dharma*[26] in society by leading children's groups, teaching them values such as *satya* (truth), dharma, *śhānti* (peace), and *prēma* (love).

Because of this, we didn't see Amma for many years. I even forgot my mantra. At the beginning, I felt sad and alone. Later, I tried to become happy in the material world, but something was missing. Sometimes when others pursued something with great interest, I felt only emptiness. Something was missing, but I didn't know what.

From my mother, I learned that a true devotee is always protected by the grace of God. She was never worried, and we witnessed miracles happening in her life. My father, who didn't have strong faith in God, never understood her optimism. However, out of his own conviction to do good, he spent many years committing his time and energy to working in a community of people with special needs.

When I was seventeen, I was standing in our meditation room one day when suddenly, one of the pictures we kept there became radiant and alive. It was a photo of a young Indian woman with long, black hair. She was smiling at me with a very joyful expression, as if saying, "My dear child! I am so happy that you are coming back to me!" I didn't recognize Amma at first.

Then my mom reminded me, "Don't you remember when you were with Amma as a child, and one of the people from Amma's group asked you, 'Will you come to India when you are grown up?' You replied, 'Yes!' and promised that you'd come?"

I had to wait another year to see Amma when she came back to Europe. After finishing high school, I went to London to see Amma, and asked her if I could come to her āśhram and stay

---

[26] Literally 'that which upholds (creation)' generally refers to the harmony of the universe, a righteous code of conduct, sacred duty or eternal law.

for six months. Amma replied with only one word, "Yes." This made me very happy because it confirmed that my inner feeling was in tune with Amma's will.

When I first arrived in Amritapuri in 1998, I stayed in the women's dorm above the *Kāḷī Temple.* Amma walked through our dorm every Tuesday, on her way to the temple for group meditation, and often swam with us in the āśhram swimming pool. I was so touched by how Amma accepted us first-time visitors as members of her own huge spiritual family.

I became very attached to Amma's physical presence. My *sēvā* on Dēvī Bhāva nights was working in the kitchen making chapatis. Sometimes I became very sad, missing Amma, so I'd run to the Kāḷī Temple where Dēvī Bhāva was being held, and immerse myself in the beautiful atmosphere there for a few minutes before returning to the kitchen.

My memories from that wonderful time with Amma sustained me through the years I was far away from her. During my yearly visits, I was often allowed to stay in the temple building with the āśhram residents. This always made me feel as if I had come home. Amma says that no matter how far a bird may fly, it always remembers its nest. Living with the memories of Amritapuri while still living out in the world, I felt like I was part of the āśhram family long before I finally moved to the āśhram.

Back in Germany, my thoughts were always on Amma, and my family couldn't understand the changes that had happened to me. When I next saw Amma during the Europe Tour, she told me many things about the nature of the world and said, "Everyone wants to receive love, but no one is ready to give it! In this way, you can never really become happy." I contemplated this. If no one is ready to give love, how can I change that and become someone who is able to give love selflessly?

While working in a big city, I spent some time volunteering at a soup kitchen run by Mother Teresa's nuns. Here I was able to practice Amma's teaching, and experienced a joy that does not depend on any object or person. When I told Amma about this, she was very happy and looked at me with so much love. She said, "Do what you really want, and live accordingly!" So I made the inner decision to follow Amma and support her charitable projects.

***

In 2003, Swāmī Śhubhāmṛitānandajī's first retreat in Germany took place in a barn that is now part of the German āśhram. During the retreat, a storm hit; heavy rain fell. The barn got a bit wet, and part of the altar fell down. The storm quickly disappeared and everyone helped to clean up and rebuild the altar in a different place. Amma's picture now hung opposite the main door. When the sun was shining again, Swāmī wonderfully commented, "Amma just wanted to see the beauty of nature!" We felt Amma's invisible presence when he said that.

In 2004, some of Amma's devotees and disciples opened the āśhram in Germany. I wanted to participate, and so moved to a place nearby. From then on, I spent all my weekends at the āśhram, engaged in sēvā activities. The next year, the āśhram manager informed us that Amma would be visiting the āśhram after the Europe Tour. We were surprised and felt very blessed.

Previously, the German āśhram was a horse farm, located in a beautiful, remote area surrounded by nature. Horses are still stabled there, and Amma used to visit them, feeding, and taking them for walks whenever she came.

Amma is at home wherever she goes. The day Amma visited, she led one of the horses by rope as if she had been doing it every day. We felt that Amma was our very own. Remembering those unique experiences, we were able to do sēvā with great enthusiasm all year, without ever tiring. Many years later, a large hall was built at the German āśhram for Amma's programs, and people from all over the world have been coming to attend programs there ever since.

In the West, we often give over-importance to the external aspects of our sēvā. We tend to work too much without remembering the divine.

***

When Swāminī Amṛitajyōti Prānājī came for a visit, she told me, "If we want to serve the world, we need strength. We gain strength by doing spiritual practices." Later, I experienced the truth of this.

Doing *sādhanā* helped me to free my mind from external distractions and remember the true reason why I had come to the āśhram. Once I realized this, I always tried to make my spiritual practices a priority. Once a week, I would go to a place where I could be alone to spend half a day in silence.

For many years I had a heartfelt wish to move to Amritapuri. However, because there was so much to do at the German āśhram, I stayed there doing sēvā for fourteen years. When I told Amma that I would like to serve God while working, She encouraged me to stay at the German āśhram. Amma said, "Everything you need will come here." In this way, She was guiding me to trust that if we dedicate our work to God, he will take care of everything we need.

Serving others and seeing all as part of the extended Amma family; working in the garden; feeling in harmony with nature; remembering God while preparing the altar and singing *bhajans*; in these things, I found some contentment.

Usually, before the Europe Tour, some people from Amma's tour group would arrive early at the German āśhram to help with tour preparations. Whenever they left to follow Amma, I felt extremely sad and asked myself, "Will I miss the golden opportunity to be with Amma in this lifetime?" I learned to observe the emotions rising up in my mind, watching as they appear and disappear. Once when I went up to Amma in a sad mood she told me to earn money and come to India.

I experienced this same sadness every year when the tour staff left. However, I was able to overcome these negative emotions by seeing Amma in everyone in the tour group. Now I just feel thankful because they inspire me by their tireless work and dedication. I took on more paid work in addition to doing sēvā, so that finally I was able to join the āśhram in Amritapuri.

In Amma's bhajan *'Bhaktavatsalē Dēvī,'* Amma sings:

> *"O ocean of mercy, let me join the group of thy devotees who live serving thy holy lotus feet. O Dēvī, goddess of the three worlds, where must I go to get relief from my misery?"*

Some time after joining the āśhram as a renunciate, I asked Amma how I can overcome the differences that I still see between me and other people, and the feeling of separation from the divine? Amma told me to let go of all preconceived notions, and instead of focusing on the outer differences, focus more on the essence of spirituality, and go deeper into that. As a practice in my daily life, I should love others as I love myself.

In closing, I'd like to share a recent experience of how I was able to overcome a situation that kept me trapped within my limited self — within the body and mind.

It happened the first time I was in Covid quarantine. I felt completely separate from nature, from other people, and from Amma. It felt like being in prison. Then Amma gave darśhan for the first time in many months but I couldn't go. I was really sad. When I came out of quarantine, I felt totally cut off from everything. What helped me overcome this negative state was being in nature with awareness, speaking with others about my experience, and of course, Amma's presence.

Three months later, I was asked to translate a very inspiring text about nature into German. As I was very busy with my various sēvās at the time, I replied, "I would only have time to translate this if I were in quarantine!" The very next day, I had to go into quarantine again, because I had come in contact with someone who tested positive for Covid, so I was able to start working on the translation.

It was Amma's divine play. And that text was her teaching for me. It said, 'We are not alone. When we connect with nature, we can come out of that notion. When we look around and love all of creation, a higher frequency of love opens in our hearts.'

I tried to practice connecting with nature by looking at the coconut tree in front of my window; seeing the birds that came near; the squirrel that jumped up and down the tree; the sun's rays playing in the branches — and I felt at peace. Immediately I felt connected to everything else, thinking, "I am not helpless and in a prison. I am not limited to the body and mind, my Self is far beyond that. I can use this time in the best way possible."

I almost enjoyed my time in that room, considering it a retreat, and felt a lot of gratitude towards my sisters who brought me food every day. It became clear that my mind had created it all — the prison as well as the retreat. Changing my attitude towards the situation was possible because of Amma's grace. If I ever have to be in quarantine again, I may become sad, but now I've learned how to come out of the feeling of separation. Amma showed me the steps, and now I just have to follow them.

May all of us find ways to connect to Amma even in challenging situations. May we remember our eternal bond with God and discover our true Self.

18

From Untruth to Truth, Darkness to Light, Death to Immortality

Varenya - Spain

In Spanish there is an idiomatic expression that describes my situation: '*Por la puerta grande*,' which literally means, 'Go through the big door.' The implied meaning is, 'I have no idea what I'm doing, but here I am, sitting next to the Divine Mother herself, and in front of an audience that knows much more about spiritual topics than me, including the little children.'

My *satsang* today is based on the following *Vēdic mantra* — a sacred Sanskrit phrase of deep spiritual meaning from the ancient scripture called the Vēdas:

> *asatō mā sadgamaya,*
> *tamasō mā jyōtirgamaya,*
> *mṛityōrmā'mṛtam gamaya*

This *pavamāna,* or purifying mantra, is found in the *Bṛihadāraṇyaka Upaniṣhad*. It means:

> 'Lead us from untruth to truth,
> From darkness to light,
> From death to immortality'

asatō mā sadgamaya — 'Lead us from untruth to truth'

In the context of this line of the mantra, let me tell you how I met Amma.

I was born to an open-minded family whose members are intellectually inclined. I was raised to use logic, to be independent, and make my own decisions based on reason. My mother's younger sister was really interested in meditation and spirituality from a very young age, and she was soon involved in Transcendental Meditation (TM).

My mother, though not that drawn towards leading a fully spiritual life, or a life in an āśhram, also started meditating, followed by my grandmother as well. In this way, like beads strung on a golden thread, spirituality came to my family one by one.

I received my personal *mantra* when I was six-years old, and was initiated into meditation as well. Though I enjoyed meditation, I could never go really deep with TM or practice it much. There's nothing wrong with the technique; I felt deeply that it was just not the right time for me. Instead, I was very drawn to nature, to being alone, and reading books instead of watching TV. I was not a conventional child.

It was only many years later that I understood how the TM mantra sowed a seed in me, how it protected me from many dangers, and how it prepared my mind to receive my Guru — my Amma, when the time was ripe.

I heard about Amma when I was a teenager. My mother used to go to see her every year in Barcelona, and my aunt and my cousins became really involved in organizing her yearly visits to Spain. Many times I was invited to join, but I was a teenager... What? A lady that gives hugs?!? Are you kidding me?!? No way! I don't want anyone touching me!

Years went by like that. I finished my BA degree in Journalism; then a postgraduate degree in Corporate Communication; got a dream job in an advertising company; beautiful clothes; a motorcycle; an active social and cultural life in Barcelona; a nice flat with a private terrace... and I was only twenty-five. But then suddenly something started bothering me. I was not happy. There was no reason for this. I had everything that you are supposed to have to be happy.

When talking about this with my close circle of friends, they all said the same thing, "Happiness is something that doesn't last, it's not meant to last! It comes and goes. You buy a new car and you are happy for a while but then it goes, and you have to do or find something else. This is the nature of happiness."

But somehow, there was a tiny but very constant voice, an intuition stronger than any logic, inside of me saying: *Eternal happiness exists.*

I have a very inquisitive nature, and I studied journalism, so I started doing some research: reading books; making new friends; going to some Buddhist events; reconnecting with my meditation practice; attending yōga classes; taking homeopathic medicine instead of allopathic; eating organic food; caring for Mother Nature; recycling... in short, I started to open my heart and change my lifestyle.

After reading a few spiritual books, I was convinced that I needed a Guru. Like a flash, Amma appeared in my mind. She takes advantage of every opportunity. She knows really well when to show up.

I thought, "Actually, Amma has already adopted part of my family, so why not me?" That same day, I sat for meditation, closed my eyes, and called to her...and Amma came. I saw her as perfectly as I see her now in physical form. She was sitting with her legs crossed in lotus posture in front of me, beaming with golden light, eyes closed, meditating. She looked so peaceful, and so happy at the same time. She was radiant. Amma won me over totally without saying a word. So I said to her, "Ok, do what you have to do."

Now I understand what it means to give Amma a blank cheque. At that moment, I had no idea what I was doing. After saying that to her in my meditation, I just couldn't do all the things I used to do, go to the places I used to go, have the same friends I used to have, work in the same company, dress in the same way...very quickly, the world I knew was crumbling around me. I wanted change...but did it have to be that fast?

Within a year, the life I had before was over. I quit my job, gave away my clothes (to a few very happy girls), left my beautiful flat, sold my furniture, kept only a few things in some boxes at my grandparent's house, and flew to *Amritapuri.*

That was more than ten years ago, and by Amma's immense grace, I have hardly ever left this place since then. The few things I left in Spain before coming here were eventually given away too. They didn't mean anything to me anymore. Looking back, I realize that only her grace allowed me to keep it together and not be overwhelmed while such big changes were happening to me, within such a short period of time.

The fact was, I had been living a lie; a completely materialistic life, without any foundation or goal. It didn't make any sense anymore.

Conversely, Amma was pointing to the truth, the changeless truth, the eternal beauty that we really are. This is how Amma led me for the first time from untruth to truth...From Barcelona to Amritapuri.

tamasō mā jyōtirgamaya — 'Lead us from darkness to light'

What is darkness? Darkness is ignorance. Not knowing who we are makes us live in ignorance, and makes us not understand the nature of the world which in turn causes suffering. Amma says that in our ignorance, we judge what is wrong to be right and what is right to be wrong. Let's see how this applies to me:

After being in Amma's Amritapuri āśhram on and off for a couple of years and going on a few tours with Amma, I saw very clearly that this is the only life I wanted. There was no way I could go back to the world.

However, before moving into the āśhram full time, I wanted to ask Amma's permission, since I was also having many health issues. During the Europe tour, in Milano I gathered enough courage to ask Amma for this permission. Milano is my favorite stop on Amma's Europe tours. It's very crowded, but people show a lot of love and *bhakti* (devotion) towards Amma. The Milano programs remind me most of the programs in India. So from my perspective, Milano was the best place to ask about moving to the āśhram. However, it turns out I was blinded by my ego.

I inquired with Swāmī Amṛitaswarūpānandajī who was translating for Amma that day about asking my question, but he replied, "No questions today... maybe tomorrow." I nodded in disappointment, and went to sit on the stage. Amma had just started giving *darśhan*. After a while, I saw Swāmījī standing next to Amma, and he motioned for me to quickly come over to him. I immediately went and sat next to Amma's chair near Swāmījī. There was no line of people waiting to ask questions that day, and so I found myself sitting there, thinking, "I am so lucky!"

But then I observed Amma giving darśhan, and soon realized why it was neither a good day, nor a good city to ask my question. Milano is one of the busiest stops on the tour, and on top of it all, it was a weekend darśhan when even more people show up. The rhythm of the darśhan was hectic and fast-paced. Amma was not even looking at me — nor at Swāmījī. I sank behind Amma's chair with only my two eyes peeking out a bit. But what could I do? I was already there and couldn't go back.

Swāmījī started trying to get Amma's attention. "*Amme*," he said... and again, "Ammeeee." He was really trying, but Amma was not even looking at him. Nor was she slowing down the pace of the darśhan either. Finally, because of Swāmījī's persistence, Amma turned to look at him with a fierce expression. She seemed to ask with her eyes, "What's so important?"

I didn't feel like my question was relevant or important anymore.

I thought, "Maybe I can just slide completely under Amma's chair and disappear, and Swāmījī can sort this out by himself..."

Then Amma turned her gaze towards me. In an instant, her expression completely changed as if she had seen the most beautiful little kitten in the world, a kitten trying to hide under her chair! Amma gave me the most compassionate look, and Swāmījī took that moment to translate my question, "Can she live fulltime in Amritapuri?"

Amma was beaming, and gave a very big and happy, "YES!"

We tend to superimpose our shortcomings and deluded mental states onto the *Guru*. We don't understand her at all. She is pure light; we are in darkness. And this was exactly what I was doing. First, I didn't show any discrimination when choosing the appropriate day to ask. Secondly, once I was there, I assumed that with Amma being so busy, with such an influx of people rushing into her arms, many of them newcomers, she wouldn't want to take the time to answer my question.

How many times has Amma said that her children are everything to her? Her children are the most important thing for her. Her children are the reason that she is here. For Amma, each one of us is like a drop of her own blood.

After asking my question, I got up quickly, ecstatic and full of gratitude to Amma and to Swāmījī, who in my eyes had risked his life to translate my question!

Later that same day, however, a person whom I was good friends with, approached me angrily and for no reason, shouted at me accusing me of many things that I had never done, nor had even thought of doing. I was stunned.

I saw this as Amma's teaching: there is no happiness without sorrow; there is no light without darkness; nothing is permanent in this ever-changing creation. You have to accept both, even if they come on the same day.

***

I am a good example of not only misinterpreting Amma's facial expressions, but also Amma's words.

Years later, in another darśhan with Amma, she looked directly in my face and said, "You are very young; this is why your mind has many thoughts, and runs here and there. But eventually, you will understand the nature of the world, and then it will not be a problem for you anymore."

If Amma said this to me today, I would be so happy to think that in the end, I will understand something...At least something!

Back then, due to my lack of perspective and arrogance, I interpreted her words as follows: she was telling me that I was not fit for āśhram life, and that eventually, she would send me back to the West, and maybe even make me get married! This is what darkness can do. It can turn joy into sorrow.

Practicing śhravaṇam, listening to the Guru's words with an open heart, is the beginning of dispelling darkness, not by removing it, but by adding light. To practice śhravaṇam, we need humility. We need to understand that in many situations we are wrong, and that Amma is always right.

Amma's immense patience is the only reason why this darkness is being dispelled. Amma has said that it is through the patience of the Guru that the disciple is ultimately liberated. This is one hundred percent applicable to me, and I can only express gratitude for Amma's divine patience.

mṛityōrmā amṛitam gamaya — 'lead us from death to immortality'

What is immortality? The scriptures tell us that we are the eternal Self. In the *Bhagavad Gītā*, Kṛiṣhṇa describes this Self in Chapter 2, verse 24 as follows:

> *achchhēdyō'yam adāhyō'yam aklēdyō'śhōṣhya ēva cha*
> *nityaḥ sarvagataḥ sthāṇur achalō'yaṁ sanātanaḥ*
> 'The Self is unbreakable and cannot be burned; it can neither be dampened nor dried. It is everlasting, all-pervading, immovable, stable, and ancient.'

How is Amma leading me, and all of us, to understand this? On the day of *Guru Pūrṇimā*, I went to the *Kāḷī Temple* to visit the Kāḷī statue in the inner shrine early in the morning. When I arrived at the temple, I noticed a small, dry tree branch with some leaves still attached to it lying there on the temple floor. Since it was a windy day, I thought that it must have blown in from outside. I had the strong intuition to place it at the feet of Kāḷī. So I picked it up and took it with me.

It was quite big and the leaves on it were still fresh, fanning out in such a way that it made it look like a rough broom. The inner shrine was quite crowded, and being Guru Pūrṇimā, everyone there was nicely dressed and in a prayerful mood. Kāḷī was decorated with many beautiful garlands made of fresh, fragrant flowers, including lotus flowers, and all the oil lamps were lit. She looked astonishingly beautiful.

Suddenly it struck me, there I was holding that branch in my hand, with all of its leaves protruding and taking up so much space. I felt somewhat ridiculous, and wanted to hide it behind me, but the leaves were so splayed out that it was impossible... I wasn't sure how to offer it to Kāḷī. Sliding it through the doors of the inner shrine was out of the question, and making it more difficult was that there were a lot of other people in the shrine praying and doing *pradakṣhiṇa* — auspiciously circumambulating the deity.

As I was standing there, I remembered how Amma said that there is no place for pride or shame in an āśhram. Just at that moment, a space to sit opened up right next to the inner doors of the shrine. I sat there, and looking at Kāḷī, I quickly offered that dry branch with all its leaves at her feet.

When I left the inner shrine and looked back from a distance, I saw that there was a line of dry, leafy branches hanging outside the shrine. I realized that the one I had just left at Kāḷī's feet was probably one of those that had fallen down from there, and had not come from outside after all. I thought to myself, "Well, maybe hanging branches in this way is the tradition for this celebration...who knows?" Happily, I took my leave.

Later that morning when Amma was giving satsang, she explained how a disciple usually offers a dry branch to the master as a symbol of surrendering all material attachments. When I heard this, I laughed at how silly I behaved when I went to offer my branch to Kāḷī. I could have enjoyed the moment; it was quite unique. However, my sense of shame, my individuality blocked me, and I ended up offering it really quickly, looking around me self-consciously.

That was a big lesson for me that day. Ultimately, what was there for me to worry about? Even though I was ignorant of the symbolism connected to the dry branch, I ended up doing exactly what was appropriate in that situation.

Nimitta mātram bhāva — having the attitude of being just an instrument in Amma's hands... Isn't this the best way to go from death to immortality?

***

In one of the *Gītā* classes in the āśhram, the teacher explained that there are no external changes to a person when she or he attains Self-realization. The changes are internal only.

From grandfathers and grandmothers to the kids, here in the āśhram we are all awakening to our inner child. In this process, we are transformed into '*amṛita* children' — the immortal children of Amma, the divine mother of immortal bliss.

This process can be rough. While walking this path, we are learning patience. Like a toddler learning to walk, we are learning to try again and again to succeed on the spiritual path, cultivating the innocent faith that a baby has in its mother. Our hearts are opening so that in the end, we can become instruments of grace.

What happens when our inner child finally starts to awaken? While our body may be the same, the mirror will give us a different reflection... the world will look completely different to us. When we rediscover our inner child, we just feel like dancing. We rediscover our lost innocence, and are happy for no reason. We become drunk with love.

The Persian poet Shams Tabrizi said so beautifully:

"We believe God sees us from above... but in fact she sees us from within."

May Amma guide us to become her immortal children of love, and may all of us be able to live in love, expand in love, and eventually merge in that love.

19

Arise, O Scorcher of Foes

Rudran - USA

Towards the beginning of the *Bhagavad Gītā,* Lord Kṛiṣhṇa asks Arjuna,

"Whence has this blemish, alien to honorable men, causing disgrace and opposed to heaven, come upon you Arjuna, at this crucial moment? Arjuna, yield not to unmanliness. It is unworthy of you. Shake off this faint-heartedness. Arise, O scorcher of foes." (2.2 – 3)

In these verses, Lord Kṛiṣhṇa speaks harshly to Arjuna, even calls him a eunuch. But Lord Kṛiṣhṇa's insults are not gratuitous. He insults his disciple with a clear goal in mind — to cut through Arjuna's mental fog and knock him back on the right track.

And that's my theme for this talk. If we are really lucky, God hones in on us, shakes us up, and pushes us out of our comfort zone. He does this so we can evolve; he does this as an expression of his love supreme.

I met Amma twenty-eight years ago at the Rhode Island Retreat on Amma's 1995 U.S. Tour. In those days there were no tokens for Amma's *darśhan*, you just joined the line twice a day, when you felt the inner call for a hug.

That first evening when I was finally face to face with Amma, I said, "AAAaaarrrrggghhhhhh!'

She looked straight into my eyes and responded back in exactly the same manner.

Amma met me right where I was, came all the way down to my level, and shared my existential frustration right alongside me.

Years later, on the banks of the Kallai River, Amma would name me *Rudran*, which means howling — Lord Śhiva in his destructive mode. But back in that program hall, where I first met Amma, I had no name, I was just another guy who wanted to be successful and famous.

On the second night of the retreat, as Amma was meditating with us, a huge industrial fan crashed to the floor. It fell about two meters from the platform it had been resting on. I saw the whole thing because, unlike everyone else, I wasn't meditating. I was watching Amma like a hawk, eyes wide open, trying to figure out whether she was a real master or a fake. When the fan hit the floor with all the noise and force of a small bomb blast, everyone in the hall jumped in fear, everyone that is, except Amma. I knew in that instant that she was a true master.

On the last morning of the retreat, Amma hugged me, and I felt this incredible love wash over me. After darśhan, I slumped against the wall of the gym, looked around and felt love for all of the devotees I had been so busy judging for the past three days. For a half hour or so, Amma let me see with eyes of love. Then for some reason I went over to Amma's picture on the altar and prayed to it, rather than to Amma herself. "Amma, I am going to miss you so much."

Her voice answered clearly in my mind, "Don't be sad, son; you will come visit me in India." I doubted that voice. Going to India seemed impossible to me, as impossible as going to Mars or the Sun.

Back then, I didn't understand that a *Satguru's* words always come true. Three years later, I found myself in a small boat, crossing the backwaters towards *Amritapuri*. In those days, there was no bridge. As the boat pushed off from the shore, time slowed down and peace and calm washed over me. It was like traveling hundreds of years back in time.

All at once, the stillness was shattered. Throngs of people jostled here and there as bhajans blared over a loudspeaker. I found the reason for this tumult on a simple banner tied between two coconut trees. 'Happy 45th Birthday, Amma.' I had arrived on Amma's birthday itself. Little did I know this lost child had just set foot in the abode of his eternal Guru.

***

Before I met Amma I was devoted to Śhirdi Sai Bābā, the great 19th century saint. My favorite quote from Bābā's biography is relevant here, "At times his eyes would become red and roll round and round in rage. Then who would dare to approach him?"

Every time I read Bābā's biography, I gravitate to quotes like this, to the idea of being close enough to the Guru that he would rough you up, break apart your false concepts, really get in there to destroy the ego, until only divinity remained.

Amma of course knew this about me, and that's why she threw in just enough *masālā* (spice), in the form of wild experiences, to satisfy my thirst for this type of treatment. She knows each of us through and through and perfectly customizes our spiritual training to suit our individual temperaments.

During several of Amma's North Indian tours, my job was to pull people away from Amma's arms after their darshan to clear the way for the next person's hug. I experienced so much grace doing this *sēvā*. Somehow or other, I ended up being one of the pullers for Amma's longest darśhan ever — the historic Mangalore program.

That darśhan lasted a full twenty-three hours. Amma did not take a single break. I was standing on the ramp, two people away from Amma for much of that program. After a devotee received Amma's darśhan, I would help to pull them away from Amma's arms, guide them down the ramp a bit, and try to hand them Amma's *prasād* — a blessed packet of sacred ash with a candy tucked inside.

Often the line went much too fast for me to give the prasād directly, so I would pass it to the person behind me, who would pass it to the person behind him and so on. There were seven backup prasād-passers to keep pace with Amma's hugging that day.

The power and beauty of Amma as she gave darśhan in Mangalore is absolutely impossible to put into words — that iridescent smile, those flashing eyes, that palpable force-field of pure love. While doing that sēvā, I felt like a part of Amma, like one of her thousand hands.

It is said that there were over 80,000 devotees present that day in the fully packed sports stadium. Before the darśhan began, a big parade marched through the town center to celebrate Amma's arrival. A sage had predicted long before that Mangalore's bad luck would turn good when a *mahātmā* came to visit. The town collectively knew that Amma was that mahātmā.

The darśhan was going at an absolutely super-human speed, when someone from the camera team, which I was supervising during that tour, came to ask me a question. I was rude and dismissive and scolded him. Darśhan stopped. Amma turned and stormed at me... full force... it was beautiful, like a series of lightning flashes and thunder claps. The brahmachāriṇī, next to Amma translated, "Amma says that while you were arguing with that camera boy, a poor old man who had traveled two days to come to see Amma did not get his prasād. Look in your right hand." I looked down. The old man's prasād was still in my right hand. "Amma says you will suffer his karma for one year, one year! GO!"

Reluctantly, I slunk away and went to the dorm to lie down. I couldn't sleep; every cell in my body was electrified, shaking from the scolding. But the magnetic attraction to be near Amma again became overwhelming. I got up off my mat, snuck up the ramp, reclaimed my spot, and started pulling devotees away again. Darśhan stopped. Amma glowered at me, her eyes full of gorgeous fire.

"One year!" she shouted in English.

I really was going to suffer that gentleman's karma for a year. And I felt so proud that Amma felt close enough to me to treat me that way, that I was playing the game at that level with the greatest of Satgurus. This little experience taught me so much – it showed Amma's complete love and concern for that old gentleman, and for each and every one of the 80,000 souls who received her darśhan that day. It taught me to respect Amma's prasād as a tremendous individual blessing, with a *saṅkalpa* (intention) customized for each recipient. And of course, once again, it showed me that I needed to be much more aware.

Then my luck changed. I ended up back in America. In retrospect I wish I had stayed and planted myself in Amritapuri in the 1990's like so many of my friends did, but I wasn't ready yet. I started *normal* life again, and got a teaching job.

No one raised a question when I put a picture of Amma on my teacher's desk, or when I disappeared into the bookroom at 10 a.m. every morning to do my *IAM (Integrated Amrita Meditation™)*, or when I disappeared for four out of the thirteen years I was supposed to teach at the school, so I could be in India with Amma.

Amma was with me in every single class I taught at that school, blessing my students in all sorts of unbelievable ways. Like most devotees around the world, I talk to Amma in my mind throughout the day. When issues arose with my colleagues or students, I would ask Amma for help and then watch the magic unfold. Let me share one story:

During my last year at the high school, a young lady, Kaleigh, transferred into our 12th grade class mid-year. She was a Goth kid and wore all black. I could tell she was feeling isolated and alone. One Friday afternoon, she arrived before all of the other students.

"Are you okay?" I asked.

"No," she responded flatly.

"Can I make you a cup of tea?" I asked.

Just to be clear, I am not like this. I am not kind like this. Amma flashed across my mind. I went to the teacher's room where one of my colleagues suggested I make ginger tea to help settle Kaleigh's nerves. I handed her the tea and started teaching the class.

A few moments into the lesson Kaleigh started gasping for air. "Mr. D, this tea doesn't have ginger, does it?" It turned out Kaleigh had a deadly ginger allergy. A couple of football players carried her to the nurse.

I called the nurse from my classroom, "Is she okay?" I asked.

"No, she's not okay," the nurse snapped. "She's in anaphylactic shock. Her throat has closed, and she can't breathe."

The phone went dead. I faced a classroom full of students, terrified. I remember earnestly praying to Amma, but other than that I don't remember a single word I said to that class that day.

I called the nurse several times over the weekend, but she wouldn't return my calls. When I went to school on Monday, I was summoned to her office first thing. "This is it," I said to myself. "The girl is dead, and it's my fault."

As I walked into the nurse's office, she shot me a no-nonsense look. "Please sit" she insisted. "After Kaleigh was rushed to the hospital, they managed to stabilize her. Just so you know, it was a very, very close call. Don't ever give a student food or drink ever again."

She continued more gently: "Her father rushed to see her at the hospital. They'd had a tough relationship ever since Kaleigh left her mom to live with him. But when the father saw his daughter in crisis at the hospital, his heart burst open, and he expressed to his daughter just how much he loved her."

Amma says that for most of us love is like honey trapped inside a rock. Sometimes it takes a hard wallop to crack that rock open. The nurse looked at me, "It's unbelievable how this turned out; you are very lucky."

I knew it wasn't luck. I knew that what was meant to be a tragedy had been transformed by Amma's grace into a reconciliation and a sharing of hearts. As the school year went on, Kaleigh became happier and better adjusted. She started making friends. And thanks to Amma, she now had the healing influence of a loving father in her life.

***

Amma is a nurturing mother, but she also loves playing the role of a disciplining father. During those years when I snuck away from my teaching job, I got to spend several hours during each tour darśhan pulling devotees out of Amma's embrace. By some amazing grace, every time I returned to India, Amma had saved my spot for me. Twenty years later, I can still hear Amma's nectarean, father-like words echoing in my ears.

"*Saipe*, (common word for foreigner) too much force!" This was Amma's continual refrain when I pulled devotees from her arms. My inability to attune to Amma's inconceivable balance of sheer power and featherlike gentleness almost ended in disaster one beautiful afternoon.

As usual Amma was hugging at an electric pace. I was doing my best to pull people away respectfully, but as quickly as possible to protect Amma's body. Well, a very heavy man, who must have weighed 180 kilos, finished his darśhan, and I pulled with all my might to free Amma for the next hug.

Unfortunately, I couldn't see the people I was pulling because the *brahmachārī* standing in front of me was much taller than I. So, I just reached my arm around him, tried to judge the weight of the person by the size of their arm, pulled and hoped for the best. After this heavy man, I took the next arm, it was the same thickness.

The reason the arm was so thick was because the lady's sāri fabric had somehow become bunched up on her left arm. I pulled with great force, and she went flying down the ramp. The tour ramps are set at a pretty steep angle, so at one point this lady was at least a meter and a half in the air.

Everyone's jaw dropped in disbelief as the skinny, elderly lady flew through the air like Lord *Hanumān* on his way over the ocean to Lanka. Like a skilled gymnast, she landed gracefully, spun around a complete 180 degrees, and flashed the most gorgeous smile at Amma and me. Amma beamed at the lady, pointed at me and shrugged her shoulders as if to say, "I apologize for this son of mine."

Then Amma raised her hands, grinning from ear to ear, in grateful prayer that disaster had been averted. This is one of my very fondest memories, and that lady is one of the most wonderful teachers I have ever had. She took an incredibly dangerous situation and turned it into a thrilling adventure.

If someone had thrown me one and half meters in the air immediately after my darśhan, I would have been really angry. But this lady was alive in the present moment, intimately attuned with Amma's spirit of joy and spontaneity.

After that tour, I returned to the U.S. to resume my teaching career, but my tenure as a teacher was running out, for during Amma's 2012 U.S. Tour when I went up for darśhan, Amma blindsided me: "Crazy boy," she said, "Quit your job and come to Amritapuri by the end of this year." My friends who saw that darśhan said I looked like I had been hit in the face with a shovel.

I was in total shock. I kind of obeyed Amma's instructions. I did leave my job, but three weeks later than Amma had instructed me. Then I went to Śhirdi, not Amritapuri as Amma had instructed me, and spent three weeks paying my respects at Śhirdi Sai Bābā's grave.

Had I listened to Amma, I would have been with her when she went swimming in the Ganges during the *Kumbha Mēla* festival in North India. Because I didn't obey Amma, I missed an unbelievable, once in a lifetime opportunity. I have no one to blame but myself. The lesson I learned — always, always, obey Amma.

Blissfully unaware that Amma was up north swimming in the Ganges, I did have a wonderful experience in Śhirdi. Every morning I chanted a bunch of *Hanumān Chālīsās*[27] in front of a huge statue of Hanumān. The rest of the day I spent reading Bābā's autobiography. Bābā's recurring description of Self-realization as a salt doll merging into the ocean settled deep in my heart.

When I finally got back to Amritapuri at around 5 p.m. on a Friday afternoon, I was told Amma was meditating at the beach. I dropped my luggage by the sand near the Kāḷī Temple, and sprinted to the shore. When I arrived, Amma was just settling into meditation.

After meditation, when Amma opened her eyes, she turned her head towards me and said, "What's the point of chanting endless Hanumān Chālīsās in front of a huge statue of Lord

---

[27] A devotional hymn on Lord Hanumān by Gōswāmī Tulsīdās comprising 40 verses. 'Prayer of 40 verses' = chālīsā.

Hanuman if you don't even know what the words mean? Anyway, Self-realization is just like a salt doll walking into an ocean and dissolving."

Amma welcomed me home by summing up my entire trip to Shirdi in two sentences, proving her omniscience to me yet again. And my heart knew exactly what she was saying beneath those words, "Saipe, why did you go to my grave in Śhirdi when I am alive right now in Amritapuri?"

Sometimes when things are really close to us, they are hardest to see. We see Amma every day. She banters with the little ones in such a humble, natural, unassuming way that I forget. I forget that she is *Bhagavān* (the Lord).

One of the brahmachārīs recently told me that Amma once said, "I've put Saipe (Rudran) through so much over the years." And it made me so happy. Happy that I have been able to hang in there with the sometimes rough, sometimes bumpy, always sublime journey with Amma. Somehow when things get really rough, she reminds me in one way or another to hang in there. She reminds me that if we are really lucky, God hones in on us, shakes us up, and pushes us out of our comfort zone. She does this so we can evolve; She does this as an expression of her love supreme.

Amma by your grace, may the peace of our meditation and spiritual practices extend into our daily lives, accompanied by patience and humility; dispassion and discrimination; *śhraddhā* (alert awareness) and pure love. Like that amazing elderly lady whom I sent flying through the air after her darśhan, may we too fly to spiritual heights, embracing whatever situations we find ourselves in as your perfect prasād, custom designed to help us evolve.

20
Humility

Malathi – France

Amma says in the book *Awaken Children*, 'To be truly humble is to bow down, not only with our body, but with our entire being. We should feel with our whole being that we are nothing, not only before the master or a few selected souls, but before all of creation. Humility is the only way to God.'

If I am here today at Amma's tender lotus feet, it is only due to her infinite grace and compassion. If I am able to say a few words, it is only due to her boundless patience and unconditional love.

Amma is the embodiment of perfect humility, simplicity and sacrifice. This is her real beauty. She often says, "If we develop at least one divine quality in our life, all of the other qualities will follow."

Humility is the divine quality that I would like to make the subject of this *satsang*.

Lord Kṛiṣhṇa says in Chapter 6, verse 30 of the *Bhagavad Gītā*:

> 'He who sees me in all beings, and all beings in me, to him I am never lost, nor is he lost to me.'

A real devotee never loses sight of Amma or God, nor does God or Amma lose sight of their child. Seeing God or the Divine Mother in everything and everyone, and understanding that all creatures and all creation belong only to the divine, is a simple practice which will slowly lead us to eternal freedom.

The 702nd name of the *Lalitā Sahasranāma* is:

> *ōm sarvagāyai namaḥ*

> 'Salutations to you who pervades all the worlds and all beings; who is omnipresent.'

Amma says, "It is the experience of the Self that makes you naturally humble in all situations. When you behold everything as God, you are always in a worshipful mood. When there are no more feelings of otherness, your whole life becomes an act of worship, a form of prayer, a song of praise. In that state, nothing is insignificant for you; everything has its special place. You behold the supreme light shining even in a blade of grass."

Amma came to Earth fully conscious of her true nature, as an infinite ocean of pure nectar. She offers her whole life, her every cell and breath as heavenly nectar — *amṛita* — for the upliftment of all.

The 99th name of Amma in the *108 names of Amma* is:

> *ōm śhaśhvallōka hitāchāra magna dēhēndriyāsavē namaḥ*
> 'I bow to you whose body and senses are always acting for the good of the world.'

Amma the Divine Mother, showers the immortal light of true knowledge and real wisdom on us, to release us from the clutches of our own minds; from the endless miseries of the impermanent world; and from the ocean of *saṁsāra* — the cycle of birth and death.

The 993rd name of the *Lalitā Sahasranāma* is:

> *ōm ajñāna dhvānta dīpikāyai namaḥ*
> 'She is the bright lamp that dispels the darkness of ignorance.'

Amma says, "Life is a mystery. You cannot understand it, unless you surrender, for your intellect cannot grasp its expansive and infinite nature, its real meaning and fullness. Bow down low and be humble; then you will know life's meaning."

***

When I was a child, I liked to enthusiastically run around our apple trees, chanting three distinct syllables out loud — TI-LA-MA.

Those same three syllables compose the name '*Mālatī,*' given to me by Amma thirty years later.

Time does not exist in the realm of God; time is God itself. What is happening now was already written, however the presence of a *mahātmā* in our lives can change our destiny. How then to describe with our limited words and comprehension, Amma's impact in our lives, who is the universal mother in human form?

We need to make constant effort to develop discernment, alertness and awareness; to be able to perform right action at the right time, with the right attitude, if we want to reach our goal. Only then will divine grace flow to and through us.

My mother visited Tamil Nadu twice when I was ten-years old, traveling there with her NGO (non-governmental organization), to bring material support to orphans in a few very poor villages. I decided to give all of the small allowance that I received every Sunday to those poor children.

I was fourteen when my parents chose to live a simpler life closer to nature. So I had to leave school, and my former life in Belgium behind, to move with my mother and brother to the south of France. The move also allowed my mother to help my older brother start an organic farming project.

In France, I started taking yōga classes, and was very interested in meditation. I was initiated into Maharishi Mahesh Yogi's Transcendental Meditation (TM), and spent a lot of time participating in a small TM meditation center. I would listen to satsangs and stories about the *yōgis* and sages of India. I met a musician at the TM center, and married at a very young age.

Even after I became a mother, spirituality remained at the center of my daily life. I spent my free time meditating and reading spiritual books about saints and sages from all traditions. I was also part of a small prayer group. We spent time in silence in monasteries, and visited many holy places where great souls had lived blessed lives in silence.

We lived a very simple life in a small hamlet, at the feet of the Pyrénées Mountains near Lourdes. It was in Lourdes in 1858, when a beautiful young lady, clad in pure white, holding a rosary in her right hand, and with a single yellow rose placed on each foot, appeared to an illiterate 14 year-old girl in a small grotto. She appeared to this girl a total of eighteen times, and gave her a message of prayer and sacrifice for the world.

After the visitations, a miraculous spring of pure, sacred water flowed out from that same grotto. It still flows abundantly today, and is taken as holy water by thousands of people coming from all over the world.

Immersed in that peaceful atmosphere, permeated by the subtle presence of the beloved mother of the universe, one day with deep longing in my heart, I prayed to her. On a piece of paper I wrote, 'In this life, I want to see you, I want to touch you, I want you to answer all my questions.'

I prayed and cried to meet the one who would guide me. I thought, "Where are all the saints and sages? Are they all gone? Are there none left on earth these days?"

Then I had a very vivid dream like a vision. I was walking in a field full of brightly-colored flowers, when I saw at the front of this fragrant field, a beautiful statue of the Divine Mother dressed all in white. When she saw me she became alive. She smiled at me and started moving slowly in my direction with her arms wide open. I also walked towards her. When we reached each other, she took me tenderly in her divine arms and softly pressed her divine face against mine...I became hers...

Soon after this dream, I heard about Amma, a living saint from Kerala. Someone gave us Amma's biography, *archana* book, Amma's *bhajan* cassettes, and a picture of Amma smiling. I met Amma physically for the first time in 1992, in the south of France in a site surrounded by natural beauty.

Everything was so simple, so clear, I had found my Divine Mother! Now I will never let her go, she will give me everything I need to complete my quest and she will never let me go!

All four of my daughters were with me when I had my first *darśhan*. After I received her divine embrace, I sat under a tree and cried and cried...

I thought, "How can I continue living in the world now that I have found my mother? So I asked Amma, "Can I come and live with you in your āśhram?" Amma looked at me deeply with a lot of concern and compassion. She asked me a few practical questions, and then said, "Come and see."

As it turned out, for many years we could only see Amma physically once a year in France for a three-day program; often we received two darśhans a day. There was no token system in those days. We just quietly sat in a queue on the grass, as the program venue was held outdoors under a large open-air tent.

During the evening bhajans, behind Amma, we could see the dark blue sky full of stars that were enjoying the enchanting night too. After the *Dēvī Bhāva* program, a storm came and refreshed the whole atmosphere, and all of nature bathed blissfully in Amma's divine energy.

Amma gave me a *mantra*. I repeated it all the time, and the beloved divine names and forms that I knew from before, all joyfully merged into one.

***

With Amma's blessing, we formed a small satsang group in our home that met every two weeks for fifteen years. Following Amma's instructions, we would start the satsang with an Amma video; then meditate; then read a few pages from one of Amma's *Awaken Children* books; sing bhajans; and finish with the *ārati,* final prayers, and sharing *prasād* with everyone.

In 2000, a devotee couple offered me a ride to visit Amma in Belgium. It took two days to get there. I was so moved, I could not eat anything before reaching the venue. When we arrived, I sat in Amma's presence, and could not take my eyes off her. Amma made a sign in my direction ... go and eat ... she knows.

That day, with infinite love and tenderness, Amma gave me the name Mālatī. The spiritual meaning is 'beyond sorrows.' Again, I cried and cried... A rebirth had happened, and only five kilometers from my original place of birth.

Real birth happens when we realize our true nature, when we realize that we were never born and will never die. Only then all our sorrows will fade away...

In the bhajan *'Rāga Vairikaḷ Nīṅgiḍum,'* Amma sings, "If the mind merges in the mother, the dispeller of all sorrows, then all of the foes in the form of desires will vanish, and all sorrows and miseries will disappear. The sinful shadows of the heart will lift, and one will abide in the truth. O embodiment of consciousness, may my thoughts subside forever. Will you put an end to my sorrows and remove my feeling of separateness? Then this birth of mine will be fulfilled. O Mother, you are the giver of the bliss in my mind."

I remember the deep impression it made on me when my feet touched the sacred soil of India — the mother of *Sanātana Dharma.* I could finally breathe deeply; I felt at home. It was July 2001, and I stayed for three weeks in the *Amritapuri* āśhram.

When I reached the āśhram, the most sacred place on earth, someone told me that Amma was giving darśhan in the *Kāḷī Temple* and that I should go immediately.

I entered the crowded temple. I was extremely tired after two long travel days without sleep. Suddenly, a wave of doubts filled my mind; "There are so many people here... I will not understand anything... Does she really know me?... Is she my mother?"

With that dark, clouded mind, I reached Amma. She looked straight at me, kindly held my shoulders, and started shaking me gently while telling me very strongly, "My daughter, my daughter, my daughter...Ok?" Instantly my mind became calm and all the dark clouds vanished... I am her daughter, there is no room anymore for any doubt.

The next Tuesday, I joined the prasād line[28]. Some emotional purification was taking place, and I had very little appetite. When I approached Amma, she reached behind her, and took a child-sized plate of food that she gave to me, proving she knew exactly what I needed. In this way, many times Amma has clearly shown me her omniscience. She knows everything, and sees our past and future as well.

One afternoon, I was floating in the swimming pool, gazing at the ever changing white clouds above me, thinking deeply that I would love so much to be in the pool with Amma, at least once...

With that longing in my heart, I was about to leave, when I heard a huge commotion, with someone saying, "Amma is coming." My little dream came true, and I had the great pleasure of Amma pushing me into the pool, and into the cool waters of her delightful presence.

---

[28] On Tuesdays in the āśhram, Amma traditionally holds a mid-day program for the āśhram residents. Part of the program includes Amma passing out plates of food for lunch, which by her touch becomes prasād.

***

When I returned to France, I started reading the *Valmīki* version of the *Rāmāyaṇa* — one of the great epics of India. I enjoyed the beauty of each and every verse, and learned about the noble spiritual principle that is called *dharma* — the very subtle and eternal law which sustains harmony in the entire universe. To be in tune with it, we need to renounce our likes and dislikes, renounce all egoistic thoughts, words, and deeds, learn to serve all, and share selflessly. Amma is our dharmic role model; her whole life being a perfect expression of unconditional love and compassion in action.

With Amma's blessing, I started working with elderly people, taking care of them and their needs in their own homes. Often while driving, I would chant the archana along with Swāmījī's (Swāmī Amṛitaswarūpānanda) recording of it, and a stream of tears would flow abundantly... Only Amma knows how I was able to reach my destination and accomplish the tasks given to me. I also practiced the *IAM (Integrated Amrita Meditation™)* at home every evening.

"It is a misconception to think that those we love, will always love us back, in truth we are always alone." This affirmation by Amma confirms my own experience. It is when the most difficult times arise in our lives that we realize we are always alone. We dream of an eternal true companion who we usually, desperately, search for outside, when the whole time, that one is patiently waiting within us.

The Divine Mother is the vast ocean of bliss and we are the infinite waves. Forgetting our narrow body-mind identification, we melt in her beatific effulgence which is our true nature, our real Self.

Amma says, "Humility is the gateway to real discipleship, and the master will himself set a perfect example of humility."

In 2004 and 2008, I again traveled to Amritapuri with my daughters. As I had been involved in the sēvā of making flower garlands for Amma's program in Toulon for many years, in 2009, the local organizers offered me the great opportunity to do the pāda pūjā to Amma's feet. I was able to worship her soft holy feet. Afterwards, I sat somewhere and observed; my mind was totally calm and quiet.

Amma says, "Humility means accepting the will of the supreme. Humility means self-surrender, surrendering our will to the will of God. Then only can one be humble because one sees that whatever happens in life, whether positive or negative, is his will. In this state, all reactions disappear. There are no more reactions, only acceptance. Therefore, humility can also be interpreted as total acceptance."

I opened my heart to Amma about the fact that I was alone on my spiritual journey. Even though I was married, our lives weren't going in the same direction. Amma said that she was aware of it and added, "In the boat to cross over the ocean of saṁsāra you are alone." Later she said, "When there is too much suffering, you have to make a decision."

In 2011, I went through divorce with Amma's grace as my only support. In December of that same year, I visited Amritapuri for a few weeks. Before arriving in India, my right knee was in a great deal of pain. With the hot, humid, Indian climate, it became worse — even walking was difficult. I felt so distressed because I couldn't physically kneel before Amma. However, internally I bowed down again and again, and my heart was full of gratitude and determination. Before leaving for France, I told Amma about my knee, and asked her if I could join the āśhram as a renunciate. She answered, "Follow the doctor's instructions, and come back soon."

I had surgery on my knee and was immobilized for a few weeks. As I couldn't move much, I spent my time reading a French version of the *Bhāgavata Purāṇa*[29].

Immersed in reading about Kṛiṣhṇa's divine *līlas* (plays), my mind kept spontaneously returning to Amritapuri and Amma's last precious words to me, "Come back soon."

To earn money, I worked for nine months as a caregiver for a severely disabled person. By that time, and by Amma's infinite grace, all of my daughters had finished their studies and were working. I then joined the Amritapuri āśhram in 2013. When walking towards the exit at Kochi airport, I suddenly saw one of Amma's swāmīs standing there holding a beautiful garland of fresh flowers in his hands. A few minutes later Amma, shining like the full moon of pure love and perfect knowledge, was there walking right in front of us! Amma and I had arrived at the airport at the same time. The following day was *Guru Pūrṇima*. It was such an auspicious time to arrive at the āśhram.

***

On New Year's Eve 2013, I had the rare opportunity to sit behind Amma's chair the whole night while she gave darśhan. On that same night, my father passed away. A few months earlier I had heard he had cancer.

Before leaving for Amritapuri, I had written a letter to my parents, explaining to them about my decisions, and expressing all of my sincere respect, gratitude, and love towards them. Throughout the years, I had tried to share the sweetness of Amma, the core of my life with all the members of my family. As Catholics, I thought they would understand, but the fact was they could not accept Amma, and never expressed any desire or even curiosity to see her.

---

[29] Ancient scripture relating stories of Lord Kṛiṣhṇa.

When our ego and mind melt into the spiritual center called the heart, we can see and feel God's presence in God's own creation and recognise his divine messengers. Amma's love and compassion create the most suitable atmosphere for our hearts to blossom.

Amma says, "To become humble is the very goal of spiritual life."

Amma's physical presence is the best soil for our spiritual progress. Her voice, her touch, her form, help us to reconnect with our divine origin.

For the last eight years for my sēvā in Amritapuri, I have had to interact a lot with others. I'm grateful and, as my English was very limited when I started, I have learned a lot about the subtle art of communication, and how to be more mature emotionally in my interactions. Everyone is a perfect mirror reflecting our own self. If we can fully accept every situation as Amma's prasād, that positive attitude of acceptance will slowly clean our minds from all misconceptions and misunderstandings.

The whole process of inner purification is the ultimate surgery.

Amma, the divine surgeon, is safely operating on us all, bringing us back to our original state of innocence and inner purity. When the divine fragrance of humility arises in the garden of our hearts, the flowers of acceptance, patience, forgiveness, detachment, pure love and inner strength start blooming.

May everlasting joy fill our hearts;
May divine harmony fill our lives;
May we become white flowers of peace at her lotus feet.

21

Amma — the Guide, the Path, and the Goal

Sahaja - France

Once upon a time in Tamil Nadu, there lived a very pious man named Pūsalar. He was a great devotee of Lord Śhiva. He had an intense desire to build a temple, but could not afford to build one, even after begging for funds from the city. So one day, he laid the foundation of an imaginary temple in his heart. He followed the traditional rituals of temple-building, and sanctified the ground. Every day, he would build a small portion of the temple. After several years, the temple in his heart was finally complete, and he invited Lord Śhiva to the inauguration.

At the same time, the powerful King Rājasimha had also built a majestic temple for Lord Śhiva at Kāṅchīpuram. The King prayed to Lord Śhiva to come to the inauguration of his temple. Lord Śhiva came in his dreams and said, "I am sorry, I have another temple inauguration on that day. I will be inaugurating Pūsalar's temple instead."

The next morning, the King remembered his dream, and became furious and fumed, "How could that temple be more important than the king's own temple?" He went in search of Pūsalar's temple, but couldn't find it anywhere. Finally he came across a man who told him that in a very old hut, there was a poor man called Pūsalar. He said, "I'd be surprised if such a poor man had found the means to build a temple."

The King went to the poor man's hut, and heard the sound of a bell ringing inside. He entered and saw only a poor man dressed in an old *dhōti* (a sarong-like cloth worn by men) deep in prayer. The sound of the bells became louder and louder as the King approached Pūsalar.

Finally, he put his ear to Pūsalar's chest, and could hear the temple bells ringing from within his heart. The temple inauguration had started, and the king realized that Lord Śhiva had chosen the temple in the heart of this sincere devotee rather than his external temple! The Lord's favorite place to dwell is in our innocent hearts. Like Pūsalar, let us make our hearts a temple dedicated to Amma's lotus feet.

As we can't always hold Amma in our minds, we can tune in to her with introspection — would Amma be happy with my actions? With my words? My thoughts? In this way, whether near or far from Amma, we can stay in tune with her. May we be able to utilize opportunities like this Covid-19 lockdown to unlock our hearts, and tune into the eternal melody of Amma's all-pervading wisdom and grace.

When I first came to the āśhram, I hadn't developed this ability to tune within to Amma. I didn't want to leave Amma's side for a day, or even for an hour. I thought, as mother and child are never separated in the early stages of a child's life, I should be with her every moment. I wished I could take the form of a little mouse, and follow Amma everywhere — including to her room. I wanted to hide behind the furniture, and spy on every single move she made while meeting people, talking on the phone, eating, speaking to her attendant, sleeping, et cetera.

I also thought that if she granted me this boon I would be eternally fulfilled, and this in itself would grant me *mōkṣha* — liberation. In scripture class, I learned that mōkṣha can be attained by an inner tuning to the Guru. In spite of hearing this, I still held onto my belief in the need for close physical proximity.

A few years later, I realized Amma had fulfilled my wish to be her little mouse, but not in the way I expected. I was able to glimpse Amma's greatness and divinity on many occasions. For example, she gave me the opportunity to help coordinate the devotees' ārati[30] during the Europe Tours.

Every experience with our beloved Amma has sweetness to it. Running after her is sweet, seeing her laugh is sweet, her gentle smile is sweet, the softness of her hands is incomparably sweet... Everything about Mother is sweet.

She is '*chitta chōra*' — the thief of the mind. Just as Lord Kṛiṣhṇa used to steal the butter as well as the minds of the *gōpīs*, Amma uses different techniques to steal the minds of her children.

Amma, like *Kāmadhēnu* — the wish-fulfilling cow, fulfilled my desire to be close to her physically. She then ensured I would turn within by instructing me to meditate more, to study scriptures more, and to keep a diary and write bhajans as a *sādhanā*.

Amma told me, "The mind is like water, it naturally flows downwards. Through the fire of sādhanā, the water (mind) flows upwards, and dissolves as it evaporates."

***

I have learned so much by traveling with Amma on her tours for the last decade. From being on tour, I learned a lesson that can be condensed down to three words: surrender or suffer.

I have sometimes been an expert in resisting Amma's will. Often I have practiced half surrender, where only the body

---

30 Ārati is a traditional ritual involving the waving of a lighted lamp to the Guru or deity usually done towards the end of *pūjā* or worship. At some of Amma's programs, multiple devotees take turns waving the lighted lamp to Amma as she showers them with flower petals and the ārati song is sung.

obeys, but the mind grumbles. This doesn't bring peace. Through experience, I have learned that when I fully surrender, painful situations can turn out to be joyous ones.

Once on an India tour, out of concern for her children, Amma had requested that each tour bus be equipped with a portable toilet for emergencies. During this trip, the portable toilet had been used. We were all highly disgusted by it! People sitting in the front would push it to the back of the bus, and then the people in the back would push it to the front...back and forth it went.

I was seated in the middle of the bus, so ultimately, the portable toilet ended up next to me and another woman. We both figured, "There is no point in pushing it towards other people as someone has to bear with it anyway, and moving it might make it spill by accident." So it remained next to us. My neighbor held the lid closed so that the contents wouldn't spill when we hit a bump on the road. At first we were a little unhappy, but when we realized that we couldn't change the situation, we started to joke about it!

We imagined Amma laughing out loud about this situation. We discovered that having to keep the lid closed provided a good armrest. The rest of the trip seemed to go faster, thanks to all the jokes and laughter about it. This seemingly difficult situation turned into entertainment for us all and helped us remember Amma.

We have two choices at every moment in life: surrender or suffer... When we can't change a situation, we either see the situation as a curse and suffer, or we accept and make the most of it. Surrender can turn our journey into a pleasant one, even in extreme situations. Surrender leads to liberation.

In the *Bhagavad Gītā*, Lord Kṛiṣhṇa says in Chapter 18, verse 62:

tam ēva śharaṇaṁ gachchha sarva-bhāvēna bhārata

> *tat-prasādāt parāṁ śhāntiṁ sthānaṁ prāpsyasi śhāśhvatam*
> ‘Surrender exclusively unto Him with your whole being, O Bhārata (Arjuna). By his grace, you will attain perfect peace and the eternal abode.’

While Lord Kṛiṣhṇa advised his devotee Arjuna to surrender exclusively to him, Amma takes it a step further. Like Kṛiṣhṇa, she not only advises us to follow spiritual principles, but like a divine director, she creates situations as opportunities to put them into practice. They are tests to measure our progress. Then she consoles and hugs her disheartened children if they fail the test.

We learn that in Amma’s world, everything is a blessing, though we can’t always see it that way. Everything comes from God’s grace alone. Everything is a stepping stone towards growth, and every fall is an opportunity to get up and stand more firmly.

As Amma says, we don’t criticize waves when they are either very small or very big. We know that they are unpredictable. Some are insignificant; others may drench us. We accept them as they are, and if the sea becomes agitated, we just don’t go too close to the shore. In the same way, the waves of life may be big or small. They are the way that they are, and only by accepting them will we be able to tune into the flow of life — tune into the divine.

I used to unburden my sorrows by telling them to the ocean when I wasn’t with Amma. But then I felt guilty thinking, “Am I cheating on Amma?”

Later, when asking Amma a totally different question, she said, “Amma is the ocean, Amma isn’t a pool. You need to dive into it!” She demonstrated with her hand how I should plunge into Amma. She encouraged me to worship her with form as a way to realize her vast formlessness. She also showed me that she is not different from Mother Nature and nourished my desire to protect and care for Mother Earth.

Amma has given me the chance to work in the garden with some of the little children in the āśhram. I have been gardening with them for a few years now, and it's truly a wonder to see them in nature. Their innocence teaches me so much. Some children are so connected to nature that they can listen to the trees, and tell me what the trees need just by hugging them. One child would say, "This tree needs more space...or more water..." And what the child was saying was true. We all have this deep connection to nature, God, and the entire universe.

Amma is the guide, the path, and the goal. She is the strength that keeps us on the path. We accomplish nothing; she does all. We forget this and literally operate like thieves by lying to ourselves thinking, "I did this." The great mother of the universe — *Jagadamba* must be laughing, watching her little puppets move about, claiming that they are doing great things when she actually holds the puppet strings in her hands.

During scripture class, our teacher said, "If a person is attached to their actions, then even while seated in meditation, he or she will be disturbed by thoughts concerning the results of those actions."

This used to happen to me, sometimes frequently. As a remedy, I started surrendering my attachment to the results of my *sēvā* to our beloved Amma's feet. I would visualize mentally packing all of my sēvā into a box. I would tie it tightly with a string and offer it at Amma's lotus feet.

For how many births have we been performing actions and expecting their fruits? This is deeply ingrained in us. If we do a small action, we expect a small fruit, like a lemon. If we do a big action, we expect a big fruit, like perhaps a mango or even a papaya. As spiritual seekers, we want to break free from the cycle of birth and death. To do so, we need to surrender our actions, and stop expecting the lemon of thank you, the strawberry of a smile, the kiwi of a successful result, or the papaya of things unfolding the way we expect.

Amma, the *jagadguru* (universal Guru) who watches over all the actions of her children, provides each one of us with a personal training in detachment from the fruits of action.

This may be painful at first. However, remembering why we have come to the spiritual path, and realizing that we are under Amma's compassionate gaze will help us to overcome all difficulties, and learn the most precious lessons in life. Those lessons will ultimately help us to merge with her.

How many lifetimes have we been waiting for this chance? Out of almost eight billion people now living on Earth, how many know the true goal of life? How many have an all-knowing mother to tell them how to find it? We are so fortunate to have found the Divine Mother in this lifetime. We sip her wisdom on a daily basis, like happy babies drinking their mother's breast milk.

Here is the story of how I came to Amma:

When I was nine or ten years old, during the summer at my parents' country home in France, I would sleep under the stars, talking to them about the meaning of life, and asking whether God exists or not... I come from a traditionally religious family, but was born to parents who had rebelled against their religion. So the theme of the existence of God, to my child-mind, remained unanswered.

One day, feeling the urge to do some drawing, I drew a round form sitting cross legged — a mother, embracing her child. I drew it again and again that summer. I asked my mother, "Do you know anyone like in these drawings? I want to know who this person is."

My mother took me into our house and showed me a statue of an African woman embracing her baby. I said, "No, I don't think that's her." She then took me to the statue of the Virgin Mary standing in the living room. I was not fully convinced it was her either. It was only many years later that I realized that the form I was drawing was Amma with the head of a child in her arms.

The roundness of the lines depicted the enveloping qualities of our dear Amma. I drew that form again and again throughout my youth without having ever heard of Amma. She was calling to me from within, and I was longing for her, wondering where on Earth I could find her.

Later, I heard that during her first world tour, Amma said she decided to go on tour because she could feel her children around the world calling her. I felt so touched. Yes I was calling her, yearning for the spiritual nourishment of the mother of the universe. She was actually the one calling herself to me, through me.

By 2008, I finished my college studies, and had everything most people want in life, but I had not found happiness. I realized I needed a Guru to explain to me what the deeper meaning of life is, and why permanent happiness seemed to be out of reach.

I flew to India and stayed in various āśhrams in Tamil Nadu.

While visiting yet another āśhram, someone told me, "Go to *Amritapuri* and meet Amma. She is the Divine Mother. She is marvelous! You won't be disappointed.

I arrived in Amritapuri during Amma's birthday celebration where I received my first *darśhan.* There were so many people there that my hug lasted less than two seconds. It felt like an electric discharge, and a deep reconnection to the mother not seen in a long time. I realized that she was the form I had been drawing as a child. I had finally reached her. The child with the mother; the mother with the child.

Even the notion of mother and child seems too narrow to describe our eternal bond with Amma. Amma is within us and we are within her. She is us and we are her. We are bound in unity, in one endless love.

In the *Bhakti Sūtras* (scripture on devotion) of Sage Nārada, he says, "There is no separation between God and his devotees."

The unique bond we have with Amma is actually the bond we have with all of creation — a bond of infinite, unconditional love — *prēma.*

Lord Kṛiṣhṇa says in Chapter 9, verse 6 of the *Bhagavad Gītā*:

'Know that as the mighty wind which blows everywhere rests in the sky, likewise all created beings rest in me.'

There are not many but only one. Unity is not only something that the *ṛiṣhis* realized long ago; it is the truth that only our egos are obscuring. Amma took upon herself the task of melting our egos with her love. There are not many. There is One. She is everywhere.

May the light of this knowledge dawn within us.

May we be able to surrender all of our mistakes at Amma's divine feet.

22

Amma, the Love that Vanquishes All Fear

Vimala Purcell - USA

Recently in the United States off the coast of California, a female gray whale had become entangled in commercial crab traps and fishing lines. She was weighed down by hundreds of pounds of traps that caused her to struggle to stay afloat. She had rope completely tangled around her body...even in her mouth.

A fisherman spotted her and radioed for help. A rescue team came, and the only way to save her was for them to dive in and untangle her. This was dangerous, as the whale could easily kill a human. The rescuers worked skillfully and patiently for hours. The whale remained still. When she was free, she swam to each of the divers and gently nudged them, then swam in joyous circles.

The person who posted the story had written, 'May you all be so fortunate, to be surrounded by people who will help you get untangled by the things that are binding you.'

Amma spends every moment of her life patiently untying us from the things that bind us. She very skillfully uses her children here in *Amritapuri* as tools to loosen the ropes.

In Chapter 18, verse 30 of the *Bhagavad Gītā*, Lord Kṛishṇa says:

> *pravṛittiṁ cha nivṛittiṁ cha kāryākāryē bhayābhayē*
> *bandhaṁ mōkṣhaṁ cha yā vētti buddhiḥ sā pārtha sāttvikī*
> 'O Arjuna, son of Pṛithā! The intellect which understands what is proper action and what is improper action, what is duty and what is non-duty, what is to be

> feared and what is not to be feared, what is binding and what is liberating — such an intellect is said to be in the nature of goodness *(sāttvic).*'

I chose this verse because I feel it defines a struggle that many people experience throughout life — wanting to do what is right, but not always knowing or discerning what that is.

Fear is one strong obstacle for me on the spiritual path; it's a knot that has been particularly difficult to untie. It ruled my life for many years before meeting Amma. It influenced most decisions I made.

My childhood was chaotic and traumatic. Fortunately, my grandparents, a source of warmth and love, were a big part of our lives. We were Catholic and they took us to church.

During that time I formed a relationship with God. This faith never left me, even in my darkest times. I suffered a lot inside from the trauma of my childhood years. As a teen, I had anxiety and felt rather lost and disconnected.

I wanted to be happy, so I sought help through therapy. I wanted to overcome my past, and not repeat the mistakes of my parents. I could only do that by moving forward. I earned a bachelor's degree in psychology, then moved from a small town in Illinois to a big city in Florida where I earned a master's degree in public health. In graduate school I met my friend Deepa, a friend who would lead me to Amma.

By the year 2000, I had a good career, my own apartment, a car, pet cat, and an active social life. Materially I had everything I needed, but deep within, I was restless. I didn't want to live just for myself. I wanted to be of use to the world. This restlessness became a longing and a prayer.

One morning, when I was driving to work I was overcome with desperation and I sincerely prayed from the depths of my heart for God to reveal himself in my life.

Within a few weeks, I learned about a retreat in Santa Fe, New Mexico with an Indian saint called Amma. Curious, I registered along with my friend Deepa. She had met Amma the year before. I thought the retreat would be like a spiritual workshop.

I assumed that Amma would teach some classes and we would have a lot of free time to do other things. My friend tried to prepare me, but I had no frame of reference, so I just kept an open mind. We arrived the night before the retreat.

I didn't know what to think about it all. However, Amma's presence was comforting. When everyone chanted Ōm, I felt calm and connected.

For my first *darśhan*, I was so worried about doing something wrong that I was not very present for the hug. Before I knew it, the darśhan was over and I was a bit stunned. When I walked away, I was surprised to find a chocolate kiss in my hand, and that my hand was shaking.

The next day the retreat started. It was in a hotel in downtown Santa Fe. Although open-minded, I had a hard time with worship of Amma because in Christianity, Jesus is considered the only son of God. I always believed that there were others like Jesus, but I didn't grasp that I could actually meet such a person. Deepa was a great source of support and knowledge during this time.

***

It was at a *Dēvī Bhāva* program where I reached a turning point. I was admittedly in a bad mood that day; I can't really explain why. I didn't even want to go to Dēvī Bhāva. When I went for dinner, I saw a woman I knew from the retreat.

She had an early *darśhan token,*[31] but her husband had a late token. She was sad because she wanted a Dēvī Bhāva darśhan with him but due to his health problems, he couldn't stay up late.

I had an early token, but I was not in the mood to be generous. I so desperately wanted an early night... after all the late nights of the retreat, and also we were going to drive to Dallas the next day. I kept quiet. But soon, I felt the prick of my conscience. I could not leave without giving her my token. I returned and still quite irritated, gave her my early token. Her face lit up! She gave me her husband's late token in exchange. Seeing her happiness changed my mood completely. I too felt happy. I stayed up the whole night and my darśhan was at 5:00 a.m.

When I reached Amma for darśhan, I completely fell apart. I sobbed into her shoulder. I had no idea why I was crying, but it felt really good.

It felt like a heavy load was being gently lifted off my shoulders. If I hadn't given the lady my token — a small act of selflessness — I don't think I would be where I am now.

When I returned home, I noticed that several small attachments and habits had fallen away. I stopped eating meat, stopped wearing makeup, and stopped spending money on frivolous things like manicures and expensive hair styles.

In those first few years, I became very attached to Amma's form. I got up early and did *archana* (the recitation of divine names) and meditation. I listened to *bhajans* on my way to and from work everyday.

I used to travel to Dallas, Texas for Amma's program and I ended up becoming involved in *sēvā* for Amma's yearly visits there. I coordinated the devotees who hand Amma the *prasād* that Amma then gives to each person who comes for darśhan,

---

[31] A numbered ticket given out to devotees wishing to receive Amma's darśhan.

making sure local devotees get time to hand the prasād to Amma throughout the program in timed shifts. I felt useful. I was so busy during the program that I forgot to eat, and hardly slept. I loved every minute of it!

During one program early in my relationship with Amma, I told her I had a lot of fear inside, even of Amma herself. First, She told me that Amma is my own. Then she said, "Love and fear cannot exist in the same space. Focus on the love and the fear will naturally fall away."

One year, I made a big mistake with the prasād-handing list. On the first day of the program, which was the busiest, we could rarely get those working the hardest to come and hand Amma the prasād. They always said they were too busy. So I had this great idea... we would only sign up the hard working people on the second day of the program when they had more time.

I felt quite proud of my solution. However, on the morning of the second-day program, I woke up with a sinking feeling, realizing that the morning darśhan ended earlier than usual because of the Dēvī Bhāva program that would start in the early evening. I totally miscalculated... This meant that the hardest working people, the coordinators, the tour organizers, the kitchen staff, etc., would get a full minute less than those who had handed prasād to Amma on the first day.

When I realized my mistake, with great trepidation, I confessed it to Amma. Amma began speaking to me in Malayalam and I could tell by her gestures that she was concerned.

My mistake had compromised the local devotees' time being near Amma, but on reflection, I realized that this distressing situation was actually a form of Amma's compassion — showing me where my lack of *śhraddhā* or awareness had been. Amma often compares herself to a gardener whose job is to remove the worms and weeds so the plants may grow and flourish.

As I spoke to Amma, I only felt her love. All my fear vanished in the presence of that love. Later, I remembered what Amma told me, "Focus on the love and the fear will fall away." I felt the truth of her words. More importantly, I learned a big lesson. I realized it was my selfish need for a smooth program and my overconfidence which created the resulting mess. This experience has given me a lot to reflect upon, and has guided me over the years.

Amma says, "Receptivity is the power to believe, to have faith and to accept love. It is the power to prevent doubt from entering our mind."

***

I came to Amritapuri for the first time in 2003 for *Amṛita-Varṣham50,* Amma's 50th birthday celebration, and had a blissful three weeks in the āśhram. Then I went to Kochi for the birthday celebrations a couple of days early with friends to do sēvā.

In our hotel, we had to keep our money and passports in a safe deposit box behind the front desk, and were given a key. Two days before the celebration, I went to get the key for the safe deposit box out of my bag, but it was not there. I searched the room and couldn't find it. I enquired at the desk but they did not have it. I had no access to money, and so I became a little worried.

I searched everything in the room again. I realized it may have fallen out of my bag at the program stadium. I told the lady at the desk I couldn't find the key, and asked, "What happens when a key is lost?"

She said, "I don't know, it's never happened before, and we don't keep a spare for the safety of the guests." I quickly got in a taxi to go to the stadium to look. I prayed intensely the entire ride...Amma, please let me find that key...please let me find that key.

When I arrived, the tent we had done sēvā in was now a kitchen full of huge pots and machines. I was discouraged, but then I saw the international office being set up, and I walked over to see two people sitting at a table. I asked, "Where is the lost and found?"

They pointed to a row of metal shelves. I walked over, repeating my new chant, "Amma please let me find that key." My heart became heavy, seeing the empty metal shelves. But as I got closer, I saw something very small sitting all alone on a vast metal shelf. Was it the key? Yes!

I was full of awe and gratitude. "Amma materialized the key!" This experience feels symbolic of our relationship with Amma. She is ever ready to give us the key we thought we lost, if we only ask sincerely for it.

I returned to Amritapuri again in 2006 to stay for six months. In the back of my mind, I had hoped that I could come and live here. I started to save money and pay off debts. I lost all interest in worldly life.

In 2010, I came here again for a longer stay and during one darśhan, I asked Amma if I could live here as a renunciate. She said, "Ok *mōlē* (daughter)." She told me, "Happiness is a decision," and I laughed... because I always believed that happiness was just out of my reach.

My biological mother, on the other hand, was not happy that I decided to move to the āśhram, and she expressed her hurt feelings and anger whenever I called. She felt abandoned by me. I told her many times, Amma is the universal mother and she is your mother too. Within a year, she came to visit me in Amritapuri, and formed her own relationship with Amma.

As a new renunciate, I threw myself into life here in the āśh-ram. I forgot about my former life in America. I was immersed in my *sādhanā* routine: sēvā, scripture classes, Indian tours, and seeing Amma whenever possible. I was assigned sēvā at the Ecology Center. I was told by the sēvā supervisor that the Ecology Center manager was going on the U.S. Tour, and that I should replace her until she came back.

I had had less than one week of training, and knew nothing about managing an Ecology Center and all the details it involved. I hadn't even met the people I would be supervising. It was definitely not in my comfort zone, and....a little scary. Amma often tells us that she creates situations in the āśhram for our growth, and these situations may be challenging. They are designed to scrub us clean, to remove *vāsanās* (latent tendencies), attachments, and likes and dislikes.

St. John of the Cross, a Catholic saint from the 16th century, said to his monks, "You have not come to the monastery for any other reason than to be worked and tried in virtue; you are like the stone that must be chiseled and fashioned before being set in the building. Thus you should understand that those who are in the monastery are craftsmen placed there by God to mortify (i.e. purify) you by working and chiseling at you."[32]

In the world, I was often praised for my work, and rarely criticized. Here in Amritapuri on the other hand, there are many 'craftsmen' available and ready to point out mistakes and imperfections. Criticism is not easy to accept and it can be painful.

Amma says that when someone criticizes us, we should see if we can learn something. It is tempting to want to immediately find fault with the people who criticize us, but Amma says we will grow spiritually when we look at our own shortcomings.

---

32 *Counsel to a Religious* by St. John of the Cross, 3.

Being in a leadership role in my sēvā, I have had to take a lot of criticism from others. I do feel such 'chiseling' has smoothed out my edges...at least a little bit.

Like the whale in the story, the ropes of negativity that bind us are being loosened by people and situations in the āśhram that Amma has skillfully placed around us. We know that every grain of sand here is soaked with Amma's tears of devotion for God. In other words, this place, like Amma, is made of pure divine love. It can only purify the darkness in us, as that is love's nature.

***

I would like to conclude with a story, an incident that is very dear to my heart.

One day in the summer of 2015, all the āśhram residents gathered in the big hall for the Dēvī Bhāva webcast. At one point during the webcast, Amma turned and looked straight into the camera and smiled. I felt she was looking at me! I thought, "Am I crazy?" Then an *Ammamar,* the female āśhram elder sitting next to me, said in broken English, "Amma look Vimala!" I felt so happy inside, wondering why Amma's attention was on me.

The Dēvī Bhāva we were watching was Amma's first visit to Atlanta, Georgia. My mom was going to be there to experience Dēvī Bhāva for the first time. The day after the program I spoke to her on the phone. She relayed the following events of the evening to me:

She was one of the last people to have darśhan, and then she experienced the shower of flower petals at the end of Dēvī Bhāva and Amma's beautiful gaze. I was very happy for her. I thought the conversation was over, but then she said, "There is more to tell..."

She started to talk about my sister who still lives in the town where we grew up. It is an extremely small farming town in Illinois that no one has ever heard of.

My sister's husband was going fishing in a pond at a local park. I know the park well, having grown up there. The park was empty, so he was alone. Suddenly, he heard the sound of vehicles; then the voices of many people descending on the park. He said they were happy, laughing and chatting.

At this point in the conversation with my mom, I stood up — suddenly knowing what she was going to say next. Amma and the tour group were having their dinner stop in the park in my home town on their way to the next program!

Some tour staff approached my brother-in-law to tell him about Amma, and that he could get a hug if he wanted. He was very shy when he saw the crowd around Amma, plus she was starting to distribute prasād. He declined. Amma asked everyone to join hands around the pond for meditation. Though my brother-in-law had declined the hug, he joined hands with the tour group for meditation and the chanting of *'lokāḥ samastāḥ sukhinō bhavantu'* — 'May all beings in all worlds be happy.'

When my brother-in-law returned home and told my sister what had happened at the park, she knew immediately that the person he saw was Amma. Excited and deeply touched, she thought, "There are so many parks and towns along the way, and yet Amma stopped here!"

Perhaps it's mere coincidence that Amma had her dinner stop there, but for me it revealed the eternal connection between Amma and me, my birth family, my hometown, and Amritapuri. Physically, I was here in Amma's home, while she was there in mine! This made me feel profoundly close to Amma.

The choices I made in life that landed me here are purely Amma's grace. I pray that, like the whale, we surrender rather than resist... and in our freedom, we shall dance for eternity in joyous circles with our beloved Amma.

23

Amma, PhD, and Beyond!

Dr. Shyam Nath – Mauritius

> *ya dēvī sarva bhūtēṣhu śhakti rūpēṇa saṁsthita*
> *namastasyai namastasyai namastasyai namo namaḥ*
> 'To that goddess who lives in all beings in the form of śhakti, power, strength; Salutations to her, salutations, salutations again and again.' *(Dēvī Mahatmyam)*

I come from Varanasi, also known as Kashi, in Uttar Pradesh, a place that is famous for having one of the twelve *jyōtirlingams*[33] of Lord Śhiva. I studied Economics at Banaras Hindu University, and although I was a religious-minded student, I wasn't affiliated with any particular *Guru* lineage. However, I regularly visited the Tilbhandēśhwar Mahādēv Temple in Varanasi.

Interestingly, the seed of meeting my Guru was sown in my mind not in India, but surprisingly in the U.S. when I visited Syracuse University for my post-doctoral studies.

One day while waiting at a bus terminal in New York, I ordered a coffee and donut at the refreshment kiosk there, when the lady behind the counter, with a smile refused to take my money and instead told me that her Guru comes from India. When she said this, for the first time I felt something lacking in my life!

While still living in India, it so happened that I had to travel to Trivandrum on Government of India Planning Commission

---

[33] Jyōtirliṅgas (usually considered to be 12 in number) are temples where Śhiva appeared as '*jyōti*,' a column of fire or light. It is believed that these jyōtis later cooled into the shape of a *liṅga* and became objects of worship.

business. It was my first time traveling to Kerala. I do not consider this a coincidence, but a dedicated opportunity to pass through Amma's geographical location even without visiting *Amritapuri*. At that time in 1989, I could never have imagined that this was going to be my place of residence in the future.

That short, three-day visit to Kerala turned out to be a landmark in my life. I always dreamed of spending my life once I'd retired, in a village that was near a temple, had electricity, running water, and communication facilities.

Amritapuri is an international village with incredible facilities.

My journey to Amma came via Mauritius, where I'd been working at the University of Mauritius as Professor of Economics since 1990.

During my first ten years living in Mauritius, I never had the chance to connect with Amma, even though I was living only two kilometers away from Amma's āśhram in Quatre Bornes. In 2000, a Mauritian friend of mine wanted to receive Amma's *darśhan* as a blessing as he was ill. He asked if I could get him a darśhan token. I got a token for him and one for myself.

During darśhan, Amma looked at my friend but she talked to me which I couldn't understand. Even then, nothing happened for me, and I just didn't connect with Amma. However, I was suddenly transported to some other plane by the messages embedded in Amma's *bhajans*. My devotion and dormant spiritual curiosity were awakened.

***

I visited Amritapuri for the first time in 2002. This started a new phase in my life. The day my wife Nisha and I arrived, instead of going to Amma during the public darśhan, Amma called us to meet with her in her room. How lucky we were! This face to face darśhan with Amma was memorable. I told Amma that we would be visiting Varanasi, my hometown after Amritapuri.

Before leaving her room, Amma added a little twist. She told me to look at the photo of Ādi Śhaṅkarāchārya on top of the gate coming out from the Kāśhī Viśhvanāth temple. I had never noticed this photo before. When Amma mentioned this, I realized that the meaning of life is far beyond our petty imagination. What little I know, I know; but what more I don't know, I don't know. Amma introduced me to something that is a treasure for me, and a path into Amma's world.

Back then, every year my journey to India began in Amritapuri. Incidentally, something incredible happened for me in 2006. During a public darśhan, Amma asked the dean of the Amrita Business School in Coimbatore to take me there so that I could start a full-time PhD program in management. I was also encouraged by the vice chancellor of the university to do this. That was my introduction to the beautiful Ettimadai campus in Coimbatore.

I started teaching Environmental Economics as part of the MBA program there and traveled every year from Mauritius to Coimbatore. The PhD program eventually started in 2009, and though ultimately I never ended up working on that program, I nevertheless felt blessed that Amma used me as an instrument to initiate the process in 2006. Amma says that we are neither weak nor incapable, but by the Lord's grace are sources of unlimited power.

Amma has accorded great importance to the quality of the PhD program. Her level of care and detail is beyond our comprehension. Amma once called for a meeting with senior faculty from all the Amrita campuses in Amritapuri to give guidelines about designing course work for the PhD program at Amrita Colleges. In this way I have seen how Amma gives her direct support and guidance to the academic programs, including the PhD program.

***

In 2010, I was scheduled to go to London to attend the launch of a book I'd written on the sustainable development of small islands. As I had to go to New Delhi to get my visa for the UK, I decided to stop on the way in Kochi where Amma was giving darśhan, to get her blessing for the trip.

When my turn came for darśhan, I was impatient to get her blessings, but she didn't respond to my enthusiasm at all. I was puzzled by Amma's behavior until, to my surprise, the very next day I got a message from the British Commonwealth Secretariat that the launch of the book had been canceled due to the sudden demise of the chief publisher.

When my book was published in early January 2011, I was visiting UC Berkeley in the U.S.. I got a copy of the book, and visited India to get Amma's blessings for it. Amma was at the Chennai *Brahmasthānam* temple giving darśhan. I joined the darśhan line and showed Amma the book. She showered her blessings and gave me a huge hug along with an extra apple!

Amma gives a lot of importance to how you dress when you work at the university. One day I went for Amma's Darshan and she touched my shirt, which was not pressed well, and commented as if this was not appropriate for someone going to the college. I felt blessed. Next day, I put on a new well-behaved shirt and stood near the ramp to get Amma's attention. After darshan, Amma was passing by me, but then she suddenly stopped and took a few steps back to assess me. She touched my shirt and said now it is ok. I marvel at how much attention Amma has given to someone who has adopted simple dress.

***

Amma always discouraged me from starting any specific program in Economics. Nevertheless, perhaps driven by my ego, I designed a PhD program in Economics and presented it to Amma. The program however did not take off. This serves as an illustration of how the ego takes over insisting that the Guru supports it.

Let me narrate a beautiful story about how the Guru tackles the ego in everybody. Satyabhāmā, one of Kṛiṣhṇa's wives, was very proud of her beauty and riches and was also very possessive of him. Krishna wanted her to understand that this attitude arose from her ego. He asked Sage Nārada to create a situation in which Satyabhāmā would agree to trade all her wealth to get Kṛiṣhṇa's undivided attention. Nārada had a large scale set up to weigh Kṛiṣhṇa on one side, against Satyabhāmā's riches on the other. If Satyabhāmā's wealth was able to tilt the scale in her favor, she would get his undivided attention.

However, all her riches fell short in weight against Lord Kṛiṣhṇa sitting on the other side of the scale. Baffled by this, Satyabhāmā asked Rukminī, whom she was jealous of, to help her out. Rukminī plucked a *tulasī* leaf and added it to Satyabhāmā's riches on the scale. The weight of just a single tulasī leaf offered with devotion by Rukminī, caused Krishna's side of the balance to rise up. Kṛiṣhṇa explained that Rukminī's devotion represented by the tulasī leaf outweighed Satyabhama's ego of being beautiful and possessive. Through this līlā we can see how Kṛiṣhṇa managed the ego of those who were close to him. But our beloved Amma through her *līlās* manages the egos of her 4,000 children here in Amritapuri and thousands more even beyond!

***

Amma knows all our sorrows only through her infinite compassion. In 2016 I decided to go to Amma's retreat program at her āśhram in San Ramon California. I went to Kochi to catch the plane to the U.S., and stayed at the AIMS hospital guesthouse, as the flight wasn't until after midnight.

Suddenly I started feeling a small pain in my stomach. I had experienced this acute pain two or three times before. I wasn't sure if I could make the long trip to San Francisco. Praying to Amma, I rushed to the emergency room at AIMS where a young doctor gave me a brief examination. He prescribed some medicine, and cleared me for travel, however, I remained hesitant to go. Ultimately, with Amma's grace, I felt well enough, and after participating in Amma's programs in San Ramon, returned safely to Amritapuri with Amma.

The day after returning to Amritapuri, I went for darśhan, and Amma asked me to go to AIMS immediately for a check-up. Of course, I was terribly anxious and went straight to AIMS. I was examined and it was determined that I had gallbladder stones which were causing my stomach pain. Surgery was suggested, but I was horrified at the thought of it. However, Amma gave her divine blessing to go ahead with the surgery and afterwards, the doctors were relieved because this complicated surgery had gone very well. Recovery was slow, but Amma had saved me.

Here in the presence of Amma, all forms of God merge into one. Amma gives the example of the sun reflected in one hundred pots filled with water. Although the reflections make it seem as if there were a hundred suns, in reality there is only ONE.

Let me conclude with Amma's divine words: 'There are no mistakes in God's creation. Every creature and every object that has been created by God is utterly special.'

24

The Mystery of Faith

Janani – Poland

I offer myself at the lotus feet of the Divine Mother who is the embodied God seated among us; who was with me before my birth and will be with me after my death; who accompanied this child in the form of her parents, teachers, friends and fools, and happy and traumatic experiences.

They all fulfilled their purpose to push me further and further, until I reached the embodiment of God herself. O Amma, who other than you calls your children home? Otherwise, no merits or miracles can make one worthy enough to behold your gracious glance!

This *satsang* is about the 'mystery of faith.'

We don't know why and when God comes knocking at our door, bestowing the gift of faith on us.

I spent my childhood in Africa. One spring, the teachers from my primary school took us on a trip to the Sahara Desert. The beauty and vastness of the desert enchanted us all. But on the return flight, the airplane encountered some major technical problems, and literally started falling from the sky.

Those who hadn't fastened their seat belts were catapulted to the ceiling. People were crying and vomiting, and all were petrified. When the sea became clearly visible below, approaching fast, we all understood that we were going to die.

The screaming stopped. I was sitting next to a classmate who had a silver Christian cross around his neck. We held the cross together in our hands in silence. Suddenly all was quiet; no thoughts, no emotions, just pure peace. On that day, for the first time I experienced the witness state — *sākṣhi bhāva*. In that state, there is no fear of death; there is no death.

Incredibly, the plane recovered from the fall and we landed safely. With our legs buckling under us, the emergency rescue team assisted us off the plane. However, that instant of perfect peace remained with me as if a door had opened to a different way of being.

Today I know that Amma was already there holding me. She saved me as it was my destiny to look directly into the eyes of the creator of all. We have been given a one in a million chance to have a personal relationship with God; the untold luxury of experiencing God as the formless infinite and as the loving mother at the same time.

The Tibetan Buddhist monk Chogyam Trungpa called spirituality 'crazy wisdom,' to imply that true knowledge cannot be comprehended by the human mind. Amma often speaks of herself as a crazy mother, and that the eccentric aspect of her behavior, her ever changing *bhāvas* or moods, and her childlike simplicity create an intimate bond between Amma and her children. My heart delights when I can witness those little motherly *līlās* — divine plays.

A few months ago, Amma called us onto the stage for a group *darśhan,* after a long break due to Covid. She distributed hot tea and cooked bananas to all, which brought tears of joy and an atmosphere of conviviality.

At one point, someone offered Amma a bunch of fresh *tulasī* leaves. As Amma was wearing an N95 mask, she gently lifted a corner of the mask, and put two tulasī leaves in her mouth. Chewing them slowly, she looked at me with eyes filled with mystical bliss. Watching her, like a child peeping through the keyhole and being caught red handed, I was filled with her bliss as well, feeling deep intimacy amongst that crowd of people as if we were alone — just Amma and me. Amma takes as many forms as there are her devotees, making their hearts sing in the intimate embrace of the divine. In my crazy gypsy heart, she installed herself as this crazy Kāḷī, the mistress of illusion.

***

We have experienced Amma as Kāḷī, and we have experienced Amma as Kṛiṣhṇa too. Yet, how can we prove this to those who don't believe us? It is impossible, as all experience is subjective. It is a matter of faith. On deeper reflection, the so-called scientific facts are also just beliefs, based on the assumption that whatever we perceive with our senses is real.

Ultimately, nothing is factual. Even the universe is based on our subjective experience. It is easier to believe in the manifest rather than the unmanifest, as we are totally identified with the body. Therefore, I'm unable to explain Amma to others. Only Amma can instill faith beyond doubt in our hearts by gracing us with a vision — a realization beyond mental understanding — a glimpse into her nature. Only that kind of realization overpowers the doubting mind.

This is the miracle of grace, and the story of salvation, when God overrides the mental grip of the human psyche, and installs her image directly into the heart of her beloved. Scholars study scriptures all their lives, yet it was mother Yaśhōdā who fainted in awe when she was spontaneously granted the boon of seeing the entire universe in Kṛiṣhṇa's mouth. This is the impact of direct experience, given only by grace.

Years ago, I would have laughed at the idea of a divine form. Born into a family of atheists and raised by a rationalist father, I was always inclined towards observation rather than imagination. My parents, although not spiritual, held a high standard of morality, and raised me and my sister to seek knowledge first over material comfort, and to serve others through good deeds.

When I was in elementary school, my father was out of work for a year, but though poor, we always had enough money for our education. On my seventh birthday I received a world atlas as a gift. I would point my finger at India and say, "One day I will travel there. This is the end of this world. When I reach there, I will have reached my destination."

How could a child not knowing anything about India, utter words of such profound meaning for her future? How did she know? What is this mystic knowledge, ungraspable by the mind?

As a teenager, I reached a state where living didn't make any sense any more. Looking around, nothing seemed worth it. I asked myself again and again, "Why do I exist? What is the meaning of Life?"

Nothing could satiate my hunger for meaning, so I tried three times to end my life. Worse than suffering from emotional pain is the suffering from a life devoid of meaning. Alas, this is the experience of many youngsters in the West. As my fate unfolded, Amma fulfilled the promise she had made to that seven-year old child.

***

Following an incredible series of events, I found myself hitch-hiking from Poland to India at the age of twenty, reaching my destination and living in that holy land for a year. I visited many āśhrams where I felt a strange well-being, then spent a week with a *sādhu*[34] in his mountain hermitage.

Mother India restored my innocence and self love. I venerate her and kiss the ground whenever I return from abroad, as India

[34] A religious ascetic, mendicant (monk) or any holy person in Hinduism and Jainism who has renounced worldly life.

appears clearly in my heart not as a country, but as a conscious being, as *Bhūmi Dēvī* — the Earth goddess. To see people there who have almost no material possessions but who laugh and dance; to receive their hospitality, friendship, and simple generosity was deeply transformative.

Returning to Poland, my search for a lasting happiness and peace within that does not depend on outer circumstances took me to Zen Buddhism, then later on to an *Advaita Vēdānta* āśhram. However, a voice in my heart kept calling me back to India.

Once again in India, while absorbed in silence in a temple in Kerala, I heard that same voice distinctly say, "You will bow down to me, you will bow down to me, you will bow down to me." Then again, three times...I opened my eyes and saw that at the opposite end of the temple was a small shrine with a shiny silver statue inside its inner sanctum. Suddenly, I found myself prostrating before the idol. As I lay there in wonder of my own actions, the priest attending the shrine called me, and pushing a leaf with sandal paste in it into my hands said, "Kāḷī *prasād.*" Three days later, I arrived in *Amritapuri.*

A great master like Amma has no personal interest in acquiring disciples. It is out of her love and compassion that she showers on us whatever we need most at that moment to grow. During that first short stay, Amma did not attract me to her physical form. Even though I received her darśhan, I just could not really see her, or establish a relationship with her. Instead, she immersed me in a state of solid bliss lasting for three days, where I experienced the world as luminous consciousness emanating from within. Amma knew that she would bind me to her love through the formless. She has never discouraged me from pursuing the path of self-inquiry. Three days became three weeks, three months, then years...

Amma's presence propelled me to two major spiritual discoveries:

The first discovery was reading the *Gospel of Sri Ramakrishna*. It awoke in me a tremendous fascination with Kāḷī. By Amma's request, the Kāḷī idol in our shrine in Amritapuri was made by the same family that sculpted the Kāḷī of Dakṣhiṇēśhwar.

One day, in a state of profound inner rapture, I cried out to Kāḷī, "O mother, if the Self is the witness of all within me, does that mean that you are just a statue? Then how could Śhrī Rāmakṛiṣhṇa[35] say that you are real? Please show me the truth, and free me from this contradiction!"

At that moment, I saw the Kāḷī statue vibrating with life force — with consciousness. Simultaneously, I sensed the same intelligent presence within my heart. Kāḷī took me beyond my ideas of duality and nonduality, to the state of pure innocence, where all aspects of the infinite exist.

I learned that a childlike cry for help to the Divine Mother is always heard, and if it is intense enough, Mother showers us with visionary understanding that can surpass the fruits of our meditation practices. I learned to hold on to Amma's skirt no matter what!

The second discovery was reading *Silence of the Heart* by Robert Adams — a modern classic of non-dual philosophy. His teachings point to only one thing: do not identify with anything you perceive, even the notion of 'I.' True silence is not even in the blissful silence of being, it is in the one who perceives the coming and going of the 'I.' Observing this 'I' coming and going is real freedom. When you watch the sense of 'I,' you realize that it is an illusion — no person or individual exists.

---

[35] Spiritual master (1836 – 1886) from West Bengal, hailed as the apostle of religious harmony.

Stretched between the two paths of *jñāna* (knowledge) and *bhakti* (devotion), and having gained deep insights from both, I gathered my courage and asked Amma, "I follow the non-dual teachings of advaita, yet at the same time I experience a crazy love for Kāḷī. Can I have both or should I just choose one?"

With a mischievous smile Amma answered, "But this love for Kāḷī is there only to take you to advaita!" That day I interpreted what Amma said in a way that discarded the worship of Kāḷī. I thought she was telling me that advaita is the higher choice. Today I don't see it quite like that. I think that when Amma spoke about advaita, she didn't mean the teachings, but the actual state surpassing all teachings and descriptions — the truth as a living experience. In that way, she was telling me that all forms of aspiration for the divine given to us are wonderful tools to help us reach the ultimate.

She also mentioned that Kāḷī is the '*ichchhā śhakti, jñāna śhakti,* and *kriyā śhakti svarūpiṇī,*' and as such, she imparts the power of will, knowledge, and action, subtly suggesting that all that I see as my own effort towards God is actually her grace alone. How amazing are Amma's teachings!...in one sentence she can convey the essence of spirituality.

***

Actually, Amma doesn't even need words. A single look is enough to impart divine knowledge as an instant living experience within us. Here is an example:

Due to financial constraints, the Australia Tour with Amma was the only one I could afford to go on. I planned my travel and booked my tickets to Brisbane, leaving out Sydney, as air tickets there were much costlier. However, that night I couldn't sleep.

Every time I shut my eyes, I had a very intense and clear vision of Amma, dressed as the Divine Mother in a turquoise sāri with a specific flower pattern on it. She was looking gravely into my eyes, holding me in her embrace.

After a sleepless night, I stood up, and as if directed by some invisible power, I rebooked my flights to include Sydney. Strangely, that night the tickets to Sydney were remarkably cheaper than before.

I sat in the program hall in Sydney waiting for the *Dēvī Bhāva* program to begin. When the curtain went up, and Amma made her glorious appearance as the Divine Mother on her throne, I started laughing loudly. Amma was wearing exactly the same sāri that I saw in my vision. Tears trickled blissfully down my cheeks as I realized that Amma had planned for me to be in Sydney with her all along, that she was alive in my heart, and guiding me from within.

Amma once told me that a true *bhakta* (devotee) realizes that the God he venerates sits within his own heart, rather than as a form worshiped externally.

In bhakti we surrender completely to the divine, discarding the notion of doership. But if individual volition is unreal, if all is the will of God, why do we experience separation and suffering? How does grace work on us?

Lord Kṛiṣhṇa in his last teachings called the *Uddhava Gītā* gives an answer that in my view, reconciles both the perspective of a devotee and a *jñāni* — a follower of the path of knowledge, validating both.

Kṛiṣhṇa says, "Human life takes shape based on one's own actions. I do not conduct it, nor interfere in it. I am just a witness watching from close quarters all that transpires. That is the *dharma* of God. But, when you realize that I am watching as a witness, you cannot do wrong things or sinful deeds. Only when you forget it, do you slip into thinking that you can perform actions unknown to me."

Ultimately, we are all devotees. A bhakta worships Īśhvara (God) in physical form, and a jñāni worships Īśhvara in the form of his own consciousness. It is the uninterrupted attention fixed on one or the other that takes us across the illusion of one's individuality. And the link between them, the purpose of any spiritual practice, is to attain a quiet mind. We need a quiet mind, a subdued mind to hear God's call of love.

***

Perhaps my most profound moment of love with Amma happened during the last Australia Tour. After the Gold Coast Retreat, I made my way to the airport to board a flight to Singapore, following Amma there. My flight was running late, so I checked in my luggage and waited in the deserted airport waiting area.

Suddenly, in utter disbelief, I saw Amma with just a few devotees around her, walking up to the check-in counter. Amma left the counter, not waiting for others, and through the vast, empty check-in area, walked straight up to me. She was actually gliding, so gently, emanating a purity and innocence that left me dumbstruck. It was as if she was showing me that at the core of her universe, beyond her play as the goddess, as the mother, as the Guru, there is just silence — an eternal quiet of utmost humility, reverence, kindness, and beyond. I stood there frozen in awe. It didn't even occur to me to bow down, fold my hands in *Namastē*, or even say '*Namaḥ* Śhivāya' to my mother.

Amma approached me, looked into my eyes, and with a childlike smile, with her words resonating deeply within the recesses of my heart said, "I am you."

When I boarded the plane, my mind finally embraced the meaning of her words, and I sobbed, and laughed, and cried till the airplane landed in Singapore. It was a cry of freedom; the call of the lover. Through this short, simple exchange she bound my life eternally to hers, dwelling in her embrace, which I feel is the highest human experience.

Amma once said that devotion is even higher than Self-realization, because in pure devotion, you renounce even the desire to realize, surrendering even that to the divine. The love for God suffices, and that in itself is the alpha and omega, the beginning and the end.

Using the language of knowledge, advaita says that the Self is ever present. There is nothing to be attained. No effort can ever bring us to that which we already eternally are. We just wrongly believe we are not that. This is *māyā* — the great illusion. And yet, effort is needed. Swāmī Pūrṇāmṛtānandajī once told me, "Indeed, great effort is needed to realize that you are completely helpless. Only when one sees one's helplessness, can one at last surrender."

Out of love appeared this mysterious līlā of experience. Some will persevere lifetimes in a diligent practice of awareness, and some will be lucky enough to be shown the infinite solely through the grace of the Guru. This grace is the mystery of faith — the rarest fortune.

Amma's mouth is the *Vedas*, and Amma's eyes contain the whole universe. She is this most beautiful white-clad figure, and simultaneously she is the witness inside our own hearts. How blessed are we to live this reality first-hand, while generations of seekers before us wandered for ages in search of it. Amma is our beginning and our end.

***

Let me conclude with a story from the life of Śhri Rāmakṛiṣhṇa Paramahaṁsa:

Rāmakṛiṣhṇa's teacher of Advaita-Vedanta philosophy was a great monk named Tōtāpurī. Immersed in the nondual formless, Tōtāpurī used to laugh at Rāmakṛiṣhṇa for prostrating to an idol made of clay, and rejected his divine visions of goddess Kāḷī. One day, Tōtāpurī fell very ill with dysentery, and no medicines were of any use. His pain became excruciating, and he could find no relief.

He tried to focus his mind in deep meditation, to withdraw it from the body, but it rushed into the stomach pain instead. He tried again and again but failed. Filled with disgust for his own body he thought, "I must get rid of this nuisance. I know I am not the body. Why should I suffer pain by associating with this rotten body? Tonight, I'll commit it to the Ganges and put an end to all these troubles."

Fixing his mind on *Brahman*, he waded out into the river. Tōtāpurī had crossed almost to the other side of the river, when he realized he couldn't find water deep enough to drown himself. "What is this divine māyā! What a mysterious play of the Lord! The Ganges has become too shallow for me to drown myself," he exclaimed.

Immediately, as if a veil covering his mind suddenly lifted, he thought, "This is due to the omnipresent, omnipotent Divine Mother! Mother is the water and land; the body and mind; illness and health; knowledge and ignorance; life and death. Whatever I see, hear, think, and imagine is mother! She turns a yes into no, and a no into yes. No embodied being can go beyond her jurisdiction unless she is pleased to allow it. No one has ever had the power to die. The same mother is beyond the body, mind, and intellect — transcendent and devoid of attributes. All my life I have been worshiping this same mother as Brahman, offering my heartfelt love and devotion. Brahman and the power of Brahman are one."

Beloved Amma, may we have that strength of devotion to you, so that it becomes enough, and nothing else is required. I bow down to you eternally and surrender my life at your feet, knowing that even these words are spoken by no one other than you. May you reside in our hearts as your seat of glory.

25

Becoming an Instrument

Gautam – USA

Lately, there has been a lot of talk around the phrase *nimitta mātram* — becoming an instrument. I don't know Sanskrit, but I know the word 'instrument' in English can mean many things. Instruments can be musical: tablas, guitar, flute etc. Instruments can be blunt and rudimentary tools: hammer, chisel, shovel etc. Instruments can be very refined, advanced tools: electron microscope, energy particle collider etc.

As Amma's children, we are extremely fortunate because no matter what our stage of spiritual evolution, we can become her instruments. This is for two reasons: first, being an instrument is more about our attitude of how we do what we do, and less about our abilities and talents for doing something. Secondly, Amma is an expert at getting the most out of each and every type of instrument. She not only uses each instrument to its fullest potential, but constantly expands its capacities and redefines its limitations.

Our main job is to allow God's power to flow through us, expressing herself and using us to do her work. This requires surrender, trust, and remembrance that our ultimate goal is to become perfect instruments in Amma's hands, allowing ourselves to be nothing more than extensions of her.

Sometimes we don't have to do anything to be an instrument in Amma's hands. We just have to be ourselves, and be very comfortable in being ourself — and let Amma do the rest. If you hand the reins over to Amma, she can make the best use of us as instruments.

I had a wonderful experience of how Amma used me in this way; it was by being a clown or jester, to simply lighten the mood and make others around her laugh, forgetting their problems for a moment.

Amma knows that almost everyone that comes to her programs around the world is looking to unburden their sorrows. And as much as she wants to teach us the ultimate truth of the Self, Amma comes down to our level and teaches us like the spiritual toddlers we are. This involves sharing her teachings via jokes or funny stories.

Here is how I had the great honor of becoming one of Amma's legendary jokes for an entire year:

I was in Los Angeles teaching elementary school just before joining Amma's summer U.S. tour. I am usually very casual with my students, so after a few classes with me, the students figured out they could speak quite openly with me. In one class, there was a student who was very cute but very sassy.

Once she came up to my desk and we had the following conversation:

Student: "Mr. Harvey, we need to find you a girlfriend."

Me: "How do you know I don't already have one?"

(Assessing me with a frown and shaking her head)

Student: "No, you don't have a girlfriend."

Me (very amused): "So what do I have to do to get one?"

Student: "I shouldn't tell you. You don't want to hear it."

Me (curious): "Why?"

Student: "You will be too sad."

Me (more curious): "No, please tell me. I want to know."

Student: "Are you sure?"

Me: "Yes."

(Student suddenly becomes very animated and takes my hair in her fingers)

Student: "First of all, this hair, you need to cut it properly... it is all uneven...fix that first of all."

(Then pointing to my eyebrows)

Student: "And then these eyebrows, you need to pluck them... they look like a jungle."

(Pointing to my teeth)

Student: "And look at those teeth, get some baking soda and try to whiten them up...they are totally yellow."

(Pointing to my unshaven face)

Student: "You didn't even shave, what girl is going to want a guy who is too lazy to even shave before work!"

(Pointing at my wrinkled shirt)

Student: "And look at your shirt...it's all wrinkled, looks terrible."

(Pointing at my arms)

Student: "Look at all this hair on your arms, no girl is going to want someone so hairy...you need to shave them."

Etc...etc...etc...

As she continued, I wasn't sure whether to laugh or cry. It was so funny, and all her critiques were true.

After telling me all the things wrong with my appearance, I asked her, "So if I do all those things...then what do I do?"

Student (still very animated): "Ok, so after you do all of those things, you go to this website and create a profile and you can find a girl there."

I was very surprised that she knew about such a website, so I asked, "Why do you know about such a website?"

She looked at me like I was totally crazy and said, "Mr. Harvey...come on! I AM IN SECOND GRADE!!!"

I told Amma this story one day during the summer tour. Amma loved it and asked me to write it down for her. I did so; then forgot about it. One evening, I was sitting in one of the side offices adjacent to the program hall at M.A. Center in San Ramon California. It was during Amma's evening talk. Suddenly, I heard Swāmījī (Swāmī Amṛitaswarūpānanda) translating a story about a teacher... he said, "This teacher is here somewhere in this hall." Curious, I stepped out of the office into the hall, and as soon as I did, Swāmījī and Amma both pointed at me and said, "There! Him! This story is about him!"

Immediately every set of eyes in the hall looked up...and for the next few minutes all heads swiveled back and forth between Amma and me, laughing all the while as Swāmījī told the story as part of Amma's talk.

This story became the big joke in Amma's talks for the entire year — at every stop on the Indian tours; all next summer on the North American Tour; and for an entire tour in Europe. I was able to hear about my bushy eyebrows, hairy arms, and crooked yellow teeth in Tamil, Hindi, French, Spanish, etc.

Since I was taking photos as one of my *sēvās* during those tours, I would inevitably be on stage and very clearly visible when my story was being told, and Amma would point me out, adding to the peals of laughter throughout the crowd.

After Amma told that story, I often noticed people coming up to me, taking extra-long looks at my arms or my eyebrows or my teeth, before walking away smiling.

Amma's greatness is that she can use a single instrument to simultaneously accomplish many things at the same time. She can use an instrument (in this case me), to make everyone laugh and to simultaneously refine me, helping to remove my inner weaknesses. I'm not a shy person but like most, I have self-doubt and sometimes lack confidence.

After a year of using my story, Amma called me one day during *darśhan*, and asked if I felt embarrassed or ashamed from all this scrutiny. I told her no, I had actually enjoyed it!

Amma looked at me proudly, and said that spiritual aspirants shouldn't have any shame when it comes to superficial things like their appearance. They should remain focused on realizing their inner beauty.

***

When a perfect master like Amma uses us as instruments, rather than breaking us, she makes us stronger and even better with each use. This is because she does it with so much love, care, sweetness, and spontaneity. We cannot help but feel inspired and motivated to grow, becoming better versions of ourselves.

When we first meet Amma, it's natural to have the desire to make her happy and proud. We often feel a strong enthusiasm to do whatever we can to be an instrument of hers, even if we aren't yet quite refined or perfect in our efforts.

All of us are at various stages of evolution when we come to Amma, and we are all trying to move from lower stages to become highly evolved spiritual beings. Accordingly, we might start off being very crude instruments — simple and rudimentary. The beauty of Amma's path is that she doesn't exclude us from offering our service at these initial stages.

On the contrary, she gives us many opportunities to serve, revealing the rough and sharp edges of our instrument so that we become more aware of what we have to work on. The more we have a feeling of 'doership,' the more our flaws will be exposed.

When I first came to the āśhram, I badly wanted to become Amma's instrument. Amma was willing to indulge that enthusiasm because she knew my efforts would give me many opportunities to see that I was more of a crude caveman-club at that time, than a refined instrument.

Like most, I came to Amma full of all manner of inner blemishes and weaknesses. In my case, I suffered a lot from arrogance, a bad temper, lack of patience, etc. Amma would often call me *Durvāsā*, *Jarāsandha*, or *Vishvāmitra* — all characters from the scriptures known for their fiery dispositions.

Amma constantly creates situations to expose our weaknesses, bring awareness to them, and ultimately help us overcome them.

Many years before there was any formal security in the *Amritapuri* āśhram, some western men were enlisted to guard the area under Amma's room. I felt so honored to be asked to do such a sēvā. I had zero qualifications other than having seen many action movies, but even so, I was full of pride and was overly confident.

One time, as Amma was coming back to her room from a program, a strange woman appeared. She looked very suspicious, so I kept my eye on her as Amma walked past, and started ascending the steps to her room. Suddenly this strange lady started following Amma. How could I let this assailant follow Amma up to her room?!? Not on my watch!

I felt so lucky to be able to jump into action and be the hero! I could save Amma from this lady! Heroically, I commanded this woman to stop, and without waiting a second for her to reply or listen to my orders, I reached out, grabbed her by the shoulder and spun her around, successfully stopping her from getting to Amma.

In an instant, I went from total hero pride, to (in slow motion) seeing the shock on everyone else's faces, realizing the person I caught may not have been the assailant I thought she was. No one nearby helped me detain this villain, because everyone else knew that she was the UNESCO Chair for Experiential Learning on Sustainable Innovation & Development; Director and Professor at Amrita Center for Wireless Networks and Applications; Dean of International Programs; Dr. Manisha.

To this day, Amma loves to remind me and Manisha (who is now my good buddy) of this story; how I dragged her by the hair like a caveman away from Amma.

I hope I have paid off a bit of this *karmic* debt, as for the last fifteen years, one of my sēvās is to load Amma's camper on the U.S. tours for traveling to the next city. Since Manisha often rides with Amma in the camper, I get to load Manisha's bags as well.

***

Probably the greatest opportunity Amma has ever given me to try and continually become a better instrument, is my sēvā of giving darśhan tokens. It's a beautiful blessing to be able to facilitate people getting that magical embrace from Amma, and at the same time... incredibly dangerous. On any given day, I could be hiding in my room to avoid being hunted down by angry mobs after the token table is closed, or hiding from Amma if I haven't given out enough tokens.

I have innumerable stories and experiences from the lessons Amma has taught me through this sēvā, but I will share just one now:

Often, especially during the tourist season when the crowds are very big, I fret over giving tokens out, as Amma finishes giving darśhan very late each night. I feel the more tokens I give out, the later Amma has to sit there, and I feel responsible for making Amma sit so late. I go through an inner struggle thinking, "If somehow I can give out fewer tokens, Amma can finish a bit earlier and get a bit more rest."

Often this thinking has expressed itself as frustration with people whom I judged to be asking for tokens too often. Every night, I'd watch Amma physically sacrifice herself, sitting until two or three in the morning. A few hours later, I would be back at the token desk, and see those same faces coming and wanting to have darśhan.

I understand the undeniable attraction to Amma, and the desire to take another dip in the unbelievably blissful river that is Amma's love, but I'd also think... "Haven't you had enough?"

Deep down, I knew I was just looking at these people on the surface level, casting my judgements on them without knowing anything about most of them, or what problems they were unburdening on Amma's lap. However, inevitably I always tried to err on the side of stinginess to protect Amma's body, and as a consequence, I faced the ire of the people who were asked to come back another day, and ultimately got scolded by Amma too.

Giving tokens should be the easiest way for me to be Amma's instrument. All I need to do is surrender to exactly what Amma has directly instructed me to do. But the ego is subtle, and doership is so hard to overcome, that we often struggle to relinquish control over how we think things should be done.

The beauty of this sēvā is that I get daily, and often immediate guidance from Amma if I try to do things my way instead of her way, which is always the right way. Amma's greatest gift is using every second of her life to show us what it means to truly be an instrument of God, through her example. The more we are able to follow her instructions and her example, the better instruments we can become.

I remember the case of a couple from Europe who came during a particularly busy time in the āśhram. I was being very strict with tokens, and this couple was very upset that they couldn't come for darśhan as often as they wanted. I had several arguments with them over their short stay, and I remember them leaving quite unhappy with me.

During this time Amma called me late one night, and asked me to give tokens to people who were feeling sad. When I pleaded with her that it was so late, and that many of these people had already come often for darśhan, She lovingly explained to me what sacrifices many had made to come to the āśhram; getting time off work, saving money, etc. For some, it was the only time they would see Amma all year.

Amma ended the lesson by looking at me with a big smile and a final instruction: from now on she wanted me to give tokens while wearing a mask. This was long before Covid. She said I should wear a mask that had a permanent smile painted on it. She knew I wasn't yet capable of genuinely smiling at everyone that came to me, but she could see that capacity deep within me, and until I was a more refined instrument, Amma wanted everyone to see a smiling face when they got their tokens.

I tried my best to remember Amma's sweet advice and keep a smile on my face as I gave tokens. Sometimes I succeeded; sometimes not. Several months went by when I noticed that the European couple who had left the āśhram earlier thinking I was the devil, had come back for another short visit. I thought this would be the perfect opportunity to put on my special smile mask. The next time they came to my table to ask for tokens, I could sense they had come ready for battle... However, I had a huge beaming smile on my face...and they were totally disarmed.

I spoke sweetly to them and gave them tokens. They walked away almost in shock. Fortunately, this time when they came to the āśhram, it was far less crowded than their last visit. In fact, I was often running around late at night, looking for more people to give tokens to, and made a point of always trying to find them. By the time they left, we were good friends, and had only smiling, positive interactions.

***

Amma's love is the magnet that pulls out our inner beauty. It was always there inside, but has likely been weighed down and hidden by our inner dirt. When Amma's magnet begins to pull out this inner beauty, the first thing we may see come up is the dirt that has been covering it. Once that is removed, we can become true instruments and inspirations through the actions we perform.

For several years, I had the good fortune to participate in the *Amṛita Kuṭīram* house construction project and Amma's tsunami relief work. Every year, Japanese university students join us as volunteers. In 2006, more than eighty of them accompanied us to Nagapattinam, Tamil Nadu to help with the ongoing tsunami rehabilitation work.

There were many familiar faces in that year's group, as many students had come back to help for the second or third time. But there was one new face in the crowd that was hard to forget.

I remember when the group arrived and I saw this boy; Takaki has cerebral palsy. While a fully functional university student on the intellectual level, he was confined to a wheelchair. With very limited control of his muscles, making the simplest movements was a challenge, including speaking.

When Takaki first met Amma in Tokyo in 2003, he watched her giving darśhan for hours on end. Seeing her tireless efforts, he also had the desire to do something for others. He also wanted to be an instrument. He knew that his classmates had been coming to India for the past several years for Amma's building projects, but due to his physical limitations, it always seemed too unrealistic to make the trip himself. He felt guilty about becoming a burden to the other volunteers, taking away from their time to do relief work. How wrong he was!

Arriving in Nagapattinam, the first day of sēvā was not much different than any other day at a construction site in India; very hot, with lots of heavy manual labor...and nothing for Takaki to do. The whole first day he watched from his wheelchair, waiting for the opportunity to help.

The next day he got his wish. Some of the houses were ready to be painted. I suggested that maybe Takaki could paint. He was thrilled with the idea and immediately agreed to try. After brainstorming ways to make the work easier for him, a few fellow classmates carried Takaki on their backs up onto a scaffolding. A paintbrush was taped to his hand (he is unable to grip things) and he was ready to go.

His hand was guided into the paint bucket and then with great effort, he moved his arm back and forth along the wall. Paint was flying everywhere, spraying anyone within range, but no one minded. No one moved out of the way. A small crowd began to gather, and several people watched with tears in their eyes. One of the local site supervisors was visibly touched, and with his hands over his heart said, "This is real service."

For several hours Takaki painted that house. Throughout the day everyone stopped by, shouting encouragement to him. The joke was that he had painted himself as much as the wall. People took turns supporting him on the scaffolding, helping him dip his brush into the bucket.

By sunset, the house had been transformed from cement-gray, to the same pink color as the setting sun. Several volunteers had spent hours painting that house; but Takaki's effort was unique. In that simple act of house painting, he was able to fill the hearts of all those who were blessed to witness it. His effort made others believe that they can contribute; they can make a difference regardless of their own limitations.

Takaki is a great example of someone inspired by Amma who is able to go beyond his own physical limitations, and who in turn inspires others with his attitude and his service.

Amma shows us every day the beauty and joy of serving others and putting their needs before ours. When we do something with a selfless attitude, we automatically become God's instrument.

Amma is providing the perfect conditions we need to grow, and that will eventually lead us to realize that everything we see is light and everyone is part of ourselves. Once this happens, we will automatically have compassion for all of creation and serve it accordingly.

I pray we all have the grace to take full advantage of these opportunities and that we become perfect instruments in Amma's hands.

Glossary

abhyāsa: unrelenting spiritual practice, constant effort.

adharma: unrighteousness; deviation from natural harmony.

adhyāsa: superimposition; the error of attributing the qualities of one thing to another due to ignorance. E.g. seeing a piece of rope in dim light and thinking it's a snake.

Ādi Śhaṅkarāchārya: saint revered as a Guru and chief proponent of the *advaita* (non-dual) philosophy.

advaita: not two; non-dual; philosophy that holds that the *jīva* (individual soul) and *jagat* (universe) are essentially one with *Brahman*, the supreme reality.

advaitic: pertaining to *advaita.*

ahaṅkāra: from *'aham'* — 'I' and *'kāra'* — 'maker.' Ego or the sense of a self that is separate from the rest of the universe.

AIMS Hospital: Amrita Institute of Medical Sciences, a super-specialty hospital in Kochi, Kerala.

ammamār: Malayalam word for 'mothers.'

amṛit: nectar of immortality, a divine substance symbolizing eternal life and spiritual liberation.

Amṛitānandamayī: 'full of immortal bliss,' the name by which Amma is universally known.

Amritapuri: The international headquarters of Mata Amritanandamayi Math, located at Amma's birthplace in Kerala, India.

Amṛitavarṣham50: Amma's 50th birthday celebration, held as an international dialogue-and-prayer event at Kochi, Kerala in September 2003, with the theme, "Embracing the World for Peace & Harmony." The four-day celebrations were attended by international entrepreneurs, peace-makers, educators, spiritual leaders, environmentalists, India's foremost political leaders and cultural artists, and more than 200,000 people per day, including representatives of each of the 191 member countries of the United Nations.

Amṛita Kuṭīram: Mata Amritanandamayi Math's housing project providing free homes for very poor families all over India.

Amrita Vidyalayam: a national network of schools managed by the Mata Amritanandamayi Math and offering value-based education at the primary and secondary levels.

Amrita Vishwa Vidyapeetham: a private, multi-campus, multidisciplinary university, currently ranked among the best in India.

ārati: a traditional ritual involving the waving of a lighted lamp to the Guru or deity usually done towards the end of *pūjā* or worship. At some of Amma's programs, multiple devotees take turns waving the lighted lamp to Amma as she showers them with flower petals and the ārati song is sung.

archana: chanting of the 108 or 1,000 names of a particular deity (e.g. *'Lalitā Sahasranāma'*).

Arjuna: great archer and one of the heroes of the *Mahābhārata*. It is Arjuna whom Kṛiṣhṇa addresses in the *Bhagavad Gītā*.

artha: goal, wealth, substance; one of the four *puruṣhārthas* (goals of human endeavor).

arthārthī: one of four types of devotees mentioned in the *Bhagavad Gītā*, an *arthārthī* is one who prays for wealth.

āsana: physical posture, usually referring to *yōga* postures or sitting postures during meditation. Also, the seat on which one sits for spiritual practice.

āśhram: 'place of striving.' A place where spiritual seekers and aspirants live or visit, in order to lead a spiritual life. It is usually the home of a spiritual master, saint or ascetic, who guides the aspirants.

ātmā (ātman): Self or soul.

avatār: from Sanskrit root *'ava-tarati'* — 'to come down.' Divine incarnation.

avyakta: unmanifest.

Āyurvēda: traditional Indian system of medicine.

Āyurvēdic: pertaining to Āyurvēda.

bhaga: the six blessed qualities, viz. *jñāna* (knowledge), *aiśhvarya* (sovereignty), śhakti (energy), *bala* (might), *vīrya* (valor) and *tējas* (spiritual splendor). One who has all these qualities is known as *Bhagavān* (God) or *Bhagavatī* (Goddess).

Bhagavad Gītā: 'Song of the Lord,' it consists of 18 chapters of verses in which Lord Kṛiṣhṇa advises Arjuna. The advice is given on the battlefield of Kurukṣhētra, just before the righteous Pāṇḍavas fight the unrighteous Kauravas. It is a practical guide to overcoming crises in one's personal or social life and is the essence of *Vēdic* wisdom.

Bhagavān: God, one who has all the six divine qualities pertaining to *bhaga* (see *bhaga*).

Bhāgavata Purāṇa: also known as *Bhāgavatam*, one of the 18 *Purāṇas*, a devotional Sanskrit composition narrating the life, pastimes and teachings of various incarnations of Viṣhṇu, chiefly that of Lord Kṛiṣhṇa.

bhajan: devotional song or hymn in praise of God.

bhakti: devotion for God.

Bhakti Sūtras: aphorisms on devotion attributed to Sage Nārada.

bhakti yōga: the path of devotion.

Bhārat: India.

bhāṣhya: commentary or exposition of a text.

bhāva: divine mood or attitude.

Brahma Sūtras: a central philosophic text synthesizing the teachings of the *upaniṣhads*, also known as the *Vēdānta Sūtras*.

brahmachārī: celibate male disciple who practices spiritual disciplines under a Guru's guidance; '*brahmachāriṇī*' is the female equivalent.

brahmacharya: celibacy; see āśhrama. *Brahma* also means *Vēda*. So, brahmacharya is the stage of life in which one pursues the study of the Vēdas with self-discipline under the guidance of an āchārya (teacher).

Brahman: ultimate truth beyond any attributes; the supreme reality underlying all life; the divine ground of existence.

Brahmasthānam: 'abode of *Brahman*.' The name of the temples Amma consecrated in various parts of India and in Mauritius. The temple shrine features a unique four-faced idol that symbolizes the unity behind the diversity of divine forms.

Bṛihadāraṇyaka: principal and one of the oldest upaniṣhads.

buddhi: intellect; faculty of reasoning.

darśhan: audience with a holy person or a vision of the Divine. Amma's signature *darśhan* is a hug.

darśhan token: 'token' = a numbered ticket given out to devotees wanting to receive Amma's *darśhan*.

dēva: deity or god; divine being; celestial being. *Dēva* is the masculine form. The feminine equivalent is *dēvī*.

Dēvī: goddess; Divine Mother.

Dēvī Bhāva: 'the divine mood of Dēvī;' occasion when Amma reveals her oneness with the Divine Mother.

Dēvī Mahatmyam: also called the *Durgā Saptaṣhaṭi* or '700 verses to Durgā,' telling the story of the Divine Mother vanquishing evil in the form of the demon Mahiṣhāsura.

Dhanvantari: originator of *Ayurvēda*, partial incarnation of Viṣhṇu and physician of the *dēvas.*

dhāraṇā: 'concentration.' Sixth of the 'eight limbs' (*'aṣhtāṇga'*) of yōga described by Sage Patañjalī in his *Yōga Sūtras.*

dharma: 'that which upholds (creation).' Generally refers to the harmony of the universe, a righteous code of conduct, sacred duty or eternal law.

dhyāna: meditation.

duḥkha: sorrow.

Durgā: A manifestation of the Divine Mother, often depicted as wielding a number of weapons and riding a lion or tiger.

dvaita: duality; the philosophy that holds that God and the individual soul are two separate entities.

ēkāgrata: one-pointedness.

Gaṇēśha: deity with an elephant head, son of Lord Śhiva and Goddess Pārvatī.

Gaṅgā: most sacred river in India. Known as the Ganges River in English.

gōpa: cowherd boy from Vṛindāvan.

gōpī: milk maiden from Vṛindāvan. The *gōpīs* were known for their ardent devotion to Lord Kṛiṣhṇa. Their devotion exemplifies the most intense love for God.

Gōvardhan: hill referred to in the *Bhāgavata Purāṇa*, famously held aloft by Kṛiṣhṇa like an umbrella to shelter the people of Vriṇdāvan from the torrential rains sent by Indra.

gṛihastha: householder; member of the second of four āśhramas (stages of life), which include *brahmacharya* (celibate student life), *gārhasthya* (married householder life), *vānaprastha* (life of retirement and contemplation) and *sannyāsa* (life of complete renunciation).

guṇa: one of three types of qualities, viz. *sattva*, *rajas* and *tamas*. Human beings express a combination of these qualities. *Sāttvic* qualities are associated with calmness and wisdom, *rājasic* with activity and restlessness, and *tāmasic* with dullness or apathy.

Guru: spiritual teacher.

Guru Granth Sāhib: the central scripture of Sikhism.

guru kṛipa: Guru's grace.

Guru Pūrṇimā: the full moon ('*pūrṇimā*') day in the Hindu month of Āṣhāḍha (June – July) in which disciples honor the Guru; also, the birthday of Sage Vyāsa, compiler of the *Vēdas*, and author of the *Purāṇas*, *Brahmasūtras*, *Mahābhārata* and the Śhrīmad *Bhāgavatam*.

gurukula: traditional school where children live with a Guru who instructs them in scriptural and academic knowledge, while instilling spiritual values.

Hanumān: the *vānara* (monkey) disciple and companion of Rāma and one of the key characters in the epic *Rāmāyaṇa*.

Hanumān Chālīsā: devotional hymn on Lord Hanumān by Gōswāmī Tulsīdās comprising 40 verses. 'Prayer of 40 verses' = chālīsā.

haṭha yōga: physical exercises or āsanas designed to enhance one's overall well-being by toning the body and opening the various channels of the body to promote the free flow of energy; the science of *prāṇāyama* (breath control), which includes other aspects of *yōga*, including āsanas and *mudras* (esoteric hand gestures that express specific energies or powers).

IAM™: Integrated Amrita Meditation,™ a meditation practice formulated by Amma, one that synthesizes simple *yōga* āsanas, *prāṇāyama* (breathing) and concentration techniques.

iṣhṭa dēvatā: preferred form of divinity.

Jagadambā: 'Mother of the Universe,' a name of the Divine Mother.

jagadguru: 'Universal Guru.'

Jagadjananī: see Jagadambā.

japa: repeated chanting of a *mantra.*

-jī: an honorific suffixed to names or titles to show respect.

jijñāsu: one of four types of devotees mentioned in the *Bhagavad Gītā*, one who longs to know God; one who is desirous of knowing something.

jñāna: knowledge of the Truth. A *jñānī* is one who knows the Truth.

jñāna yōga: the path of knowledge. One of the four main *yōgas*, the others being *bhakti*, *karma*, and *rāja yōga.*

jñānī: one of four types of devotees mentioned in the *Bhagavad Gītā*, one who knows God or has Self-knowledge.

Kabīr: 15th Century mystic poet and saint. Also called Sant (saint) Kabīr.

kaḷari: temple where Amma used to hold Kṛiṣhṇa Bhāva and Dēvī Bhāva *darśhans.*

Kāḷī: Goddess of fearsome aspect; depicted as dark, wearing a garland of skulls, and a girdle of human hands; feminine of *kāla* (time).

Kāḷī Temple: main temple in Amritapuri dedicated to Kāḷī.

Kali Yuga: the present dark age of materialism and ignorance (see *yuga*).

kāma: lust, or desire in general.

Kāmadhēnu: the mythical wish-fulfilling cow.

Kāñchipūram: sacred city known as 'City of a Thousand Temples' in Tamil Nadu.

karma: action; mental, verbal and physical activity; chain of effects produced by our actions.

karma kāṇda: ritualistic portion of the *Vēdas.*

karma-yōga: the way of action, the path of selfless service.

kāruṇya: compassion; kindness.

Kathōpaṇiṣhad: principal *upaṇiṣhad* in the form of a dialogue between the teenager Nachikētas and Yama the lord of death.

kīrtana: communal devotional singing or chanting of divine hymns and names, often accompanied by music and dancing.

kṛipā: divine grace.

Kṛiṣhṇa: from '*kṛiṣh,*' meaning 'to draw to oneself' or 'to remove sin;' principal incarnation of Lord Viṣhṇu. He was born into a royal family but raised by foster parents, and lived as a cowherd boy in Vṛindāvan, where he was loved and worshiped by his devoted companions, the *gōpīs* (milkmaids) and *gōpas* (cowherd boys). Kṛiṣhṇa later established the city of Dwāraka. He was a friend and advisor to his cousins, the Pāṇḍavas, especially Arjuna, whom he served as charioteer during the *Mahābhārata War,* and to whom he revealed his teachings as the *Bhagavad Gītā.*

Kṛiṣhṇa Jayantī: festival celebrating the birth of Lord Kṛiṣhṇa, also known as *Janmāṣhṭami.*

krōdha: anger.

Kuntī: mother of Karṇa and the Pāṇḍavas, known to be beautiful, intelligent and shrewd.

Lalitā Sahasranāma: 1,000 names of Śhrī Lalitā Dēvī, a form of the Goddess.

līlā: divine play.

lōka: world.

lōkāḥ samastāḥ sukhinō bhavantu: 'May all beings in all the worlds be happy.' A prayer for universal peace and wellbeing.

Mahābhārata: ancient Indian epic that Sage Vyāsa composed, depicting the war between the righteous Pāṇḍavas and the unrighteous Kauravas.

mahātmā: 'great soul;' term used to describe one who has attained spiritual realization.

mālā: garland; rosary, usually made of *rudrākṣha* seeds, *tulasī* wood or sandalwood beads.

manana: reflection on spiritual matters.

mānasa pūjā: worship done mentally.

mantra: a sound, syllable, word or words of spiritual content. According to *Vēdic* commentators, *mantras* are revelations of *ṛiṣhis* arising from deep contemplation.

Matruvani: 'Voice of the Mother.' The āśhram's flagship publication dedicated to disseminating Amma's teachings and chronicling her divine mission. It is currently published in 17 languages (including nine Indian languages).

māyā: cosmic delusion, personified as a temptress; illusion; appearance, as contrasted with reality; the creative power of the Lord.

Mīrābaī: great female devotee of Kṛiṣhṇa who lived in the 16th century.

mōkṣha: spiritual liberation, i.e. release from the cycle of births and deaths.

mumukṣhutva: intense desire for liberation.

Ōm: primordial sound in the universe; the seed of creation. The cosmic sound, which can be heard in deep meditation; the

Holy Word, taught in the *upanishads*, which signifies *Brahman*, the divine ground of existence.

(Ōm) Namaḥ Śhivāya: 'Salutations to Śhiva, the auspicious one, the inner Self,' a famous *mantra*; greeting used in Amma's āśhrams.

Nānak: Guru Nānak, founder of Sikhism.

Nārada: wandering sage ever engaged in singing the praises of Viṣhṇu. He composed the *Nārada Bhakti Sūtras*, aphorisms on devotion.

Narmadā: One of the sacred rivers of India.

nēti nēti: an advaitic methodology of discerning between the real and the unreal by negation. Lit. 'not this, not this.'

nididhyāsana: deep and repeated meditation on scriptural statements.

nimittamātram: lit. 'instrument,' usually used with reference to *Bhagavad Gīta* verse 11.33 to indicate being 'a mere instrument in the hands of the divine.'

nirguṇa: without attributes (as opposed to *saguṇa*).

nirōdha: restraint or suppression.

Nisargadatta: Nisargadatta Maharaj, *Advaita* guru who lived most of his life in Mumbai. Author of *'I Am That.'*

pāda pūjā: ceremonial washing of the feet as a form of worship.

pādukā: traditional Indian footwear like sandals that may be used in worship symbolically representing the Guru's auspicious feet.

parābhakti: highest level of selfless devotion.

paradharma: duty of others, as opposed to svadharma.

paramparā: transmission of knowledge and practices within a lineage or tradition.

Pārtha: 'son of Pṛithā,' a name for Arjuṇa often used by Lord Kṛiṣhṇa in the *Bhagavad Gītā.*

pāyasam: sweet pudding.

pīṭham: small platform; seat for the Guru; also: a center of learning and power.

pradakṣhiṇa: circumambulating a sacred object or person, usually in a clockwise direction, as a sign of reverence and spiritual connection.

prārabdha: also known as *prārabdha karma*; refers to the part of our past *karma* that is the cause of our present birth.

prasād: blessed offering or gift from a holy person or temple, often in the form of food.

prasāda-buddhi: the attitude of seeing everything one receives as a gift from God.

prēma: deep love.

pūjā: ritualistic or ceremonial worship.

pūjāri: one who performs ritualistic or ceremonial worship.

pūjā manō bhava: attitude of worship.

Rādhā: eternal companion of Lord Kṛiṣhṇa, *gōpī* who exemplifies the highest form of devotion.

Rāmakṛiṣhṇa Paramahaṁsa: spiritual master (1836 – 1886) from West Bengal, hailed as the apostle of religious harmony. He generated a spiritual renaissance that continues to touch the lives of millions.

Rāmāyaṇa: 24,000-verse epic poem on the life and times of Rāma.

ṛiṣhi: seer to whom mantras are revealed in deep meditation.

Ṛiṣhikēśh: sacred city located along the Gaṅgā river in northern India.

sādhak (sādhaka): Spiritual aspirant or seeker, one dedicated to attaining the spiritual goal, one who practices *sādhanā*.

sādhanā: regimen of disciplined and dedicated spiritual practice that leads to the supreme goal of Self-realization.

sādhu: a religious ascetic, mendicant (monk) or any holy person in Hinduism and Jainism who has renounced worldly life.

saguṇa: with attributes (as opposed to *nirguṇa*).

samādhi: lit. 'cessation of all mental movements;' oneness with God; a transcendental state in which one loses all sense of individual identity; union with absolute reality; a state of intense concentration in which consciousness is completely unified.

samarpaṇam: handing completely over, surrendering.

samatva: even-mindedness or equanimity.

saṁsāra: cycle of births and deaths; the world of flux; the wheel of birth, decay, death and rebirth.

saṁskāra: impression; rite or ritual.

Sanātana Dharma: lit. 'Eternal Religion' or 'Eternal Way of Life,' the original and traditional name of Hinduism.

saṅkalpa: divine resolve, usually used in association with *mahātmās*.

sāṅkhya: one of the *'ṣhad darśhana'* or six orthodox philosophies of *Sanātana Dharma*. It is a *dvaita* or dualistic philosophy introduced by Sage Kapila.

sannyāsī: *sannyāsin*.

sannyāsin: monk (or nun) who has taken vows of renunciation.

Sanskrit: language of the oldest sacred text, the *Ṛik Vēda*, and the other three *Vēdas*; the language of most ancient Hindu scriptures.

Saraswatī: goddess of learning and the arts.

Sarayu: one of the sacred rivers of India on whose banks the city of Ayōdhyā is placed.

sāri: traditional outer garment of Indian women consisting of a long, unstitched piece of cloth wrapped around the body.

Satguru: 'true master.' All *Satgurus* are *mahātmās*, but not all mahātmās are Satgurus. The Satguru is one who, while still experiencing the bliss of the Self, chooses to come down to the level of ordinary people in order to help them grow spiritually.

satsang: 'communion with the supreme truth.' Also, being in the company of *mahātmās*, studying the scriptures, and listening to the enlightening talks of a mahātmā; a meeting of people to listen to and/or discuss spiritual matters; a spiritual discourse.

satya: truth.

sēvā: selfless service, the results of which are dedicated to God.

sēvite: person who performs *sēvā* (plural: *sēvites*).

Śhabarī: a woman belonging to a hunter tribe who was an ardent devotee of Rāma.

śhakti: personification of cosmic will and energy; strength; see *māyā*.

śhānti: peace.

śhāstra: science; authoritative scriptural texts.

Śhiva: the static aspect of *brahman* as the male principle. Worshiped as the first in the lineage of Gurus, and as the formless substratum of the universe in relationship to the creatrix Śhakti. He is the Lord of destruction in the trinity of Brahmā (Lord of creation), Viṣhṇu (Lord of preservation), and Śhiva. Usually depicted as a monk, with ash all over his body, snakes in his hair, wearing only a loincloth and with a begging bowl and a trident in his hands.

Śhivājī: also known as Chhatrapatī Śhivājī, the emperor of the Marāṭha Empire; disciple of Samarth Rāmdās.

śhraddhā: attentiveness; faith.

śhravaṇa: listening (to scriptural truths); often used in conjunction with *manana* and *nididhyāsana.*

śhrī: a title of respect originally meaning 'divine,' 'holy' or 'auspicious;' now in modern India, simply a respectful form of address, similar to 'Mr.'

Śhrīmad Bhāgavatam: see *Bhāgavatam.* Śhrīmad means 'auspicious'.

śhūnyatā: Buddhist term meaning 'emptiness' or the Void.

Sudhāmaṇi: Amma's birth name.

sūtra: aphorism.

sūrya namaskār: sun salutation, traditional sequence of 12 haṭha yōga postures.

svadharma: personal *dharma* or one's own duties; opposed to *paradharma.*

swāmī: title of one who has taken the vow of *sannyāsa* (see *sannyāsin*); *swāminī* is the female equivalent.

tapas (tapasya): austerities, penance.

tulasī: a sacred plant related to basil.

upaniṣhad: portions of the *Vēdas* dealing with Self-knowledge.

vairāgya: dispassion.

Vallikavu: name of the nearest mainland village where Amma grew up.

Vālmīki: sage and author of the *Rāmāyaṇa.*

vānaprastha: 'forest life;' a reference to the retired life dedicated to spiritual practices; the third of the four stages of life (see *aśhrama*).

vāsanā: latent tendency or subtle desire that manifests as thought, motive and action; subconscious impression gained from experience.

Vēdānta: 'the end of the *Vēdas.*' It refers to the *upaniṣhads*, which deal with the subject of *Brahman*, the supreme truth, and the path to realize that Truth; a *Vēdāntin* is a follower of *Vēdānta.*

Vēdāntic: pertaining to *Vēdānta.*

Vēdas: most ancient of all scriptures, originating from God, the *Vēdas* were not composed by any human author but were 'revealed' in deep meditation to the ancient seers. These sagely revelations came to be known as the Vēdas, of which there are four: *Ṛik*, *Yajus*, *Sāma* and *Atharva.*

Vēdic: pertaining to the *Vēdas.*

vibhūti: holy ash; can also mean splendor or prosperity.

Viṣhṇu: 'all-pervader,' Lord of sustenance in the Hindu Trinity.

viśhvarūpa: divine and cosmic form of Lord Viṣhṇu.

Vivēkachūḍāmaṇi: a *Vēdantic* work by Ādi Śhaṇkarāchārya.

Vṛindāvan: 'vṛindā-vana,' 'Rādhā's forest.' A region in Mathura district in Uttar Pradesh, celebrated as the place where Kṛiṣhṇa passed his early days as a cowherd.

Vyāsa: lit. 'compiler.' The name given to Sage Kṛiṣhṇa Dvaipāyana, who compiled the *Vēdas.* He is also the chronicler of the *Mahābhārata* and a character in it, and author of the 18 *Purāṇas* and the *Brahma Sūtras.*

Yama: the god of death and justice.

Yaśhōdā: Kṛiṣhṇa's foster-mother.

yōga: 'to unite.' Union with the Supreme Being. A broad term, it also refers to the various methods of practices through which one can attain oneness with the Divine. A path that leads to Self-realization.

Yōga Sūtras: 'Patañjali Yōga Sūtras,' aphorisms composed by Sage Patañjali on the path to purification and transcendence of the mind.

yuga: according to the Hindu worldview, the universe (from origin to dissolution) passes through a cycle made up of four *yugas* or ages. The first is *Kṛita* or *Satya Yuga*, during which *dharma* reigns in society. Each succeeding age sees the progressive decline of *dharma*. The second age is known as *Trēta Yuga*, the third is *Dvāpara Yuga*, and the fourth and present epoch is known as *Kali Yuga*.

Pronunciation Guide

Vowels can be short or long:

a – as ‘u’ in but; ā – as ‘a’ in far
e – as ‘a’ in may; ē – as ‘a’ in name
i – as ‘i’ in pin; ī – as ‘ee’ in meet
o – as in oh; ō – as ‘o’ in mole
u – as ‘u’ in push; ū – as ‘oo’ in hoot

ṛi – as ‘ri’ in crisp; ṛu – as ‘ru’ in Spanish ‘Peru’
ḥ – pronounce ‘aḥ’ like ‘aha,’ ‘iḥ’ like ‘ihi,’ and ‘uḥ’ like ‘uhu.’

Some consonants are aspirated (e.g. kh); others are not (e.g. k). The examples given below are only approximate:
k – as ‘k’ in ‘kite;’ kh – as ‘ckh’ in ‘Eckhart’
g – as ‘g’ in ‘give;’ gh – as ‘g-h’ in ‘dig-hard’
ch – as ‘ch’ in ‘chat;’ chh – as ‘ch-h’ in ‘staunch-heart’
j – as ‘j’ in ‘joy;’ jh – as ‘dgeh’ in ‘hedgehog’
p – as ‘p’ in ‘pine;’ ph – as ‘ph’ in ‘up-hill’
b – as ‘b’ in ‘bird;’ bh – as ‘bh’ in ‘rub-hard’

r – as ‘r’ in ride
ñ – as ‘ny’ in ‘canyon;’ ṅ – as ‘ng’ in ‘sing’

The letters ḍ, ṭ, ṇ are pronounced with the tip of the tongue against the hard palate, the others with the tip against the teeth.
ṭ – as ‘t’ in ‘tub;’ ṭh – as ‘th’ in ‘lighthouse’
ḍ – as ‘d’ in ‘dove;’ ḍh – as ‘dh’ in ‘red-hot’
ṇ – as ‘n’ in ‘naught’
ḷ – as ‘l’ in ‘revelry’
ṣh – as ‘sh’ in ‘shine;’ śh – as ‘s’ in German ‘sprechen’

With double consonants the sound is pronounced twice:
chch – as ‘tc’ in ‘hot chip’
jj – as ‘dj’ in ‘red jet’

Acknowledgments

This book is the fruit of the joint efforts of Amma's children and done in the spirit of offering. Especially in the initial phase, Br. Mādhavāmṛita Chaitanya's inspiration and mentorship put us onto a well-trodden path that we could follow. I would like to thank Anita Raghavan, Veena Erickson, and especially Rajani Menon for their invaluable support on the backend, as well as Jagannath Maas for patiently and diligently preparing the layout. Swāmī Vidyāmṛitānanda was instrumental in the preparation of the extensive glossary. Every step of the way our progress was guided by Swāmī Jñānāmṛitānanda, whose wisdom and experience has been our backbone. I am truly grateful to you all.

Julius Heyne

www.ingramcontent.com/pod-product-compliance
Lightning Source LLC
Chambersburg PA
CBHW071950100426
42736CB00043B/2722
* 9 7 8 1 6 8 0 3 7 8 9 7 9 *